THE
GREATER
FREEDOM

THE
GREATER
FREEDOM

Life as a Middle
Eastern Woman
Outside the Stereotypes

ALYA MOORO

Little
a

Published by Little A, New York

www.apub.com

Amazon, the Amazon logo, and Little A are trademarks of Amazon.com, Inc., or its
affiliates.

ISBN-13: 9781542041218
ISBN-10: 154204121X

Cover design and illustration by Anna Morrison

Printed in the United States of America

'Freedom to be oneself is all very well; the greater freedom is not to be oneself.'

James Merrill, from *A Different Person: A Memoir*

*For the culture
and for the fifteen-year-old me/we*

Introduction – Or, Why I Wrote This Book

Sometime in the months before I decided I even wanted to write this book, I typed 'Arab woman' into Google, already on a quest for some sort of clarity of 'identity', without really knowing why.

I had been in a London taxi and was answering the question that crops up in every cab ride I have ever taken, which was, 'Where are you from?' I gave my usual response: 'I was born in Egypt but grew up in London.' The driver spun around in his seat to get a better look at me and commented that he thought I was Spanish, because Arab women are always veiled.

I felt my blood boil and yet, later – as I typed, and clicked on 'images' – hundreds of eyes stared back at me, peering from beneath niqabs and hijabs. There were a few belly dancers thrown in here and there too, for good measure.

I had known subconsciously that this is the general stereotype of what an Arab woman is supposed to look like. This is, after all, pretty much all that is depicted in the media. From the reductive movie char-acterisations to the news reports on how subjugated and repressed we're supposed to be (when we're not terrorists), to the surprise on some people's faces when I tell them where I'm from and they have to reassess their preconceptions.

But I was still a little shocked that these images remain prevalent, so pervasive, when I know that there is so much more variety than the stereotype suggests. There are, for example, many Arab women – just like me – who seem to be invisible to the Google image search function. Labelling 381 million people[1] from twenty-two countries as monolithic 'Arabs' felt evasive, inaccurate and reductive, as did the assumption that this automatically meant we were all the same.

It's not something I had ever really considered speaking about, or writing about, before – being Egyptian, being an Arab growing up in London, being *technically* Muslim.

Although I am a journalist by profession and I've spent many years – if not my whole life – articulating my feelings and thoughts and experiences, as well as those of others, I had never really felt that my identity as an Arab woman or a Muslim was an integral part of the conversation. It didn't feel relevant to the stories I was telling. I had always been interested in the universal, and brandishing my ethnicity didn't feel necessary.

But the older I became, sweeping generalisations and ignorant assumptions began to jar. When the tug of two cultures on my life became impossible to ignore, I realised I needed to address it.

The more comfortable I became in reaching my own conclusions – and in expressing them – the more I realised how important it is to add to the conversation. It was happening without me anyway. Being an Arab woman today means that simply *existing* makes me a part of this conversation, whether I choose to be or not.

I was born in Egypt to Egyptian parents. We moved to London when I was eight years old and I've lived here ever since, minus one year back in Cairo when I was thirteen, and countless trips back and forth in between. I'm a hybrid. I never really thought about it growing up, but I feel it now. I am British, but I'm also Egyptian. I am both and consequently neither.

When I first told my father I wanted to write this book, he was surprised that cultural identity was a topic of interest for me. Having grown up in Egypt until his early thirties, it was never something he had had to consider and he didn't raise me to take note of our cultural differences. It had never crossed his mind that I might do so anyway.

As Amal Awad posits in *Beyond Veiled Clichés*, while the Arab world faces many challenges, 'cultural identity is not one of them'. She suggests that, while the lives of men and women in the Middle East – and how they see themselves – are influenced by class, religion and lifestyle, it's not their place in society *as Arabs* that they grapple with. They know who they are, she says, even if they don't always like who they're expected to be. [2]

Conversely, growing up in London, I was in a minority and therefore needed to consider my culture – my heritage as an Egyptian woman – far more than if I had grown up in an Arab country.

My growing awareness was all the more necessary after the tragic events of 9/11, which happened when I was twelve years old. It ushered in a new era, one full of stereotypes and preconceptions surrounding people from my part of the world. Whether or not those were categories I automatically looked like I fitted into, I technically did. Figuring out my place in all this required consideration.

Certainly, as I have felt throughout the course of my life – and have subsequently explored in this book – for many Arabs who grow up in countries other than where they are originally from and where they are a minority, figuring out who you are, what you want, where you belong and what it is you truly believe can be complicated by the juxtaposition and by your role as 'other'.

Sex is ultimately what made me want to write this book. It's what made me realise what it meant to be an Arab woman. Or, more precisely, it was my inability to have sex when and with whomever I wanted. For a long time, I would blush if I even just thought of sex. Even though I was actually having sex; even though I had disposed of my virginity at the

UK's average age for girls to lose their virginity. In London, where I'm from, it's not a big deal to sleep with a guy you like and who likes you. In Cairo, where I'm also from, it's illegal to have sex before marriage. My subsequent discomfort around sex was a very Arab thing, it turned out. Women hold the burden of a family's honour, and that honour lies between their legs.

To borrow from a piece by Salma Elbarmawi,[3] 'there are words that don't exist in the English language. Words my mother uses to describe her love for me; words like "rouhi", that translates to, "You are one with my soul." Words like "hayat alby" that mean "You give my heart its very life".

'There are [also] emotions that only exist for me in Arabic. Emotions relating to responsibility, honoring my family, and representing the country of my parents, of my ancestors.' Relating to what *should* be done, how I *should* live, what I *should* want. In reality, the thought of my family's opinions and judgement has been the scariest part of writing this book.

It can be hard to decipher your own voice in among all the others, especially when trying to construct your own ideals from around the stereotypes – both those from within the community I am 'technically' from, as well as from those outside it. As I felt increasingly as I grew older, culture runs deep and can be both a blessing and a burden. Undoubtedly, whether you choose to acknowledge it or not, it impacts all sorts of things, not least your inherited expectations and behaviour codes for yourself and your life.

Caught at times between opposing expectations, Arabs growing up abroad can often be stuck between the pressure to not become too 'Westernised' and thus lose their 'culture', and at the same time not be too 'fresh off the boat' (a term used to describe immigrants who have arrived from a foreign country and have yet to assimilate the culture, language and behaviour).

It's something that goes far beyond religion and is deeply entrenched in the culture – so strongly, it turns out, that it plays a role even when you have been raised thousands of miles from the countries in which these attitudes and expectations originate, and even when your parents don't – on the surface – think like that at all. Trying to straddle two conflicting cultures can, as I have learnt, make you question yourself, your desires and your choices.

Talking about and unravelling some of the restrictions and expectations placed on Arab women, while also trying to dispel the stereotypes surrounding us, is very hard. It's going to be impossible, if I'm honest. I'm inevitably going to end up feeding the stereotypes with one hand while I try to dispel them with the other. However, it's actually not as straightforward as that; there are many layers to everything, and indeed to everyone.

I wanted to know which aspects of my life were being impacted by this pull of cultures and why. But I also wanted to say 'Hi, Mr Taxi Driver, guess what? There are people like me too!'

And that's what brings us together now: you with this book in your hands, me examining every aspect of my life, interrogating the intersection where race, culture and universal experience meet – and, at times, clash.

It's been quite the selfish endeavour, but I know for a fact other people will find catharsis in this book, too, if not some understanding.

Some of the Middle Eastern women I spoke to as part of my research are my friends, some are those who have reached out through social media, some are friends of friends of friends. They range in age from twenty-four to fifty years old, and come from various socio-economic backgrounds and countries such as Egypt, Iraq, Lebanon and Oman. Most have grown up in the UK, several in the US or in Europe. I have changed all of their names and some identifying characteristics.

Over the course of the next couple of hundred pages, I weave together personal experience, research and conversations with these

Middle Eastern women. They spoke to me openly and candidly about many of the aspects of their lives to tell the story of the coming of age of a Middle Eastern woman living outside the stereotypes – namely me, but also partly them, and partly all women. It's something I learnt in journalism: it's never just my story; the human is always universal.

This might be #toodeepfortheintro but there are common threads that run through the lives of all women to varying degrees. Generally viewed as the 'weaker' sex, we have all been subject to the same socialisation and the same prejudice – the expectations to look and behave in a certain way. We share a language of stereotypes, socialisation and inequality. Regardless of where we live, where we're from, the colour of our skin and what we call God if and when we pray to Him.

Throughout the course of this book, I'll be exploring everything from representation, expectations of how a 'good Arab girl' looks, sounds and acts, and the effects of this on sex and relationships, as well as how it feels to live as a Middle Eastern woman – albeit an 'invisible' one – in a post-Brexit, post-Trump being elected as President world. The word 'should' will come up a lot.

I've always believed that if you don't like the story, you should write your own. So, shall we begin?

Chapter 1
When You Can't See Yourself

It's strange how often much of what you first learn about yourself comes from how others perceive you.

The first time I remember having anything other than 'human' reflected back at me, I had just turned eight years old. My parents, my younger brother and I had been living in London for a few months, and one of the boys in my class had just asked me to be his girlfriend.

The crumpled note had made its way down the line of desks in the classroom before eventually landing on mine. I remember picking it up gingerly, unsure it was really for me.

'Will you be my girlfriend?' the writing scrawled, with 'yes' and 'no' checkboxes at the ready for me to deliver our fate. I excitedly checked off the affirmative and passed it back, already mentally scribbling my first name with his last.

But our romance lasted only until lunchtime, when Katie and Lauren – the mean girls of the class – cornered me on my way out of the library, where I was apt to spend my break times. 'Uh, only we're allowed to have boyfriends,' they told me, their eyes flickering over every inch of my face and body before hammering the nail in the coffin that was my young self-esteem: 'Why would he even like you anyway . . . you're brown!'

I can still picture myself almost comically stretching my arms out in front of me as if to confirm their diagnosis. Prior to their kind interventions, I don't think I had really given the colour of my skin all that much thought.

My family and I had moved to London from Geneva, where we had lived for three years and where I had attended the International School, which was – naturally – a hub of ethnicities. At school in London, the vast majority of bodies that filled the seats were white. Equally, I had never given this much thought either.

I had always been far more concerned with what was going on in the pages of the novels I was reading, and I had always managed to find pieces of myself in characters like Elizabeth and Jessica in *Sweet Valley High*, and in *The Famous Five* and *Are You There, God? It's Me, Margaret*. It had never dawned on me that I could not or should not see myself in those characters just because they were white (or that I was not white, for that matter).

Just like me, the characters in my novels were also reckoning with their own becomings, also trying to figure out what the hell a period was, how to get a certain boy's attention and how to make their boobs look bigger. Those were the concerns of the age, and they were similarly just as important in my life as they were in theirs. Thanks in large part to my voracious appetite for reading, I learnt early on that the human experience is often pretty universal.

What's more, I had spent much of the first eight years of my life running around the beaches and streets of Egypt with my friends, all of whom looked like variations of me. When we acted out scenes from our imaginations in the Cairo heat we could all pick whoever it was we wanted to embody, regardless of any sort of enforced logic like whether or not flying was actually feasible. Our character plays were not restricted by gender or shades of skin. That was what imaginations were for, after all, and I had yet to endure a world where there were limitations to imagination.

But for many people of colour, kids in school and the media are often the first mirrors through which we see ourselves, outside of our homes and families. It's often the first time we realise that – other than the totally valid 'we are all human' argument – we're not actually all the same.

'I think the beauty of being a child is that you're so untainted and unjaded and you're not really aware of these differences,' Sarah – a twenty-nine-year-old Egyptian who was born and raised in London – told me. 'You're so unaware of the fact that prejudice exists or that different skin tones can mean different things to different people.'

Entering the real world of school – and what can often feel like the battlefield of the playground – can therefore often be a real awakening. As a child, there's really nothing you want more than to fit in with those around you, and so when you don't, it's felt far more acutely.

Growing up in London, where I was ultimately in a minority, therefore forced me to confront the differences (and the similarities) that existed between myself and those around me – starting, as always, with the olive colouring of my skin, my dark hair and eyes, and an accent that belies my origins.

I pass quite often for a Mediterranean of indistinct origin, and am what editor of *The Good Immigrant* Nikesh Shukla terms an 'invisible immigrant'.[4] That is, my family and I have assimilated easily, we speak English better than we do Arabic, and we even share many of the same cultural tastes as the British.

While stereotypical depictions of immigrant children at school often bring to mind tales of lunch boxes wafting pungent smells, parents who insist on showing up at school wearing an array of traditional outfits, and children who want nothing more than to hide rather than deal with the potential embarrassment, my experience was nothing like that.

But what I learnt that day when Katie and Lauren forced me to consider my skin colour – and countless times in the years since – is that, far from the stereotypes, there is a vast expanse of space where 'difference' resides. I learnt that, although I didn't consider myself particularly *other*, they saw any minor diversion to their *norm* as different – full stop.

It mattered less to me as I grew older and the differences started to feel more like badges of honour, like markers of uniqueness; but when I was still trying to make sense of myself and the world around me, every difference felt like a vast gulf between me and the norm.

Because regardless of how 'invisible' you may be or may feel, the 'universal' is still white, still the standard against which everything else is measured. It wasn't even about passports or religion when I was a child, although later they too would become part of the conversation.

In reality, it's not just the assumption that fair, European features are considered superior (although that is often the case, as we'll explore in the next chapter), but also that there's a certain colour blindness involved; a lazy cultural stereotyping and caricaturing of anyone who doesn't fit into a neatly predefined box. It's a caricaturing that erases differences, making you interchangeable for any and all other ethnic minorities.

It happens a lot – individuals within a race are often mistaken for others within the same race, whether they're black or Asian. It's called the 'other-race effect'[5] and is said to be a cognitive phenomenon that essentially makes it harder for people of one race to recognise or identify different individuals within another.

It's what causes the British media to use photos of grime artist Stormzy and footballer Lukaku interchangeably,[6] it's what allowed the Golden Globes' Twitter account to confuse America Ferrera for Gina Rodriguez[7] and it's what made the *Hollywood Reporter* mistake *Master of None* actor Kelvin Yu for show co-creator Alan Yang, who tweeted in response, 'Same race, different dude.'

It happened to me all the time while I was growing up. There were a handful of 'brown' people in my class, including another Egyptian and a girl whose father was Pakistani and mother Italian. They quickly became two of my best friends. We were eventually forced to get used to forever being confused for one another by our classmates. We covered up our upset by laughing at their assumptions that we weren't either triplets or – at the very least – sisters, but it was a profoundly othering experience that often made me feel very invisible indeed.

It was an experience many of the Middle Eastern women I spoke to were familiar with. Samira – a thirty-one-year-old Egyptian who was born and raised in London – told me how in high school she had been repeatedly asked to pick which 'side' she belonged to out of the black girls and the white girls.

'In my entire school there were probably no more than four Arab girls; the school was very segregated,' she explains. 'The white girls were together, the black girls were together, and the "others" had to choose if they wanted to be on the white side or the black side . . .

'The white girls would say, "Well, she's Egyptian and that's in Africa, so she's black", while the black girls would say, "Her skin isn't black enough and she straightens her hair to look white, so she's white."'

While today there's arguably much more awareness of Arabs and Arab culture (whether this is always the good kind of awareness is a different question), growing up in London in the late 1990s, it felt very much like we were the invisible middle.

When it comes to Arabs, the classification is a contentious one to begin with. UNESCO identifies twenty-one Arab states, while Wikipedia lists twenty-three; who or what falls under that category has long been up for debate.[8]

Egyptians traditionally never considered themselves Arabs. Now we (mostly) do, although some Egyptians – like my grandfather – still disagree. This is attributed to Egyptian President Gamal Abdel Nasser, who made Egypt a symbol of Arab nationalism – what was, for some, a controversial decision. Nasser's dreams of Pan-Arabism were so strong that for a few years Egypt was officially known as the 'United Arab Republic'.[9]

In the UK, and across the world, 'migration and transnationalism are changing the very idea of what or who Arabs are,' wrote Ramy M. K. Aly in *Becoming Arab in London*. 'It is in a place like London where Morocco, Iraq, Syria and Sudan are no longer thousands of miles apart but just a few doors away.'[10] And while there are differences, the cultures are not dissimilar. Growing up, I saw my life experiences and struggles mimicked across the nationalities.

When I first started needing to fill out forms, I baulked at how there was nothing I identified with in any of the categories I was required to choose from. My choices consisted of 'white', 'black' or 'other race'. Was it a question of skin colour? Of geographical origin? Was I invisible? That's often what it felt like. What I checked off subsequently depended on a number of factors, including how tanned I happened to be at the time.

Despite the sheer size of the Arab diaspora around the world, 'Arab' was only added as a category to the census in the UK in 2011.[11] In the US, which reportedly houses over a million Arabs,[12] a category was proposed in 2014 and subsequently rejected.[13] In America, Arabs have been deemed white since 1944, although of course without the 'white privilege' that affords.

The history of Arabs in London is a particularly interesting one. The influx of rich Arabs coming to London to shop, buy properties and hotels and generally spend a lot of money, after the oil boom in the Gulf, was seen as an invasion of sorts, the legacy of which still continues today.

Growing up in London, I learnt there are two prevalent Arab stereotypes: the Edgware Road cliché and the Knightsbridge cliché.

What comes to mind when most people think of Knightsbridge is an image of a wealthy, often fat individual, usually from the Gulf, who trails a smell of Oud behind them while buying up the entirety of

Harrods. The Edgware Road stereotype is often that of a man in sandals and a galabiya, sitting outside a shisha café and puffing away on his water pipe while sleazily ogling the passing girls. Neither is particularly favourable or (entirely) accurate.

I was not black, but I was not white either, and in a classroom (and a world) where white is the norm, you learn very early on that 'not white' is a minority ethnic class in itself.

It was reflected in little things, like having to relinquish my dream of being Baby Spice (even though I had the exact white platform shoes she wore!) to the reality that, to the rest of the class, I would always – *always* – be Scary Spice, the black Spice Girl. 'You kind of look like her!' they'd say, pointing to my skin and curly hair as proof. Once you realise you can't even *play* at being Baby Spice, you begin to realise a lot of other things, too.

In a piece for *Teen Vogue*,[14] Arab-American journalist Ashley Rahimi Syed wrote how, aged fifteen, she learnt that she was not white via a 'joke' her friends had made. 'I asked my friends what we should dress up as for Halloween,' she wrote. 'Almost immediately, someone exclaimed that I should be a terrorist – and the whole group burst out laughing . . .

'Only later did the full nuance of the situation sink in,' she continued. 'When I saw my friends, I didn't see their whiteness; when they saw me, almost all they saw was my brownness. That's why it was so easy to call me a terrorist, why it was so funny, and why I was so blindsided.'

While I don't remember ever having to contend with that sort of 'joke', I have long been aware of the cultural stereotypes attached to being from the Middle East. When I was younger (pre-9/11) and I mentioned I was from Egypt, I was greeted with all sorts of questions, each one tinged with wonder and magic at the prospect of the Land of the Pharaohs. Sure, most were reductive – questions like 'Do you live in a pyramid?' or 'Do you go to school on a camel?' particularly so – but they were definitely less offensive and frustrating than the assumptions of today. Now, when I say where I'm from, I'm often asked for my opinion on Islam or the latest terrorist attack. The questions are far from the wonder I used to be greeted with.

In 1978, Edward Said[15] coined the term 'Orientalism', defined as 'the exaggeration of difference, the presumption of Western superiority, and the application of clichéd analytical models for perceiving the "Oriental" world'. Forty years on and it seems the world is no closer to understanding and portraying nuanced images of 'the Orient'.

The 'Arab world' consists of a number of diverse countries, which encompass all hues of skin colour and a variety of faiths; in Lebanon alone, there are fourteen different religions.[16] Current reductive media portrayals are therefore inaccurate and limiting, serving to foster both animosity and fear from the outside, as well as pressure and fracturing from the inside.

Growing up, I saw no one I identified with in the mainstream media. Later, as more depictions started filtering through, I stopped looking for them. They were often little more than cursory, racist storylines, if not out-and-out stereotypical depictions that were painful and embarrassing to watch.

In a study[17] that asked 293 secondary school teachers to name any heroic or humane Arab characters they had seen in movies, 287 could not think of even one. 'I can't actually think of anyone, unfortunately,' echoed Shams, a thirty-year-old Iraqi Londoner when I asked her the same question. 'Princess Jasmine?' she eventually offered.

Before 9/11, Arabs were rarely portrayed in the mainstream media, with the exception perhaps of the characters on *M*A*S*H*, which was before my time. After 9/11, Hollywood's desire to portray the war on terror meant there were plenty more roles available for Arab actors, but the majority tended to equate Muslims predominantly with oppression and terrorism.

In a profile for *GQ*, journalist Jon Ronson interviewed a group of Muslim and Middle Eastern actors working in Hollywood.[18] They all told him the same thing: that overwhelmingly, the roles available to them were those of terrorist villains. The actors Ronson interviewed explained that this meant they were stuck with an unpleasant choice: either take roles that reduced their heritage to a terrorist stereotype, or stop working.

These days, there are token Arabs popping up on TV screens that stray beyond that limiting stereotype, but there still aren't really any Arab characters portrayed in a three-dimensional way. Middle Eastern actors are rarely (if ever) cast to play the hot guy or the boss at work or the popular girl at school or the nerd; they still by and large play into the incorrect notion that the only thing that someone from the Middle East can be is Muslim. Religion is their defining characteristic, the defining facet of their identity.

A recent study that analysed TV shows in 2015 and 2016 found that 92 per cent of scripted TV shows had no season regulars of Middle Eastern origins. Of those who did appear, 78 per cent appear as trained terrorists, agents, soldiers or tyrants, and 67 per cent spoke with an accent, further reinforcing the stereotype that people of Middle Eastern origin are foreign.[19]

Many other minority groups have traditionally faced the same sorts of problems in terms of negative and reductive portrayals, and have felt the subsequent results. Speaking to Buzzfeed News,[20] Alex Nogales, president and co-founder of the National Hispanic Media Coalition, made a poignant argument on the real-life implications that stereotypical images have on people's perception of Latinos: that they are mostly uneducated and perform manual labour jobs (or are thugs), that they can't speak English and have fiery tempers.

'When you have those kinds of stereotypes, and that's the only roles you have, consider what that does to our children. Our children are growing up thinking that that's who we are and the only thing that we are,' he said.

This is particularly important because research[21] has found that – especially as children – we look for examples of ourselves in the media, and that finding those examples can significantly influence our self-esteem. What happens, then, when they are absent or – at best – reductive?

Representation and diversity have become ever more a talking point. The frenzy and utter joy that movies such as *Crazy Rich Asians, To All the Boys I've Loved Before, Black Panther* and *A Wrinkle in Time* were greeted with goes some way to demonstrating the dearth of fulfilling and rounded character roles available to people of colour in movies or on TV. How sweet the relief to finally see yourself reflected on the big screen.

As actor Riz Ahmed said on *The Jonathan Ross Show*:[22] '*Black Panther* isn't just a win for black people. *Crazy Rich Asians* isn't just a win for Asians. When we stretch culture, we all have more room to be ourselves. When we see a wider range of stories, we stop seeing others as others.'

Films like these are well overdue. In a study[23] that analysed more than 21,000 characters and behind-the-scenes workers on more than 400 films and TV shows released in 2014 and 2015, just 28 per cent of characters with dialogue were not white. Of these, 13 per cent were black, almost 6 per cent were Asian and 3 per cent were Hispanic. Dire numbers all round, but also do please notice the distinct lack of Arabs.

As Iraqi-British actor and writer Amrou Al-Kadhi argues in a piece for the *Independent*,[24] 'stories onscreen have the rare ability to arouse empathy for diverse characters in audiences around the world, so leaving out Arab and Muslim voices [or simply perpetuating the already negative, reductive stereotypes] in such a context of global Islamophobia is particularly damaging.'

The media helps to inform who and what we see as important, it defines the visible options for what the world sees as possible. It affects everything – like who we think can be a politician; who is considered beautiful or smart or worthy; who belongs and who is 'other'; who can be seen to live happy, healthy, 'normal' lives.

After a portrait of former First Lady Michelle Obama was unveiled in 2018, a photo of a young black girl staring at the portrait went viral.[25] The girl's mother explained that her daughter had thought Obama was a queen, and – potentially for the first time – thought it might be possible for her to be a queen one day too.

Alongside a photo of the portrait Obama posted to her Instagram,[26] she emphasised the importance of positive representation and how that can make us feel proud, bold and confident.

Perhaps it's a similar feeling to how I feel when I see how Egyptian footballer Mo Salah – who plays for Liverpool – has seemingly made the whole world fall in love with him. While he is undoubtedly a supremely skilled football player, as a fair-weather fan of the sport my admiration for him comes predominantly from the way he owns who he is. His ability to remain true to himself, his beliefs and his culture, and his significance to other Egyptians, Arabs and Muslims, is, for me, really the best part of his success.

But his positive impact goes far beyond just allowing Egyptians everywhere to take pride and ownership in the fact that he is Egyptian (in the way Egyptians everywhere are prone to do). Headlines have been single-handedly praising Salah for helping counter Islamophobia.[27] Liverpool fans even coined a song for him,[28] the lyrics of which are arguably very different from the kind of thing you might usually hear at a football game, where racism is a pervasive reality.

> Mo Sa-la-la-la-lah,
> Mo Sa-la-la-la-lah!
>
> If he's good enough for you,
> he's good enough for me.
>
> If he scores another few,
> then I'll be Muslim too.

Certainly, the world's reaction to Salah, as well as to countless examples like him, shows the importance of humanising the 'other' and how it can help build empathy, respect and understanding.

Nuanced and varied representation can go a long way to opening up possibility, understanding and acceptance, as well as the recognition that there are multiple ways of living, thinking and behaving, none of which are better, or worse, than others.

Perhaps if the wider world sees more examples of 'others' living lives that are just as universal as white people's are, they won't be surprised when they see someone who doesn't fit so neatly into their narrow worldview. Maybe they won't be so shocked that a boy has a crush on a brown person instead of on them.

As I grew older I began to realise that I had blindly taken narrow categories and biased definitions for granted and that, while the human experience is universal, there are different human experiences and my story was valid, too. I began to realise that there are countless ways to look and think and feel – many more than the handful of options presented to me by society. It's sad that that's even a revelation I needed to come to.

This is why it is important that our ideas about what is considered normal and universal are not homogenous and limited to old-fashioned, reductive, often inaccurate ideals, but instead expand to include the full range of colour and experiences. Otherwise, the world continues to say that white faces and white stories are universal, while the faces and experiences of people of colour are not. It continues to say that the rest of the world is essentially interchangeable.

It's a lot easier to be yourself if you can see yourself. And that's what we need to see more of: people being themselves and, in doing so, giving others permission to be themselves also.

Chapter 2
When You Learn How You're
Supposed to Look

I've always prided myself on being low maintenance but, in reality, I guess I'm not. Sure, I've never had cosmetic surgery and most days I leave the house without a scrap of make-up on; I tend to live in tracksuits and, up until a few months ago, my beauty regime consisted of not much more than splashing water on my face. But I've probably spent thousands of pounds and even more hours getting the hair on my head blow-dried and the hair on my face and body waxed and plucked and tweezed. Not to mention weekly trips to have my nails painted and manicured, or all the money I've spent on personal trainers and gym memberships in an effort to slim down my naturally curvaceous Egyptian behind. I always believed these were just the basic requirements for staying presentable.

Across the world there is ample pressure on women to look good, to be attractive. Across all fields women are judged and criticised for their outfits and their appearance, often far above and beyond the focus on their work or contribution to society. In a national survey of 2,500 men and women conducted by *Allure* magazine[29] (a US-based women's multimedia brand), 64 per cent of respondents said that the first thing they notice about someone is how attractive they are. Half thought appearance defines us significantly or completely.

Being attractive can open many doors in life, and it has been proven that we are more likely to think someone is smart, funny and kind if they are good-looking. This is called the Halo Effect.[30] I'd be lying if I said I didn't have my fair share of extremely shallow moments, too.

In a highly gendered Arab culture, there is a profound and all-encompassing emphasis on being 'well put together', and a very specific version of what this might look like. Women in the region and its diaspora are often held to high standards: straight hair on our heads and smooth, virtually hairless bodies. In addition, there is an expectation to be manicured and well dressed, not to mention in good physical shape.

It's an interesting contradiction – one of many in the Arab world – that while women are warned against being in any way sexual from childhood, they are at the same time trained to be almost wholly preoccupied with their body, hair, eyelashes and clothes, sometimes even at the expense of developing their minds, personalities and other assets.

Some of my earliest memories are of my mother wrestling with my hair on Sunday evenings, trying to blow-dry it into submission in order for it to look 'presentable' at school the next day. My hair was an all-consuming concern and a thing to be 'dealt' with. As I got older, the steps required to look the way I was supposed to look became ever more time-consuming and demanding.

It's not something I ever really thought about while I was growing up; that was just the way it was. Like most women, one of the first things I learnt was how to compare myself to those around me and try to conform to those standards.

The thing is, cultural norms have racialised beauty standards. Many Arab countries, including Egypt, have some history of colonisation by the British or French. Perhaps partly as a result of this, and perpetuated by the internet and global technologies, European characteristics are often considered more attractive.

Since the nineteenth century, standards have overwhelmingly favoured stereotypically 'white' (or Eurocentric) features: straight hair, light skin, light eyes and a slim body. These ideals are perpetuated and reflected back to us by the media we consume, which has long served to inform men and women what is considered beautiful and desirable.

'I think quite early on I noticed how people would react to and interact with the blue-eyed, blonde girl and also how girls that looked like that had an innate confidence,' twenty-seven-year-old Lebanese-born, London-raised Daria told me.

It was a sentiment echoed by Samira, who added that whenever she went back to Cairo on holiday, her family would ask to see pictures of her and her school friends, forever gushing about how pretty her blonde, blue-eyed friends were. 'This only reinforced the belief that I would never be as pretty and cute without fair hair and fair skin,' she said.

Celebrities and models featured across all media, all around the world, are – even today, with all the focus on diversity – mostly white women of a specific age and body type. What's more, they're mostly sporting particularly unattainable ideals of beauty, often photoshopped beyond recognition. These days, some models aren't even human at all but created entirely by computer generated imagery (CGI).[31]

For Middle Eastern women, many of these ideals go against what our biology naturally allows. The hair on our heads usually grows curly, on our legs and elsewhere dark and thick; our bodies are often pear-shaped, bigger on the bottom. These are the shapes our mothers gave us with one hand and, with the other, tried to change.

While watching *The Illusionists*[32] – a critically acclaimed documentary by Italian filmmaker Elena Rossini, which looked into the globalisation of beauty ideals and the dark side of advertising – I baulked but was not surprised at all when I heard a Lebanese woman saying, 'I come from a culture where people say, "You have a beautiful face! Haram [poor you] your body . . . what are you going to do about it?"' It's a culture of perfection I am all too familiar with.

The top beauty-related Google searches in the Middle East are 'how to whiten skin' and 'how to slim your nose',[33] and the first recorded case of cosmetic surgery in the world was reconstructive nose surgery, reportedly carried out in Egypt in 3000 to 2500 BC.[34]

Today, Lebanon has the highest rate of plastic surgery in the world, with one out of every three women going under the knife.[35] Banks even provide loans to help women achieve their desired looks and there are tourist packages for people from other Arab countries who wish to travel to Lebanon to have cosmetic surgery. We are supposed to look good and we are encouraged to do whatever it takes to achieve that.

'I got my nose done when I was nineteen because my mum suggested I should,' Dunya, a twenty-seven-year-old Iraqi who was raised in London, told me. 'I'm happy I did it. It was a good decision but it was due to her encouragement. I was always self-conscious about my nose, and my parents would say things like, "You're beautiful, the only thing you could fix is your nose", so they started saving and I did it.'

To keep yourself looking 'well put together' is an imperative placed on women around the world, but Arab women in particular, regardless of where they live, are held to especially high standards by their families, by society and – perhaps most importantly – by themselves.

When it comes to make-up, spa treatments, trips to the salon and other forms of self-care, Arab women are winning. Or losing, depending how you look at it. The Middle East's share of cosmetics alone amounts to 20 per cent of the total global market.[36] Ahead of the game is Saudi Arabia, which ranks top of the league for Middle Eastern countries. Despite their lack of visibility in the public sphere, Saudi women spend more on cosmetics than women in the West do,[37] with the amount nearly doubling from $280 million in 2005 to $535 million in 2015 (around £393 million).

While many Saudi women cover their faces and hair with black veils – and are required by law to wear long, loose black robes known as abayas over their clothes in public – many of the wealthier Saudi women, as well as those from other Arab countries, wear designer clothes under their abayas.

A few years ago, while writing an article for *Refinery29* on the rise of global fashion brands catering to Muslim consumers, I came across a mind-boggling statistic from 2015, which stated that Muslim consumers spend an estimated $230 billion on clothing. The report estimated that this would reach $327 billion by 2019, which is more than the UK ($107 billion), Germany ($99 billion) and India ($96 billion) spend combined.[38]

At parties and weddings, where women are segregated from men and can therefore remove their outer coverings, many women take the opportunity to show off the latest fashions and out-there make-up looks, often opting for brightly coloured accessories in a bid to add some personality to their black veils and abayas. It is hardly a discouragement that men won't see these displays; just like elsewhere in the world, women most often dress for themselves, and to impress other women.

'The constant primping and preening was the hardest thing about moving back to Egypt,' Selina, a thirty-two-year-old who has moved back and forth between London and Cairo numerous times, tells me. 'I had a blow-dry every day, waxes every fortnight and nails every week. It wasn't expensive to do by UK standards, but what bothered me was that if you missed an appointment, or got a chipped nail that you didn't immediately fix, someone would always notice and comment . . .

'I'd never go out in Egypt and not have my hair done,' she continued. 'Sometimes I go out shopping in London and just have my hair up, but in Egypt I wouldn't be caught dead [like that]! You would get judged, and if I'm honest, I probably would judge someone in Egypt – not judge them but I'd think, "Oh, they're not really bothered about taking care of themselves."'

Low maintenance as I claim to be, Selina's beauty regime sounds a lot like mine. I haven't done even one important thing – whether in my work or public life – with my hair in its natural, curly state, and my nails and eyebrows are almost always done to perfection.

I had always thought this was the bare-minimum level of upkeep required from women. I thought this *was* low maintenance. Never mind that my schedule was governed by the weather forecast and the availability of hairdressers and other beauty professionals.

Like many Middle Eastern women, I have coarse, curly black hair that kinks right from the root, complete with baby wisps that curl at my forehead. Growing up, my hair caused me a lot of grief (and still does today). At school, I would come up with any number of excuses to avoid the swimming pool during PE, because I just couldn't trust how my hair would dry afterwards and it would make me feel so self-conscious.

Most of my formative years were spent in the hairdresser's chair, at the behest of my mother. Even today, she still makes comments about my appearance – in particular what my hair looks like – every single time I see her.

'My mum said to me once – it was in jest, but it stuck with me – she said, "I don't think you can get away with not making an effort",' Selina told me. 'I've had it ingrained in me about keeping myself looking well groomed. A lot of people at work say, "Oh my God, you always look so glamorous!" but I don't feel like I do; it's just the basic and if I did anything less than that you would not want to see me.'

When I recently took to Instagram to lament my mum's seemingly endless obsession with my hair, I received an influx of messages confirming that hair discrimination is a very real thing, and by no means limited to just me or my family.

'My grandmother would call my hair *mankoosh* [messy] and the rest of my family would tell me I don't look elegant unless it's straightened or treated,' Egyptian-born, London-raised Mariam told me. Twenty-six-year-old Aya said her family would often ask her if she'd been 'dragged through a bush' when she wore her hair curly.

Comments like that, or questions and assumptions such as 'Are you going to straighten your hair for that job interview/first date/night out?', suggest that, ultimately, curly hair isn't beautiful or sophisticated enough to be seen in these kinds of settings. Pop culture and movies such as *The Princess Diaries* and *Miss Congeniality* parrot the same ideals, with the main characters transformed from unsuccessful 'ugly duckling' to beauty queen thanks to makeovers that more often than not include straightening their naturally curly hair.

One of my best friends – an Egyptian who has grown up in London – recently almost missed a mutual friend's destination wedding because she couldn't find a hairdresser to tend to her locks in time. After a few frantic phone calls and a lot of stress, she turned up with her hair blow-dried straight and sleek. I had had my hair straightened in London before getting on the plane, fearing a similar scenario. Turning up late (or not at all!) was a preferable option to being there punctually with our hair in its natural state.

A quick Google search for 'Middle Eastern hair' and 'Arab hair' throws back a multitude of articles all about how to 'deal' with curly hair. Even the wording is telling: it's only problems that need to be 'dealt' with.

The Good Hair Study[39] (conducted in 2016 and the first of its kind) affirmed that 'good hair' in the Western world – and consequently in the rest of the world, too – is hair that is straight or wavy in texture. The study – which showed 4,000 participants photos of black women with both straight and curly hair, along with rotating word associations – found that black women's natural hair was rated as 'less attractive' and 'less professional' than when it was straightened. It concluded that the majority of people asked, regardless of race or gender, held some bias towards women of colour based on their hair.

Dove's recent 'Love Your Curls' campaign[40] also found an implicit bias. It concluded that only four out of ten curly-haired girls think their hair is beautiful, with children as young as five expressing their desire for 'smooth' hair.

While the conversation around natural hair and the studies conducted in this field have until now pretty much centred on black women, there are some parallels that can be drawn. Arab hair may not have quite the same texture or be able to grow to quite the same level of afro but, for many Middle Eastern women, hair grows curly and frizzy, not straight and down. Adhering to European hair standards therefore requires a lot of effort, everything from spending hours brandishing a hairdryer to the fear of working out or getting caught in the rain without an umbrella. It's these sorts of things that contribute to what the Good Hair Study concluded were 'high levels of anxiety' most commonly felt by black women. Middle Eastern women face similar anxiety – believe me.

The term 'good hair day' goes some way to substantiating the extent of the connection. As psychologist and author Vivian Diller notes, 'the role hair has played in people's self-image goes way back to ancient history. As long ago as Greek and Roman times, elaborate wigs were signs of status and wealth . . . [while] Samson's long hair symbolised supernatural strength.'[41]

I was around thirteen when I began the first of the debilitating relaxing treatments that would try to change the natural texture of my hair. (Relatively old, it turns out. According to Chris Rock's *Good Hair* documentary,[42] which looked into the prevalence of relaxing treatments and weaves for black women, some girls start having their hair relaxed from as young as two years old.)

I didn't have much choice to begin with. The options my mum presented to me were either doing the Yuko system[43] – billed as 'the leading brand of chemical hair-straightening that gives you low-maintenance, shiny, hassle-free straight hair' – or missing out on that year's summer vacation. She was probably joking, but in a #jokingnotjoking sort of way.

The treatment did a good job of straightening my hair, to be fair, and made maintaining it while on that beach holiday (and countless others) far, far easier to deal with. And so for years, every few months, I would resign myself to up to eight hours in the hairdresser's chair, where the stylist would divide my hair into sections and apply the thick ointment with a mask over my nose and mouth to protect them from the toxic fumes the product would emit. Even when my eyes would literally stream tears and my scalp would tingle and itch and burn, I just shrugged. Even when the stylist got pregnant and refused to apply the treatment any longer, it didn't really click. Long term it gave me straight hair, and straight hair was the priority.

But studies have found that chemical relaxers often include compounds that affect reproductive pathways, can lead to early puberty and uterine fibroids as well as to an increased risk of premenopausal breast cancer.[44] Research also suggests that chemical relaxers can lead to hair loss.[45] I didn't make the connection at the time, but the first time I got alopecia was a couple of years after I started the Yuko system. Despite the evidence, so strong was my denial that I'm still not entirely convinced that one was related to the other.

'I got my first chemical straightening treatment when I was in my early teens,' forty-nine-year-old Egyptian-born Duha, who lives in Manchester, told me. 'I felt excited, like I could finally be like the rest of the girls and wear my hair down and have cool hairstyles.

'The process itself – the smell of the chemicals on your hair – is not nice,' she continues, 'and there were a few other things, like a little of my hair fell out, but I didn't care. I still wanted to continue doing the treatments in order to have my hair straight.'

So narrow the ideals, so strong the pressures to conform, so few role models proudly rocking their natural hair, and so little insight into how best to get your curly hair to thrive as opposed to just 'dealing' with it, that it's no wonder so many of us resort to whatever it is we need to do to manage.

While it's increasingly becoming more of a 'thing' for black women to wear their hair in its natural state – with blogs and YouTube channels increasingly dedicated to showing others how to care for and style natural hair – it's still far from normalised, and in the Middle East and its diaspora we're still a long way off.

Half-Moroccan, half-Egyptian model Imaan Hammam – who has appeared on the cover of American *Vogue* three times (natural hair and all!) and modelled for everyone from GUESS to H&M and Chanel – wears her curly hair beautifully. She is one of a growing number of women who increasingly give me courage to attempt to style my hair in similar ways rather than just scraping it back into a ponytail as the only possible alternative to a blow-dry.

Varied and nuanced ideals have long been found to have an impact on negative bias, and having positive role models can help counter this. Dove's 'Love Your Curls' campaign concluded that girls are seven times more likely to love their natural hair if the people around them do. I'm trying. While I still have some way to go in terms of embracing my curly hair, getting blow-dries has now become the exception instead of the rule. I've increasingly started wearing my curly hair with pride, no longer prone to feeling sheepish and self-conscious while doing so.

These days, when I'm in Egypt, I see more and more women wearing their hair naturally and there's an increasing number of Facebook groups dedicated to the cause, which post 'how to' videos about cutting and styling curly hair. I've subscribed to many of them and they've helped me realise that many of the challenges associated with curly hair are because mainstream haircare products are not designed with curly hair in mind, not necessarily because curly hair is that much more difficult to manage.

In recent months I've stocked my bathroom with a variety of different products I hadn't even heard of before. New shampoos and mousses and curl-defining creams by brands I hadn't known existed. And they actually make a difference! I increasingly catch myself admiring my curls instead of freaking out about them; I'm starting to realise they have a charm of their own.

The hair on my head is just the tip of the iceberg. For Middle Eastern women, grooming regimens and requirements extend far beyond just that. While we might be generations from the Ottoman harem – where, according to orientalised narratives, women would only leave their hair, eyebrows and eyelashes, waxing everything below the neck every three weeks – my own hair-removal routine is actually not too far off that, or from that of most Middle Eastern women I know. The only Middle Eastern women I know who don't think about body hair are those who have had laser hair removal on their entire bodies.

A smooth, hairless body is still the ideal dictated by the media around the world. In Arab culture, this is reportedly linked to Islam, which associates a lack of body hair with increased hygiene.[46] Regardless of the reasons behind it, the removal of body hair is a rite of passage, and one that is practised by all Middle Eastern women, everywhere. And often from a young age. While ripping burning wax off my pubic bone the other week, my waxing lady told me how the client just before me had been a nine-year-old Middle Eastern girl and how she had removed the hair from the girl's arms, legs and underarms, and threaded her upper lip and eyebrows.

My first thought was, 'woah, so young!' My next was a flashback of how insecure I had been at nine years old when I had first begun to notice how my body hair was so much darker and thicker than that of my majority white classmates. If I had been allowed, I surely would have done the same.

My memories of school swim classes are particularly vivid. I can still remember feeling marooned by the side of the pool in my black one-piece, overwhelmed by embarrassment while attempting to contort my body in a multitude of ways in an effort to hide as much as possible of the seemingly unrelentingly sprouting black hair. I remember being acutely aware of how different my furry covering was to the see-through blonde hair twinkling softly in the sunlight on the legs of my white classmates.

It would have been bad enough if I was the only one to notice, but it was pointed out every so often by other people. On a school trip around the age of twelve, I remember one of my friends pointing to the back of my neck and asking why I had hair *there*. She had hair there too, obviously, it's just that hers was blonde. I didn't realise that at the time, though, and I doubt she did either. I just felt like a gorilla. Mortified, I spent the rest of the weekend with my hair down and my arms and legs covered, trying to avoid giving her any further ammunition.

'It scars you for life when people point out these things to you,' says twenty-eight-year-old Iraqi-born, London-raised Haifa. 'I had a Croatian friend at school and I don't think she had one hair on her body. I used to always be jealous of that, to be honest, growing up . . . other girls just didn't have as much hair.'

'I was always really conscious about hair on my legs but, compared to other Arab girls, I wasn't even very hairy, which I was very lucky with,' Shams echoes. 'One of the girls with me in Arabic school was really hairy. [One day,] she was wearing shorts and this guy was like, "Ewwww, why do you have man legs?!" We were only thirteen and that hurt me and stuck with me, even though he didn't even say it to me. After that I thought, "I can never wear skirts again."'

As I soon learnt, the removal of body hair in the Middle East and its diaspora is a policed rite of passage. Removing my body hair, therefore, was a lot more complicated than just popping into Boots and buying myself a razor like my English friends had started to do. In fact, when I attempted to do just that, my mum cornered me with a rage that definitely didn't match the severity of the situation, shaking me awake in the middle of the night after unpacking my suitcase upon arrival in

Cairo, where she had discovered the contraband that was a pink Gillette razor. Like many people, she believed slicing the hair with a shaver would only cause it to grow back thicker – basically the worst thing that could happen, in her eyes.

Many Middle Eastern women are still devoted to ancient waxing practices dictating that the only appropriate way to remove body hair is via a plate of amber-coloured hard wax called *halawa*, which is often made at home out of sugar, lemon juice and water. Outside the MENA region, this is often called 'sugaring', although the pain it delivers is far from what that name implies.

Women have been removing their body hair for as far back as history is recorded. Across the world there have always been countless rituals and superstitions associated with body hair and its removal. As an article in *VICE* attests,[47] 'Ancient Egyptians used razors made of flint or bronze. They used beeswax as we use wax today. As far back as ancient Greece, pubic hair was seen as uncivilized, and hair removal was a class identifier. Women would remove their body hair with pumice stones, razors, tweezers and depilatory creams.' It continues: 'the painting of Venus by French painter William-Adolphe in the 1800s . . . depicted [the goddess] with no pubic hair, or body hair for that matter', while 'Charles Darwin's 1871 publication *The Descent of Man* linked body hair on humans to sexual, mental, and criminal deviance'. Indeed, a hairless body is pretty much always what has been considered desirable or 'sexy'.

Today, 99 per cent of women are said to have removed their body hair at one point or another,[48] but the numbers appear to be dropping. *Mintel* found that the number of young women in the West aged between eighteen and twenty-four who remove their underarm hair fell from 84 per cent in 2014 to 77 per cent in 2016, and those who removed their leg hair dropped from 91 per cent to 85 per cent.[49]

While 'feminist body hair' is becoming increasingly more of a 'thing' in the West, from pubic hair on American Apparel's mannequins[50] to the likes of Madonna and Miley Cyrus unabashedly flaunting their underarm hair, much emphasis is still placed on women around the world adhering to the hairless standards asserted by the media and the porn industry. Even today, when a model bares her unshaven legs in an advertising campaign she gets rape threats;[51] when Emma Watson says she has an oil that she uses on her pubic hair, seemingly all the news sources pick up on it like it's really important news[52]; when a picture is posted on social media of a line of hair snaking down from a woman's navel, Instagram bans it.[53] There is still uproar whenever women try to deviate from these hairless norms. For Arab women, however, deviating is rarely if ever an option. Undoubtedly, connotations of body hair among brown women are different to those for white women, due perhaps in part to the fact that the hair is dark and therefore visible, as opposed to what is often fair body hair on white women.

I have grown out my body hair only once in my life, aged nineteen, after splitting with my first long-term boyfriend. Actually, twice: I haven't even looked at a grooming product while writing this book. Both times it felt like a rebellion of sorts. But both times less so, perhaps, for the fact that I knew I would *never* let any potential partner see me like that. The best form of contraception, for me, has always been being unwaxed, as it automatically results in abstinence. Even with long-term boyfriends, in the inevitable growth period in between waxes, I will do everything in my power to prevent them from seeing me naked. I don't even really know who I'm doing it for anymore. I don't think it's for them. I'm not sure they would really care that much.

Having now had some moments of body-hair growth, I personally do find it more hygienic to be hairless, but it feels more of a conscious choice now I've tried both ways.

Growing up, it was alienating to not see myself or anyone who looked like me reflected in the world around me, neither in or out of the classroom. This feeling of being 'other' grew as my body started to develop into a shape that was not widely catered for in the high-street stores I liked to frequent with my friends. Fashion and make-up brands the world over, the advertisements that promote them and the stores that stock them have long perpetuated narrow, Westernised beauty ideals. It didn't take me long to realise that the popular styles, sizes, shades and shapes in the stores catered to a European body type, i.e. not me, not mine. A universality had been assumed, and I was not included.

Looking through old photos recently, I found some that well encapsulated the struggle; white concealer glaring in patches on my face, weird eyeshadow colours that did nothing but further muddy the dark brown of my eyes, and too-tight trousers that threatened to burst at the seams in my attempt to spill my Middle Eastern, 'bottom heavy' self into them.

'Growing up (and to this day) I was very self-conscious of my body shape, as it was very different to everyone else's,' Shams tells me. 'Miss Sixty had the coolest jeans at the time, and I could never find the right size! When it comes to dresses and different styles of clothes, I still to this day face an issue.'

It was only in my mid-twenties that I began to master the art of online shopping or getting dressed without panicking that the clothes never looked quite the same on me as they did on the size-zero girls who were without fail chosen to advertise them. Growing up, the size of my bum, thighs and legs was my biggest concern. My attempts to get them to resemble anything like the seemingly endless, skinny legs that featured in magazines, advertising and on the TV were all futile.

Offset by Jennifer Lopez's ascendance to what was considered desirable circa 1999, it was at least another ten years before – aided massively by the likes of the Kardashians – that body image really hit the mainstream. And while, as of late, the Kardashians have become caricatures of sorts, barely able to keep up with themselves, in the years since they first emerged on to our TV screens, half-Armenian Kim and her sisters have pushed the culture and the aesthetics of beauty far away from the standard fashion-model look that was so pervasive when I was growing up.

As journalist Charlie Brinkhurst-Cuff writes in a piece titled 'My body shape may be in fashion just now, but for how long?',[54] 'Although . . . I don't believe that body parts should be seen as fashionable or unfashionable commodities, I know that part of the reason I've become more accepting of my own body shape is because it's become societally desirable.'

Testament to the power of nuanced representation, the Kardashians and others like them have ushered in ideals that have helped me and thousands like me find beauty in the colourings and shapes we were born in.

Like Charlie, I can't remember when I stopped hearing 'Does my bum look big in this?' but these days it seems you can't have a butt too big (the likes of Primark even facilitate with their padded underwear), and thighs like mine are now considered 'thick' instead of 'fat'. Lyrics serenading big butts feature pretty much in every popular song, Thicc Thursday has become a commonly used hashtag, and there are tons of influencers with followers numbering in the millions who have found fame simply for 'flaunting' their bubble butts.

Social media has, as with everything else, done a lot to democratise the ideals, increasing the scope of what is visible and, as a result, of what is considered beautiful. In a study Dove conducted on the impact social media has on beauty standards,[55] they concluded that women are increasingly becoming their own media creators and influencing the beauty conversation, whether that's by 'rating beauty products, giving each other advice or sharing personal beauty/body image stories, or posting their own images'.

Following the trend, fashion has started catering for more diverse body shapes, with an increased focus on high-street to high-end brands catering to all shapes and sizes. Diversity is the buzzword of the day, and during fashion weeks and in beauty and fashion campaigns, models are more diverse across the board. A growing number of brands are catering to a wider range of skin tones, and different body types and women of all ages are increasingly being celebrated.

But the opposite could also be said to be true. In reality, these new ideals can in turn become unattainable and dangerous. Butt enhancements, for example, have been rising by as much as 15 per cent a year since 2013,[56] and the word 'diversity' has seemingly turned into a corporate buzzword in and of itself, often used to the point of redundancy. Certainly, much criticism is levelled at brands for what are often regarded as disingenuous PR stunts and token castings.

We may still have some way to go, but that's not to say that real change has not already been achieved. The rise of social media allows people to hold everyone accountable. What's more, the more 'minority' gatekeepers there are across all levels and industries, the more accurate, varied and nuanced representation will become an afterthought rather than something that needs to be so mathematically calculated.

The world's ideals of beauty have undoubtedly shifted. Scientists from the Boston University School of Medicine compared *People* magazine's 1990 'World's Most Beautiful' list to 2017's list, placing particular emphasis on features like age, sex, race, skin type, hair and eye colour. Results found that the list progressively included more people with darker skin, as well as older people. The proportion of celebrities of 'non-white races' increased from 24 per cent in 1990 to 40 per cent in 2017.[57]

A few years ago, I realised the tide was truly turning when, standing in line to board a flight with my boyfriend at the time, I overheard a group of girls in the queue behind us saying, 'Look at that black guy with his "commercial girlfriend".' It was around the time Kim Kardashian and

Kanye West married and it made me laugh that almost fifteen years after the popular girls in my class had found the fact that someone found me desirable so confusing, my brand of beauty was now considered 'commercial'. It's certainly not something I could ever have imagined when I was growing up and being told I was not attractive for those very same characteristics and colourings. But I do wish I had known then what I know now: that the concept of beauty holds too much power; that it doesn't really matter what my classmates or what anyone else thought of me; that feeling comfortable in my own skin – regardless of what the outside world says or does or thinks – should always be the overriding ambition.

Of course, it's easier to say that with hindsight; to say that now I am the 'commercial', now that I am older and not held hostage by the judgements of others. But as I've become more comfortable with who I am and what it is I have to offer, I can say that I have stopped caring so much about what I see in the mirror.

That's not to say that I don't like to look good, that I don't enjoy taking selfies or posting them on social media, or that I don't take pride in my appearance. I do. But I take pride in far more than just that.

Over the years I have become a better friend and daughter, a better sister and human. I've realised that I have far more to offer the world than just what I look like; that what I look like is actually the least interesting thing about me. And I am increasingly thankful for that. Indeed, I am shallow *and* deep, and it's the time I spend in the deep end that keeps me from drowning.

Chapter 3
When You Learn Who You're
Supposed to Be

I was twelve and my family and I had been living in London for five years when my mother announced that my brother and I would be moving to Cairo with her at the end of the year, leaving my dad behind. She didn't say how long we would be away, just that her own mother was ill and she wanted us to be close to her.

I was devastated. A middling human on the scale of popularity, I was by no means killing it at pre-teen life in the way I had hoped I would be, but for the most part I was still happy with the way things were.

The last time we had moved country – from Geneva to London for my dad's new job – I was eight years old and I had hated it. Hated saying goodbye to my friends and packing up all my things to travel across continents to a country where I knew I'd have to start over.

It's a special kind of uncomfortable when you're outgoing but also very, very shy. Starting over as the new girl at school has therefore always been my idea of actual hell. It never got any easier. I have done it five times. The hardest part was always the beginning, the first few weeks or months where you had to figure out who everyone was, who would be your friend and who would just pretend while twisting your words and starting fires with them in the hallways. It felt like a jungle every time.

I had wished I was a boy. It would have been so much easier to make friends, I thought, if I could just run on to the football pitch and dribble around a ball to make friends, rather than having to take part in the strange courting rituals between girls that seemed to be a constant no matter which school or which continent.

At my current school, it had started to feel like I had just about made it out the other side. I knew my way around now; knew which teachers would let me give my homework in late and which would not take any shit; I had a close group of friends who made the jungle feel a little less savage; I had my beloved books and a Nintendo 64 games console in my room; I had parents who fought with each other *all the time* but who loved me just the same.

While I was familiar with Cairo, due to the fact we had been there every school holiday, I was still livid at the thought of leaving my life in London behind. In defiance, I refused to eat, researched boarding schools and came up with 101 different reasons why I should stay behind in London with my dad. Nothing worked.

Eventually weakening in hope and resolve, I asked if I could at least visit the school I was due to attend in Cairo on my next school holiday, to see what the hell I was getting myself into. Despite my initial reservations (and my very best stubborn efforts), I remember feeling immediately struck by a sense of home as soon as I walked into the British school in Cairo, a private school that occupied a building in Zamalek, just ten minutes from the Nile. I already had a few family friends in Cairo, most of whom attended the school, so it softened my initial trepidation at the visit. But I still hadn't been expecting to feel quite as comfortable as I did.

Walking through the gates of the school, I looked around to see a playground filled with hundreds of kids, all of whom looked a bit like me. In London, I had almost grown accustomed to looking like an anomaly; I hadn't realised how nice it might be not to feel like one.

Slowly, eyes swivelled to take me in: the new girl. Smiles glimmered on faces and within minutes I found myself enveloped in hug after hug, kids from all grades introduced themselves to me, telling me our mums were friends or that they had seen me on the beach that previous summer, always adding that if there was anything – *anything* at all – I needed, I should come and find them.

I spent the day attending classes and quickly and seamlessly bonding with my future classmates, many of whom I soon learnt were my extended cousins or had family histories that intertwined with mine as far back as hundreds of years. Many even had great-grandparents who had been raised with my great-grandparents. It was a heady, humbling, grounding experience that made me feel like my new friends were my family and I was immediately theirs, just through the simple fact of also being Egyptian. It filled me with a sense unlike anything I had ever felt before. Like all the things that had made me feel 'other' in London were the same things that, in Cairo, I didn't need to explain. My point of difference here was my exposure to a life in London; in the UK, it was *everything*.

Holiday over, I returned to London to spend the remaining months of the school year hunched over the family computer, exchanging messages with my future classmates on MSN Messenger.

I had made friends and even a boyfriend of sorts – my first one. We were still children and they were all childish pairings, but in London none of the boys had ever reciprocated any of my feelings. One of them had even come up to me after class one day and emphasised that I should *please* stop telling people I liked him: 'You're ruining my reputation,' he said. It now felt amazing to have so instantly been deemed one of the popular crowd in the Cairo school; one of the girls desired by the boys and 'cool enough' to be friends with the popular girls.

But it was a tough year. My grandmother was not well and her illness was taking a huge toll on my mum, who idolised her. Mum was also finding it difficult to be so far away from my dad and having to deal with my brother and me on her own. She took it out on us often, and so – in an attempt to avoid her, as well as to revel in my new life – I spent a lot of time outside the house, making up reasons I needed to stay late after school so I could hang out with my new friends, growing into a newer version of myself.

It wasn't all smooth transitioning, though, and differences came into focus quickly, as did the stereotypes that came with the fact that I had grown up in London. It was something experienced by a couple of the Egyptian girls I spoke to, who had also moved back to Egypt in their teen years.

'I was twelve or thirteen and it felt like everyone just automatically thought that because I had lived in a country where people openly had sex, I was like that too,' Selina told me.

'I was one of the only girls in my grade and I was like a white girl; pale, blue eyes, blonde hair, in the middle of all these sexually frustrated guys,' Sondos said. 'There was one guy who spoke English so we chatted a bit in the classroom, then the next week people were making up rumours that we had had sex and he had come to my house and we had done all of these things.

'There were so many rumours made up about me and it was so easy for people to do, because there were already all of these assumptions that because I was from London, I must have already had sex with five guys,' she continues. 'They thought they would get away with it, or that I would like it.'

⚊

Ramadan, which that year was only a few months into the school year, was also particularly illuminating and alienating for me. My family don't fast, nor do we celebrate Eid (or Christmas, for that matter; growing up, I'd always make my birthday a huge deal because it was the only thing I got). Mine was a pretty secular household. I remember one year, I asked my dad if I could fast and his response was, 'How are you planning on concentrating in class if you haven't had anything to eat or drink?' I saw his logic. I had tried once and had fainted almost instantly; so I didn't fast that year, either. Or any year since.

People at school took it badly. To be fair, I probably shouldn't have taken to the playground at lunch break with my slice of pizza and can of Coke and appeared to enjoy it so very much, while the rest of the school was starving and staring at me, but I genuinely did not even think about it.

Fasting had never been a thing at school in London, and it hadn't even occurred to me that everyone else might be adhering. I spent the rest of the month fielding questions from kids asking me if I was Muslim. I started telling them I was Christian so they would leave me alone.

It was my first glimpse of the judgement that would come from those around me; opinions on how I should live my life; on what I should do or refrain from doing. In the Middle East, society and culture are often their own governments. They have their own judge and jury, and its citizens – both men and women – are expected to abide by the spoken and unspoken rules that dictate everything from what you should want to how you should behave and your place in the world.

The word '3aib', which starts with a guttural sound present in much of the Arabic language (and is almost impossible to say, let alone spell out, if you're not Arab), can be pronounced sort of like 'ahhyb'. It became a familiar word in my vocabulary; a catch-all term used to describe behaviour that is 'shameful' and frowned upon by society. It's often used interchangeably with 'haram', which means 'forbidden'. It's a real, almost tangible thing, the judgement, and it lays thickest at the feet of women. As Egyptian feminist Nawal El Saadawi wrote in *The*

Hidden Face of Eve,[58] 'The education that a female child receives in Arab society is a series of continuous warnings about things that are supposed to be harmful, forbidden, shameful or outlawed.'

In patriarchal societies like many in the Middle East, as a woman, you're guilty by the pure fact you have a vagina. You learn that you should be demure, in case you offend; cover up, in case you turn on; be quiet, in case you overstep. Behaviour is policed militantly through gossip, or even just the fear of inciting gossip. Everyone is the jury.

I didn't notice it immediately, of course, nor really until much later. My concerns that year and for most of my adolescent years centred around my social life, and why in the hell my parents wouldn't stop shouting. I can't say I cared about anything other than the thoughts and feelings churning inside of me.

My first hint of this jury was when, to my maternal grandfather's shock, I appeared to always have plans after lunch at his house. 'What cabaret are you going to now?' he'd ask me, looking at my mum in confusion.

'In Jordan, to be a firstborn female child came with added pressure – to be *m'addaleh* [spoilt], *sitt el-banāt* [a lady], *btiswi thuglik dhahab* [worth your own weight in gold],' wrote Diya Abdo in an article for *The Paris Review*.[59]

'Whenever my grandmother uses this phrase to describe some woman or other, I keep a tally of the qualities she admires,' she continued. 'When she uses it to describe my mother . . . it means that my mother had listened, obeyed, self-abnegated – the butter would not melt in her mouth . . .

'When she uses it to describe her daughter-in-law, it means that daughter-in-law is content with her lot, her dirty laundry unaired – her secrets in a well,' she wrote. 'When she uses it to describe her neighbour, it means that the neighbour is chaste, never flirting, never yielding to men's plying compliments and denuding gazes – as pure as yoghurt.

'But most importantly, to be worth your weight in gold means that your *seira*, your narrative, your story, is not on every tongue.'

It's a heavy burden I am well familiar with, and one that is placed on Middle Eastern women everywhere: to be a 'lady' and ultimately the guardian of a family's honour; a well-raised, respectable, 'good' Arab girl. It's considered a reflection of our entire family lineage.

'Family members have a collective responsibility for protecting the unity and honour of the family,' wrote Rawan Ibrahim in *Bad Girls of the Arab World*.[60] 'The actions of an individual reflect not on that person alone but the family as a whole, and therefore the reputation and needs of the collective take precedence over individual needs,' she added.

As journalist Katherine Zoepf, who lived in Syria for a number of years, concludes in her book *Excellent Daughters*: 'The lines that separate the individual from the society to which he or she belongs are drawn differently here. People were assumed to be responsible to one another in ways that would be difficult to imagine in much of the West.'[61]

The threat of society's judgement and the fear of what people might say – especially in regards to women – is so strong that it can impact your own behaviour and reaction to things, even if you don't really care yourself. My mum has perhaps a million times given me 'What will people say?' as a reason for why I can't or shouldn't do something. To her mind, it is the most valid of concerns.

Living in Cairo that year, I learnt that my parents weren't the guardians of the universe, that ultimately it didn't matter what they thought or what they themselves would be OK with me doing – the opinion of *society* mattered more. It trumped them.

I learnt that, as a girl, it was a weird tightrope to walk because your behaviour (as well as what you wear, who you talk to, how you talk to them, if you swear, if you smoke, and on and on) all impacts your reputation, and your reputation is *everything*.

'It was way more intense in Suez than in Cairo because everyone there is very old school and family orientated,' Sondos told me. 'Some girls didn't even shake a guy's hand for the mere thought of, "He's going to think I'm a slut because we touched hands", or "If I squeeze his hand too hard maybe that's like how I'd squeeze his dick." Really intense thought processes . . .

'I went from being so comfortable in my skin and so confident to being almost a recluse,' she continued. 'Growing up in London it was like: yes, I'm a girl and you're a boy – that's cool, whatever, whereas in Suez it was: "You're a girl. That means that you can't drink, you can't smoke, you can't wear a short skirt, you can't kiss guys on the cheek . . ." There were all of these restrictions just because I was a girl.'

Many of the Middle Eastern women I spoke to told me they are often given that line as valid reasoning for why they can't do a multitude of things – from going out at night, smoking, or swearing, to hanging out with certain people and more.

Curious, I took to my Instagram story to ask my female Arab followers if, while growing up, they had felt like their male family members were allowed to do more than they were. Of course, it's not the most representative sample in the world, but the results were interesting: 78 per cent of respondents to my poll said yes.

'My brothers would go out and come home at 4 or 5 a.m. and no one would say a thing, whereas if I or my female cousins get home a minute past ten we'd receive lecture upon lecture,' Sarra, a twenty-year-old Tunisian told me.

Rahma, a twenty-five-year-old half-Egyptian, half-Polish Londoner told me she had faced similar double standards with her older brother. 'My dad openly says, "He's a guy", and that really hurts because obviously I respect my dad and the things he does, but that's just such a barrier. No matter how kind or loving he is – that's just a disagreement we'll always have.'

Some women told me that their parents often allowed them extra freedoms if they were with their brothers or male cousins, considering them safe and protected and free from gossip. I know many girls who use and have used this loophole. One of my friends in Egypt recently brought her brother along to a bachelorette party we were on, because it was the only way she was allowed to come.

In reality, the same cocooning safety you get from the fact that everyone knows everyone and has done so for generations is the same thing that can make you feel stifled, because everyone also knows everything about everyone. And has opinions on it. Wherever you are there is someone watching you and judging your conduct.

'The inevitable battle with the bawab [doorman] was one of the things I found weirdest about moving back to Cairo,' Selina told me. 'As anyone who has lived in Cairo would know, the bawab is central to your life; he guards your building, will run any and all nearby errands for you, and also knows every single detail about your comings and goings. He felt the need to ask me every time I left my apartment what time I would be back.'

The bawab is part of this invisible jury. Just the knowledge of his presence and scrutiny is enough to impact how you live your life and the sorts of things you do (or don't do).

Nothing is more policed than women's sexuality and virginity. There are tons of sayings in the region that reflect the importance placed on a woman's chastity. Things like: 'A woman is like a piece of candy; if you threw it on the floor, would you still want to eat it?'

While slut-shaming and sexual double standards are not just prevalent in Arab culture but all around the world, in the Middle East the burden that falls on women to abstain from being sexual creatures is an overwhelming one. Sex is illegal before marriage in Egypt and in many other Arab countries, a rule that is policed by law, by the media and by local gossip.

In a study looking into attitudes towards pre-marital sex in the region, a third or more of young men said they are sexually active before marriage, while upward of 80 per cent of women said they are not.[62] This firstly raises the question of who these young men are having sex with; secondly, it proves that not only are people indeed having sex before marriage, but that women are far more reluctant to admit it.

For men, being sexual is considered a positive attribute of masculinity. As Samira told me, her older brother was always allowed to have girls sleep over. 'My mum used to say things to him like, "I know you're a man but please don't [have sex] when I'm at home." But for me? No way! It would be impossible.'

For women, losing your virginity before marriage can have dire consequences – although, of course, many do. In the most extreme examples, husbands are urged to display the bed sheet after their wedding night, to prove their wife was actually a virgin and had therefore bled (even though it is largely a myth that you bleed when you lose your virginity), while gynaecologists are also often asked to provide certificates of virginity to a bride's future husband prior to the wedding.

While these sorts of extreme bloody requirements are these days not practised so much outside of rural villages and in the more conservative sectors, the after-effects of the ideologies behind the practices still linger. Sex is cloaked in a degree of shame, even when you are having it.

Many Middle Eastern girls get around the issue of their virginity by engaging in what Shereen El Feki calls[63] 'alternative forms of sex: anal sex, oral sex or "superficial relations"', which come with their own set of ironies, including creating quite a few pregnant virgins because, as sex education would teach you, pre-come is a 'thing' too.

Living in Cairo that year, aged thirteen, myself and many of the girls were very conscious of our interactions with the opposite sex. It had long been drilled into us that our virginities were something we were supposed to keep for our husbands, and – although I was always allowed to run around freely with my friends, many of whom were boys – many girls' interactions with the opposite sex were severely restricted.

It was a weird sort of hypocrisy, though, because we did want to be 'sexy', to a point. Most of the girls, including me, would undo the top buttons on the shirt of our school uniforms, stuffing the pockets with everything from our phones to cash and chewing-gum packets in an effort to weigh it down and show some cleavage.

The boundaries were invisible, and often pretty inconsistent. If you were to stray beyond them, you were in trouble. On one particularly memorable occasion, a girl in class got called a whore for the entire year, because of a rumour that she had given a guy a hand-job on the staircase after school one day. Who knows whether it was true or not, but she never lived it down. It was mostly the girls doing the name-calling.

In another interesting contradiction of Arab life, it was in Cairo that I experienced many teenage rites of passage for the first time. I drank alcohol and smoked a cigarette for the first time that year, followed swiftly by my first joint. I kissed a boy, lied to my parents, got grounded, and witnessed my friends in physical fights – all for the first time. (Fighting was a thing the boys liked to do in Cairo, I soon realised. As I saw more and more fights, I began to see the connections: it was almost always something to do with their pride, an important aspect of masculinity in the Arab world.)

I had just turned thirteen the summer before moving to Cairo, so my age had more than a little to do with these rites of passage, of course. Whenever I'd go back to London to visit my dad that year, my friends were getting up to many of the same sorts of things. But there were undoubtedly a few other factors thrown in, too, including that it's always more fun to do something when you're not supposed to do it. In fact, in Egypt, as in many Arab countries, there is a thriving, roaring underbelly of debauchery, particularly in the more affluent sections of society.

As Lea, who has moved back and forth between London and Lebanon numerous times, puts it: 'It makes sense to me that the most repressed, closed-minded and backwards places are the wildest. It's a reaction.'

I was also very angry at my parents, and subsequently at the world, which made it very easy to throw myself into doing all of those things, and with relish. Mere months after we had arrived in Cairo, my mum told me we would be moving back to London at the end of that school year. I was furious that she seemed to be treating me and my life like a piece of luggage. Life overdramatically felt forever torturous and unfair, and I often acted accordingly.

I had boyfriends throughout the entire year we lived in Cairo but, at thirteen, they were mostly just boys I spent hours talking to on the phone or sitting next to at shisha cafés, holding hands. There was nowhere really to do anything more than that, and even the thought of taking it further felt so wrong and made me feel panicky. In Egypt, as in many Arab countries, even a kiss or any public display of affection is illicit, and illegal on the streets, so even harmless interactions and natural rites of passage with the opposite sex are hard to come by, making the whole thing feel quite sordid at times.

I can't really remember my first kiss, only that it happened. It was during a game of spin the bottle, the first time I ever smoked a joint of hashish, the first time I had ever played, the first time I was alone in a house with my friends and our friends who were boys. I almost swallowed my tongue in panic as the bottle slowed its spin and settled on me. That's all I can remember. Panic. Not even who was on the other end of the bottle. Then it being over already.

My second kiss was in the elevator going up to my apartment where my boyfriend was dropping me off, the week before I moved back to London. We had been dating for months but had never kissed. We rode up and down in the elevator as we gained courage and he tentatively leant over to brush his lips against mine. The creaky old elevator was dirty and made me feel dirty in a way, too. It was not at all how or where I imagined my first proper kiss would be.

In Arab culture, it's definitely not a thing to be able to go to your boyfriend or girlfriend's house, and in many countries it's illegal to stay in a hotel room with someone of the opposite sex who isn't your brother, father or spouse. The rules are strictly enforced, leaving few options.

As we got older, many of my friends took to faking marriage certificates or renting out two hotel rooms, only to leave one abandoned in the middle of the night so they could spend a night with their partners. A lot of sneaking around needs to be done so you can do what you want to do. And that's if you have the money, the means, and the relative freedom.

I didn't fully realise it at the time, but you feel it acutely living there. The shame, the secrecy; people publicly abiding by societal rules while privately rebelling or burning up inside. The censorship is everywhere.

I remember the first time I went to the cinema in Cairo. Cosying down in my seat, a bucket of popcorn in my lap, I was just getting into the movie when there was a sort of jostle on the screen and the sound cut, just for a split second. I looked to my left to see if my friend's expression would reveal whether anything weird had happened: nothing. Except that the man and woman who had just now been on screen and had looked like they might be about to kiss were walking down the road. Had they kissed? 'Is something wrong with the movie?' I asked my friend. 'Oh yeah,' she said. 'They censor movies in Egypt.'

When an Egyptian TV presenter recently discussed the possibility of a woman becoming a single mother on her show, she was jailed for three years and the show suspended, accused of 'outraging public decency' and promoting 'immoral ideas that are alien to our society and threaten the fabric of the Egyptian family'.

Indeed, the censorship and painting of normal desires and needs as dirty and morally corrupt is everywhere, and it inevitably leads to sexual repression, which plays out in all sorts of nasty ways. In Egypt, you can't walk in the street without getting whistled at or cat-called; sexual harassment is ever-present, with 99 per cent of women saying they have experienced it at one point or another.[64]

I'm well accustomed to dodging the calls of 'ya 3asal!' (oh, you're sweet like honey) and the expressions on the faces of the men watching my every move when I walk in the Cairo streets. Their mouths hang almost comically open, despite the fact that I always make sure to dress conservatively, as well as to actively limit my time outdoors. It happened the year I was living there, too, aged thirteen – age is no restriction. I never wear tight-fitting clothes or have my shoulders, cleavage or legs bared. But it makes no difference. In a country where an increasing number of women are putting on the hijab (many just in an effort to avoid these everyday affronts), any amount of female flesh on display is too much.

But, just as with everything else in Egypt and in the Arab world, there are two sides to reality. Enter into any of the luxury hotels or take a drive to Egypt's north coast (or numerous other stunning beaches) where my family and many of our family friends have beach houses, and you'll find bikinis and skin and 'debauchery' (or overexcited displays of semi-freedom, whatever you want to call it) everywhere. In some spaces in Egypt – like on many of those north-coast beaches as well as in high-end venues the country over – women with hijabs are increasingly refused entry.[65] Being in Egypt can literally feel like being in two parallel, opposing worlds simultaneously.

If you have the means, and know where to go, being in Egypt can feel like being anywhere else in the world; maybe even the *best* place in the world. The houses and beaches are beautiful, you're surrounded by friends who feel like family, and absolutely everything you could ever want is at your disposal. It's there where it can feel like you're free from the constraints, momentarily.

'Even moving to Cairo from Suez for university was a culture shock for me,' Sondos told me. 'I thought everyone in Egypt was like everyone in Suez and then I go to uni and my first encounter is my roommate who I'm sharing a bathroom with crying to me about a guy that she had had anal sex with the night before! I was so confused as to where I was.

'For a while, going from such a closed-minded place to such an open-minded place made me feel really uncomfortable,' she continued. 'I didn't know how I was supposed to behave, how to talk to people. Can I say I smoke and drink? In Suez, when I had thought people were open-minded and I would open up to them, the next thing I knew everyone in school would be talking about me.'

The opposing messages are disorienting. The sense of two completely different worlds can often make you feel as though you're in a little bubble being chauffeured from one gated community to another, through the streets, into clubs where you can get drunk and spend the equivalent of your driver's monthly salary on shots, then back into the car and back home to sleep it off.

A few years ago, I went to a club in Cairo with a few of my friends. We got drunk and danced like we could have been anywhere in the world. A few hours later, I stumbled out and ordered an Uber with another friend, who was staying with me that night. We folded our limbs through the doors of the car, reeking of alcohol, and repeated the address to the driver. As soon as we got into the car, he blasted the Quran through the car speakers, turning the volume all the way up as if the recitations would drive the alcohol from our bodies. They almost did. As he sped through the streets I held my hands over my mouth so I wouldn't vomit my tequila shots back up all over his car.

Although alcohol is considered haram by most Muslims, a significant minority do drink, often drinking enough to make up for the ones who don't. When adults who never drink alcohol are removed from the equation, Chad and the United Arab Emirates – both Muslim-majority countries – rank highest on the global table of alcohol consumption.[66] Egypt must surely be somewhere pretty high up on that list too.

Of course, 'getting fucked up' is common parlance across the world, in teenage years and beyond. Britain was a boozy country, and I had seen my fair share of people throwing up outside pubs and swaying barefoot down the street. But in Cairo it looked and felt different. It wasn't allowed so it happened more discreetly and more desperately, with a certain kind of urgency.

The drinking culture in Egypt has, as with much else, become a little more haram, and is regarded differently now to how it was in the 1940s and 1950s, when Cairo was considered a cosmopolitan city ranked among the likes of London, New York and Paris, as my grandparents like to tell me. But buying and drinking alcohol – in affluent neighbourhoods especially – is still socially acceptable and effortless. My friends and I often frequent restaurants, nightclubs and bars that serve your chosen poison at a high price. It's just a little harder to get and a little more expensive.

Alcohol is just the tip of the iceberg, though, when it comes to debauchery in Egypt and in many other Arab countries. As of 2018, the rate of drug addiction in Egypt is said to be twice the global average, with 10 per cent of Egypt's almost 100-million-strong population said to be addicted to drugs.[67] Hashish in particular is very common. A report published by the *Daily Telegraph* in 2017 ranked Egypt twenty-fifth out of the thirty countries with the highest rate of cannabis consumption worldwide. Over 6 per cent of the population were considered regular smokers.[68]

'There's not much else to do here,' one of my friends in Egypt confided. 'We don't have that many bars, and the ones we do have are super-expensive,' she said, adding that her group of friends often take cocaine or MDMA on the weekends and smoke hashish during the week.

Growing up in Cairo, we'd wait until our parents went out, then roll joints and make our way to the balconies that overlooked the roaring city, lighting up and chatting. Often, we'd hang out on street corners, lifting our bodies on to the roofs of strangers' cars where we'd spend hours talking and laughing. Everything seemed like a good idea. We'd put hash into shishas, create bongs out of plastic water bottles or apples. It seemed almost like it was a part of the culture. Everyone was doing it, young and old.

But despite it being so common, there are often strict laws around drugs in the Middle East. Dubai famously has a death penalty, and in Egypt there are no formalised custodial sentences, meaning that time served is set at the judge's discretion. If you get caught with larger quantities, it can be perceived as dealing, which can lead to twenty-five years in jail, or death.

In Egypt, as with many Arab countries, there are very clear class divides, meaning that if you have money, you can mostly get away with anything by using a 'wasta' – essentially, utilising well-connected people your family may know, if not a good old-fashioned bribe. I've heard plenty of stories of people getting caught smoking, and escaping arrest by simply breaking off a piece of their stash to give to the policeman, who would gratefully accept it and be on his way.

Even in Saudi Arabia, arguably the strictest country in the region – where women have only recently been allowed to drive and can be jailed for socialising with men outside their family – there is a thriving, throbbing party culture.

Across the region, I have seen, experienced and heard plenty of stories. The full range of worldly temptations is available: alcohol, drugs, sex, whatever you want, and often in excess, just all behind closed doors. What you're supposed to be doing and what you are actually doing are worlds apart. Implicit here is that as long as you're not too obvious about what you get up to, you can get away with it.

For women, this can be particularly confusing because the lines are not clear-cut and the rules tend to vary. For example, if you have a boyfriend you are automatically expected to start behaving in ways that 'respect' him. This isn't in terms of obvious things like refraining from cheating on him or anything as straightforward as that, but consists of a far more complicated set of variables. Even some of my most open-minded male friends in Egypt often change when they have a girlfriend, suddenly expecting her to stop smoking, standing too close to men while talking to them or being 'too friendly', as well as wearing 'revealing' clothes, simply because she is now his girlfriend. Many speak openly about finding a 'good' girl to marry, as if those things could be mutually exclusive. Sadly, in the minds of many, they are – and virginity is the first and most important indicator of this. My friends and I jokingly call this being 'Masry', which translates to being 'Egyptian' and essentially refers to men who have restrictive ideas of what a 'good' woman, 'good' girlfriend and 'good' wife should be – the same ideas that the invisible jury lives by.

It's not just limited to Egyptians, though, and is in fact an Arab mentality. It's actually a topic that comes up again and again with my Middle Eastern friends in London: where to find an Arab guy that isn't 'too Arab', that isn't 'Masry' in that way.

Certainly, these judgements all felt very important when I was younger, and I remember being extremely conscious of who was around me when I did things like light a cigarette, aware that this was something 'bad' girls did. (I'm not sure if the eye of judgement is less severe these days, or if it just matters less to me, because now that I live in London I am less indebted to the opinions of Egyptian society. Having grown up here, I suspect I am considered British enough to get away with crossing these invisible lines of what is and isn't socially acceptable.) At the time, I was too angry and too young to really understand. I wasn't yet able to gauge why or what these rules were that impacted my social life or my perceived sense of freedom, let alone differentiate between who was setting those rules – my mother or the invisible jury.

Moving back to London from Cairo felt like absolutely the worst thing that could ever happen to me. It is only now I look back with gratitude, both for my move to Cairo and my return to London.

As Sondos put it: 'I'm glad I moved there because I would never have met any of my friends who are literally my family, I would never have had friendships like I do now if I had not moved to Egypt . . .

'Arab friendships are different, there's something about being born into Arab blood that just makes you more loving and caring and nurturing,' she continued, echoing my thoughts with every word. 'Friends are like extended family and you always feel welcome in their houses and their parents are so generous. Even if you don't have money . . . even people in the streets. If there's a car crash in Cairo, you don't need to worry about dying alone because the whole street will stop and run to your car and die with you. There's a sense of nurturing and caring and loving people and we're all a team, even if we're not a team.'

I agree. There's a certain family bond and loyalty inherent in Arab culture that plays out in the most beautiful ways in its friendships. As Gamilla put it: 'No one is ever left alone. You'll never have no one call for your birthday or end up in a hospital alone. You always, always have your friends and family.'

Living in Cairo that year gave me that. It further instilled in me many beautiful proponents of Arab culture: to be kind and generous, hospitable, to have good manners and to respect family and elders, among other things. But it simultaneously made me all the more aware of the invisible jury, the one that to this day informs me what Egyptian society expects of me. It's ever present, even if these days I mostly choose to ignore it when its ideals don't chime with my own.

Chapter 4
When You Can't Be Who You're Supposed to Be

The desire to be 'popular' altered the course of my adolescent years on numerous occasions, but definitely when it came to deciding where I would go to school when we moved back to London. Because after gallivanting around Cairo with all my friends, I just couldn't bear to go back to a school in which I had felt that hiding out in the library was the best option for surviving.

So while my brother slotted back into the school we had both attended before moving to Cairo, I asked my parents if I could go elsewhere. And that's how I found myself at a Church of England, all-girls' private school, not far from where my dad had been living for the last year, and where we would soon join him.

I often compare my years at that school, which I attended from the age of fourteen up to my graduation at eighteen, to the movie *Mean Girls*, released the summer of my first year of attendance. I was the Lindsay Lohan character. There are numerous parallels that can be drawn. I had just moved from Egypt (read: Africa) and, shortly after my arrival, I was inducted into the Mean Girls crew until I was harshly spat back out. But that's a story for the next chapter.

I spent the first few months crying. That's how I remember it now, anyway. A notebook of old poems I had written that year confirms the memory. I spent all my time on MSN Messenger with my friends in Egypt and went back to visit every few months. I hated my parents for making me move back to London. I could barely stand to look at them. I couldn't have cared less about making new friends – I already had my friends, and they were a five-hour flight away. I couldn't bring myself to pay attention in class, to care about anything other than how furious I was to be back in London. I could have killed someone.

Time passed and I eventually connected with a few girls. Most of my class was English but there was a smattering of other ethnicities, and my first friends were originally Polish, Chinese and English, respectively. Having exchanged email addresses, I would tentatively message them on MSN from the safety of my room at night, forging digital friend-ships that would naturally extend to the classroom and the playground the next day. I've always felt braver online, behind a computer screen, where I could measure my words, layer them one on top of the other in a way that would safely and accurately convey what I wanted to say.

We'd take the bus home from school and I would detour at least half an hour out of my way for us to go to McDonald's for a cheese-burger and fries, or to buy Krispy Kremes from Harrods.

At some point, the ringleader of the Mean Girls – let's call her Regina George in a nod to her movie namesake – extended her talons, pinging me a message one evening. 'Come back to mine after school tomorrow,' she wrote. 'Sure, babe!' I answered. 'My name is not babe,' came the response. My heart flip-flopped.

She had blonde hair and was from Kuwait and she often littered her sentences with Arabic. Being in her house made me feel a little bit closer to Egypt in a way, and we bonded over being Middle Eastern. We wrote each other letters, long odes we'd spend entire classes pen-ning, and soon I ate my lunch on the Mean Girls table and I laughed with them about the other girls in the class and made plans for what we would do over the coming weekend and what we would wear and which boys we might meet. She had a cousin who was a few years older and we often hung around him and his friends, smoking weed and drinking Bacardi Breezers, rolling our T-shirts up into crop tops and hanging on the rude boys' every word.

After school and before exam period we'd go to the local library. This was a fiction we'd sell our parents (it wasn't that the library didn't exist, but more that our time there was actually spent on its steps, killing far more brain cells than we were nurturing). They would drop me off and I'd go upstairs to lay out my books, minutes later flopping down on the steps below to light a cigarette and talk about nothing.

While my parents became increasingly laid-back as I got older, at the time it felt like they were unreasonably strict. As in: they weren't OK with me going out late at night, smoking, hooking up with boys or any of the other 'bad behaviours' my friends were getting up to aged fifteen. My curfew was consequently much earlier than those of my friends – even my Kuwaiti friend. I had to be home for dinner by 7.30 during the week, and on weekends I could stay out until 9 p.m. This got later as I grew older, but while my curfew was always quite late compared to most of the Arab girls I knew and met later, it was ridiculously early compared to my friends at the time, most of whom didn't have a curfew at all.

I was usually late for curfew but it wasn't that I didn't care; I felt the burden of it, all the time. As the hours ticked by I would begin to feel the pressure of my parents' deadline. I could never outpace it; it was always there, lurking at the back of the enjoyment. One minute late counted as late, full stop. It often equalled a grounding. As the minutes would tick past, my phone would start buzzing, vibrating almost in tandem with my pulse. I acted like I didn't care but, in reality, I was constantly terrified. Especially of my dad. As soon as I saw his name on my phone I would feel physically sick. He could always tell when I was lying, could always smell the cigarettes and alcohol on me from the other side of the house, always knew how to push my buttons, never let me get away with anything. He had veins that popped out the side of his neck when he was very angry, and I seemed to make him very angry very often.

He was frequently away for work, and even when he was in London he worked late a lot, so it was usually my mum setting the rules. When she would greet me at home she'd make me hold out my hand so she could smell my fingers for smoke. I'd often carry tangerines in my bag, which I'd hastily peel and squash into my hands in the elevator in an effort to mask the smell. But my mum was a lot easier to manage, and I could sometimes manipulate her into keeping my secrets for me. The only threat I'd heed was that she would call my dad.

Many of the Middle Eastern women I spoke to told me that their fathers were also predominantly the scary authority figure. Lamis, a twenty-nine-year-old Iraqi who was born and raised in London, told me how even after her father moved back to Iraq, just the threat of her mother calling him was enough to terrify her. 'I remember one time I got caught stealing from Boots and my mum called Dad. He came on the phone and even then, through the phone, I was shitting myself,' she told me.

There were house parties or under-eighteen raves every weekend, and my parents would let me go on the condition I was home for curfew. It was a non-negotiable that burdened many of the women I spoke to.

'My mum, in her mind, thought she was really laid-back, but she was comparing herself to back home,' Samira laughed. 'So, she's like, "I'm letting you out until 9 p.m., do you know what that means?!" And I said, "At 9 p.m. people haven't even left their houses yet! They're still getting ready!" I used to challenge it a lot, and we'd argue every single time.'

'My best friends were allowed to do all sorts of things that I wasn't,' Shams told me, her voice still laced with irritation. 'I'd be out with my friends who didn't have a curfew and I remember feeling: "*Why* do I have to go home? Why is my mum calling non-stop and telling me the Addison Lee is outside, from eleven o'clock?!" I'd try to tell them that the party didn't start until ten and they'd say, "Either you go for one hour or you don't go, *khalas* [finish].'"

The Addison Lee debacle was one I was familiar with, too – a compromise of sorts that ensured I was able to attend some of the things my friends were going to, even if only for the first couple of hours. It allowed my parents to keep tabs on where I was, and make sure I was getting home safely and on time. And that they wouldn't need to come and pick me up themselves. I was happy that I was allowed to go, of course, but leaving when the party was just getting started felt heartbreaking, every time.

In an effort to get around all this, I'd often make plans to sleep over at my friends' houses, friends whose parents were often far more lenient than mine, and it felt like we were able to wear whatever we wanted, go wherever we liked and stay for as long as the party lasted. Most of my Middle Eastern girlfriends were never allowed to sleep outside the house, for precisely this reason.

I had – ingeniously, I thought – scanned my passport to the computer and used the 'rotate' tool on Microsoft Paint to flip the last '9' in the year of my birth (1989) to a '6', making me eighteen. Lots of us had fake IDs. We'd take full advantage, and get dressed up half-naked to go out to the clubs in central London. It must have been obvious that we were underage, but the bouncers let us in just the same. There, we would join the tables of our Arab friends, who would keep the drinks flowing. Certainly, while horribly faked IDs like mine would never make the grade today, in my teenage years the rules were rarely enforced.

Going to house parties in particular always scared me, though. They felt like the embodiment of all the things we weren't allowed to do, in an arena in which everyone was keen to do them publicly and in excess. While parties in Egypt could also be wild, the things that happened there were always done in secret and therefore far more subtly. In Cairo, I might walk into a room to find a couple kissing and then have the girl insist to me later that what I saw wasn't what I thought it was. In London, I could just as easily see someone getting fingered with abandon mid-party, mid-room. It's not that one was necessarily better or worse than the other, it was just different. At times, and at first, overwhelmingly so.

I had drunk and smoked in Egypt before, and I had even kissed a couple of boys, but something felt different about doing those things so openly in London. In Egypt, I had always felt safe. I had felt like I was constantly surrounded by people who – regardless of whether they were friends or strangers – were basically my family, and would have my back no matter what. I didn't feel like that in London; these were strange houses on strange streets, overflowing with people whose names I barely knew, let alone those of their entire family lineage.

It was with my Middle Eastern friends that I felt most comfortable and I'd always tell my parents I was with them, even when I wasn't. There was an intrinsic understanding between us of what was at stake, a mutual belonging of the same world. They understood that when my parents called them looking for me, they had to take the fall for me, even if I hadn't given them prior warning. They had to pretend I was in the bathroom (or similarly preoccupied), then call to tell me to contact my parents immediately. They knew I'd do the same for them.

'We all just understood each other and that we had to have each other's backs. I remember even when we were hanging out in the library you'd tell your mum that you were with me even when you weren't and she'd call me and I'd say, "Uhhh, yes, she's right here!"' reminisced a friend who I often used as a scapegoat.

Naturally, it saves you from even trying to explain to someone why you can't do something or go somewhere. It's a shared understanding of the way things just sometimes *are* in Arab culture. Even though I have friends of all different ethnicities, most of my best friends – especially as I get older – are Middle Eastern. The same was true for many of the women I spoke to.

'I actually don't have one English friend, which is really weird . . . Not a single one,' Haifa told me. 'I think it's more a relating thing. I had a few English friends in school but they'd say things like, "Oh my God, I can't believe my mum, she's such a bitch; she shouted at me because I came home at 3 a.m.", and I'd think, "Uhh, girl, I have to be home at 10 p.m., are you kidding me?"

'I have so many rules and regulations and sometimes it's hard to hang out with people or speak to them about your problems when they just don't get it at all,' she added.

Of course, exploring boundaries and testing the limits – your own as well as those imposed on you – is a natural part of growing up. My teenage years were rife with rebellion, as they are for the majority of teenagers, and I often wonder now: were the things I got up to really *that* bad or did the actual experiences feel doubly naughty because I was forbidden to have the same sort of social life as my friends and therefore had to think up all sorts of ludicrous ways to get around my parents' rules?

While parents' imaginations can sometimes conjure up stories of all sorts of mischief – and while of course sometimes we *were* actually getting up to that mischief – sometimes it's the simplest, most innocent things that you're barred from doing. Such as simply going to dinner with friends, or to watch a late-night movie, or to dance to good music. Those rigid rules and regulations are often, in turn, met with lies.

'I compare my life to that scene in *Bend It Like Beckham* where Jess, forbidden to play soccer by her very traditional parents, hides her uniform in the bushes where she later dresses herself, along with guilt, as she secretly plays on a soccer team,' wrote Jordanian-born, US-raised journalist Nadine Sulz in an article for *Elite Daily*.[69] 'I always find myself questioning things that most people my age have never had to. When my friends want to go away for a weekend, go to a midnight movie, or even go out after 11 p.m. (God forbid), I'm always the one who has to think of a lie days in advance to even be considered by the jury that is my parents,' she continued. 'And when they do allow me, because a twenty-one-year-old apparently needs to be given permission to do anything, the combination of their terms and my paranoia almost makes it not even worth it.'

It was a common sentiment among all of the women I spoke to. 'As a teenager I just had to lie so much,' Daniah, a twenty-seven-year-old Kuwaiti, told me. 'I'd say I was at a friend's house and their parents were there, or that they were going to drop me home, but I'd just be getting the bus home,' she laughed. 'You get so used to lying . . . I just wanted to be a teenager and do what my friends were doing but I couldn't really, or I had to beg and lie and fabricate things massively to be able to.'

In an effort to get around what at the time I considered to be my parents' unreasonably strict rules, I became something of a master liar, inventing any number of activities I needed to do after school to cover up what it was I was actually doing. I often used to say I was going to the cinema because it would afford me a few hours free of suspicion when I didn't have to answer my phone.

Once, shortly after I had turned fifteen, I told my dad I was going to watch *Supersize Me* but I was actually at my boyfriend's house. When I got home my dad told me he had watched it too, and asked me what I had thought of it. Without having researched the movie at all, I went into a ten-minute monologue on how much I loved it and how sad it was to see how obese the guy got. My dad let me finish and then slapped me. He told me that the guy hadn't, in fact, become obese at all.

It became a running joke that I was grounded, and it felt like I was forever in trouble. I was so angry at the world that getting caught didn't concern me in the least. I think I actually wanted to get caught. Between the usual adolescent turmoil and my anger at having been forced to move back to London, I often took it out on my parents.

They, in turn, continued their usual tirades with one another, still many years away from their eventual divorce. Bad vibes in our house were the norm.

As I learnt, anything you're not allowed to do seems all the more appealing, all the more tempting for the simple reason that you are not allowed to do it. Research backs this up: experiments show that children want to play with a toy more after they're put under severe rather than just mild pressure not to play with it,[70] while people are more likely to watch violent TV shows when labels warn against them.[71] There are countless examples of books becoming more popular after they're banned.[72] It's hard, I guess, not to be intrigued: what could be *so* bad about this?

The rebellion was something I saw play out time and again with many of the Middle Eastern girls I knew, some of whom had mind-bogglingly strict rules imposed on them. One of my friends didn't even have keys to her own house until she was twenty-five. Her dad wanted her to have to ring the bell so he'd know of her comings and goings every time. She was the wildest person I knew.

'A lot of my friends couldn't go out growing up, so at university they would just go nuts,' Shams told me. 'When you're told you're not allowed to, you just want to do it a lot more.'

My resistance was often met with a slap . . . or a few. Many of the Middle Eastern women I spoke to told me how they were often chased with slippers. You could get a hit for a number of offences: for answering back, for doing something you shouldn't have been doing or for watching someone doing something they shouldn't have been doing and not stopping them. At least, those were my main offences. It's very common in Arab culture to slap your child if they are being disrespectful or misbehaving. According to a 2014 UNICEF study, Arab nations have the worst record of corporal punishment in the world, with Yemen and Egypt registering the highest rates of physical punishment of children aged two to ten.[73] About 1.1 billion caregivers around the world think it is necessary to physically punish a child in order to properly raise or educate them. It's only really in the last ten years that it's become frowned upon to spank or cane children in the UK and in many Western countries. Only sixty countries have actually prohibited corporal punishment – neither the UK nor the US are on this list.[74]

For me, it wasn't the slaps that fostered change in the end, nor the groundings, nor the therapy my parents sent me to – although that might have helped indirectly. It was communication. I can't remember what my latest transgression had been, only that it had been one in a long line of a seemingly never-ending tirade of fucking up, of lying and getting caught and shouting on shuffle and repeat.

My dad sat down on the edge of my bed as I glowered at him from the furthest corner. And he cried. I can't remember what he said exactly, only that it marked a turning point. The conclusion we reached, ultimately, was that I should tell him whatever it was I was going through, and he'd help me. 'Just please don't lie,' he said. The line I still remember is: 'Even if you get arrested just call me, I'll help you, and then we'll deal with it later.'

When I asked him about this exchange recently, he told me he couldn't remember the conversation. Ever the rational one, he said a lot of it was likely due to my hormones as a teenager and the normal rebellions. Whatever he said worked, though, because I did start to open up to my parents, and now I consider them two of my best friends. I tell them pretty much everything. It was a relationship that gradually improved and then blossomed when I moved out of the house to go to university aged nineteen. As I became more honest with them, they afforded me greater freedom – and the more freedom I had, the less I felt the need to lie.

'We had rules, and you knew what they were, and you still didn't give a shit. That's why I used to get mad,' my dad told me recently. 'You were still a kid.'

Certainly, as I evolved and became an independent adult, and as I started to actually make better decisions (my judgement was definitely lacking for many of my teenage years), my parents began to trust my ability to make good decisions and therefore increasingly allowed me the freedom to enjoy them.

'I don't give a shit what other people think – zero,' my dad told me. 'A lot of the Arab "shame", if you will, is, "What will my neighbours think? What will people say?" I don't give a fuck about any of this, to be honest . . .

'I gave this a lot of thought when I was growing up – what's right and what's wrong. Good judgement is what I care about, not sticking to a norm just because other people decide something is right. It's something I wanted to instil in you and your brother,' he continued.

In truth, I am grateful every day for it. For a while I felt the claustrophobia and frustration that can result from the need to unceasingly fabricate lies and live a double life, and I am unutterably thankful I don't need to do any of that anymore.

The thing is, most teenagers are rebellious to a degree and, no matter where you're from, it's always difficult trying to grow into your own person; you have to push and cross a lot of lines to know where your own boundaries lie. The friction this causes is heightened when parents are overprotective (as Middle Eastern parents often are) and when your behaviour is seen as far more than just decisions about who your friends are or what kinds of things you do or wear, but as an indication of who you intrinsically are as a human, of which culture you are choosing to side with.

To be sure, certain actions, desires and ways of being are assigned to certain cultures; therefore your life choices are often seen as more than the sum of their component parts. The choices are often made to feel like 'East' vs 'West' rather than 'right' vs 'wrong'.

Being an Arab growing up in the West, therefore, your wants and behaviours are constantly set in opposition to the supposedly immoral 'other'. They're considered reflective of the extent to which you manage to retain your 'culture'. For me and many like me, at least, it's more 'what will your aunt think?' than 'what will God think?'

'I couldn't help but feel that "we Arabs" and particularly females born and raised in Britain, were torn between competing ways of life,' wrote Ramy M. K. Aly in *Becoming Arab in London*.[75] 'Between the demands of our families and communities on the one hand and the wider society on the other, not being able to live a full life in either one or other realms or indeed between them.'

Writing about the pressures his sister, who had ended up running away, had faced, he wrote: 'The pressure not to make "mistakes", the feeling of being constantly watched, evaluated, moulded and judged, were exacerbated by her role as a daughter. The symbol of honour, the ultimate measure of whether our parents had successfully raised us despite and in spite of the "England" that surrounded us.'

Whereas, in Egypt, my mum's rules were considered among the most lenient, in London they were decidedly less so. This was due in part to the fact that I was now comparing them to the very relaxed rules of my English friends' parents. But it felt like she also became a lot stricter, for a while, at least. When I'd get caught doing things I wasn't supposed to be doing, my mum would often say things like '*We* don't do these things', emphasis on the 'we' and on the need to distance myself from the cultural norms I was constantly surrounded by and yet was not meant to absorb. Growing up, it was a logic I struggled with. Why was wanting to grow into your own version of yourself restricted to people from a specific culture? Why was it something *they* could do, and *we* could not?

What's more, I found the notion that I might be infected by exterior, negative influences quite offensive. It didn't take into consideration my ability to make autonomous, conscious decisions. Also, to state the obvious, my Arab friends were often no 'better' than my British friends; in Egypt, we had been doing much of the same. As Haifa told me, laughing, whenever her mum used to say things like that to her, she'd always wish to respond: 'What things? I'm the one making them drink shots!'

When I sat down with my mum recently to talk about those years and why she thought things had unfolded as they had, she told me that when we had moved back to London, she had been seized by a panic that I would 'lose my way'. It was something Aly had touched on in his book, where he explained how parents are often gripped by a 'moral panic' regarding the society their children are being raised in.

In reality, just as the West stereotypes all Arab women as being oppressed, the East's stereotype of Western women is often that they are all morally loose. Author and humanitarian Zainab Salbi suggests that these stereotypes are often shaped by images from the mainstream media depicting nudity or near-nudity everywhere, explicit discussion of sexual acts and behaviours as well as an over-consumption of alcohol and other substances. Both assumptions are, she says, clearly unfair to women and 'based on a small minority being generalized to whole cultures and countries'.[76]

My mum explained that she worried she would 'lose control of me' and I would lose my identity as an Egyptian woman. 'What even is identity?' I asked her. 'Do you think it's the limitations you put on yourself . . . how you ultimately behave?'

She went silent for a minute. When she met my eyes, her own were sad. 'Yes,' she said. 'Sometimes I think I failed, a little bit.'

I did sort of know what she meant. It's something I felt in the form of imposter syndrome when I was pitching the idea for this book. I found myself asking if I was 'Arab enough'. I worried that the fact that I drink and smoke and have sex and tattoos disqualified me from 'being Arab'; that others might not consider me Arab enough because of these 'transgressions', although my DNA is Egyptian through and through.

'Identity *is* the limits you put on yourself,' Dunya said when I raised the subject with her. 'My parents didn't want me to do a lot of things, but they happened in any case because we're in England, not in Iraq anymore. There's only so much you can stick to in terms of identity and stuff, you do lose it . . . The fact that I go out and I've had boyfriends in the past – you forget who you're supposed to be, but it doesn't mean it's a bad thing.'

For some reason, culture and identity seem to be inherently bound up with behaviour. It's something that came up in a study that found that Arab girls who lived in the West and had sex before marriage subsequently felt 'less Arab' as a result. They considered themselves either the 'good Arab girl' or the 'bad American(ised) whore'.[77]

It's ultimately very difficult to craft an identity and gauge your own moral compass when faced with all these burdens of external perception, and when each of your decisions seems to carry so much weight. In truth, it's about a lot more than just what your parents let you do or not do, but is a concern that stays with you for life. Because your choices are forever considered more than just flippant decisions, throughout your whole life each one – how you dress or spend your time, who you date, whether you drink and smoke, and on and on – are all considered indications of who you are, on which side you fall.

'Over the last few years I've often wondered how different my life would be if my family and culture had been less controlling, or if I felt less controlled by their beliefs,' Lamis told me. 'Would I have done more things, would I have been with totally different people? It's made me feel very suffocated.

'There's a half-Iraqi girl I know,' she continued. 'The way she was so liberal and free and confident around her family; she could wear what she wanted, she had tattoos and piercings. Every time I saw her I thought, "God, how fucking cool." No wonder she's so confident, because she's allowed to just fully be herself.

'I always remember thinking how amazing that must be, to have that kind of openness where she could talk about sex and all of these sorts of things. What a beautiful sense of freedom to be able to have that.'

It was a sentiment that was expressed again and again with many of the Middle Eastern women I spoke to. 'For years I felt like I was leading a double life,' Rahma told me. 'I never wanted to lose my dad because it's such a common thing to have to distance yourself from your family in order to be who you want to be . . . But from the age of, like, sixteen I started to stand up for what it was I wanted to do.

'I walked out one time when he wouldn't let me go out and we didn't speak for a while. I've had stints where I haven't spoken to him for a year . . . He wouldn't let me grow up, whereas my mum was really supportive. It was a shame because I didn't want to be that person. I still to this day feel like he doesn't know who I am.'

The thing is, having to exchange the love and respect of your family and society in order to obtain personal freedom is a very difficult, if not impossible, choice to make or idea to get your head around. What's more, in the Middle East and its diaspora, you never really grow up.

It's pretty unusual that I have my own apartment and live by myself, or that I have such an open relationship with my parents; my friends often baulk at the sorts of conversations I have with them. It's something my mum told me she was asked about many times when I first moved out, aged nineteen. It's not really the done thing. In Arab culture, it's customary for both men and women (although particularly women) to live at home until they marry. Even much later, you can still expect to be welcomed with open arms if you were to move back to your parents' house, and be helped out financially for as long as needed or is possible. You are financially and emotionally dependent on your family for a lot longer than may be the case elsewhere – and therefore also subject to their approval.

'Family is so important in Arab culture,' Rahma attested. 'Family is everything, which is a beautiful thing, but it means that no matter how open-minded you are, those family values are always going to be there and dictate our lives and the way that we do things.'

It's something I think about often. I'm very lucky that my family – especially my dad – has bestowed upon me a freedom beyond the fifteen-year-old me's wildest dreams. I live alone and I am independent and can do what I want when I want. Not everyone has that luxury, I'm well aware. But I still know what Egyptian society expects of me, even when my mum isn't around to remind me. It's always there in the back of my mind. Sometimes I wonder how many of my life choices have been dictated by the invisible jury. How much of what I think it is I want is actually just me following the assumed ideal? How many avenues have I closed off before taking even one step, because it's not something 'we' do?

The considerations only become more pronounced the older you become, when you start to make actual grown-up, life-altering decisions. It's a weird surprise when you don't consider yourself wedded to tradition in the least, but then still find yourself left with a layer of guilt.

What's more, I'm well aware that if my family – and especially my dad – didn't think the way they did, it would be far more difficult for me to be able to be who I am today. If my dad disapproved or disagreed with my life choices – instead of being proud, as he is – it would be much harder for me to make these choices.

If he didn't encourage and facilitate, would I have been free to have had the life and the experiences and the space and the relative freedom to even develop these thought processes? Would I even be writing this book? I don't know. Probably not. Or rather, it would have been a far more difficult, painful and risky process.

Ultimately, my dad allowing me to be myself is what allows me to be myself. That is a humbling realisation. That even where I am free to live my life by my own rules, it was still a man – still my father – who was the gatekeeper to my freedom. If he had wanted to enforce a different reality upon me, he could have. He can.

Chapter 5
When You're Supposed to Be a Virgin Until You Get Married

'The honour of a girl is like a match; it only lights once.'
– Egyptian proverb

When I look back at my teenage years – at some of the things I did and felt – it's hard to believe that that person was actually me. My fifteenth year particularly stands out. It feels like a movie I watched once. It's incredible to realise that, with enough distance, you can make light of and then compartmentalise even the most scarring of experiences.

Amid the rebellion of the last chapter, I lost my virginity under what can be considered, by general consensus, really shitty circumstances, and it caused chaos in all aspects of my life.

I wish I could go back and tell the fifteen-year-old version of myself that all of what followed would be just one chapter in my book, but she probably wouldn't have listened to or believed me. It felt like the end of the story, at the time – as though I was all out of 'to be continued's.

In the same way that I can't remember my first kiss, I can't really remember the first time I had sex either; only that it happened. It was my second year living in London and I was fully immersed in the Mean Girls crew. Or maybe by now, I had become one of them. I had not settled back into London life – nor life in general – and my house was basically a war zone, definitely not somewhere I called 'home'. I felt everything deeply.

Having sex was pretty normal among my friends and the girls at school, despite the fact that we were technically underage. Many of the girls in my year, particularly within the popular crowd, were already sexually active, either with their boyfriends or having casual sex.

Our experiences chimed with the rest of the UK; the average Brit loses their virginity at fifteen, despite the legal age being sixteen.[78] Boys were always the topic of conversation at break times. The claim to fame of one of our friends, a gorgeous if slightly ditzy brunette, was that she had given a blowjob before ever even having kissed a boy. The girls whispered about it but it was almost to applaud it rather than to criticise. In a game that included 'pulling competitions' – in which teens would descend on under-eighteen parties with pretty much the sole intention of hooking up with as many people as possible – she was leagues ahead. She had already jumped some 'bases'.

By contrast, I was always the awkward one at the party, crawling out of my skin when guys would try to dance with me. I wanted to enjoy it – was enjoying it – but felt so uncomfortable at the thought that I might be that I just wanted to get out of there as quickly as possible. The idea of sex – the thought of it – occupied my mind all the time, but it was always with an underlying feeling of discomfort. While people were hooking up casually all around me, I found myself already burdened by the invisible jury, by the messaging that I had apparently absorbed by osmosis: that the only acceptable, socially acknowledged context for sex was marriage. That sex (and subsequently desire) was dirty and bad and *wrong*. To be essentially devoid of sexual desire, to refrain from sexual activity, sexual jokes and sexual clothing, are all requirements enforced on Middle Eastern women in all sorts of subtle and not-so-subtle ways. For many, the concept of the opposite sex in general is immediately dismissed as 3aib (shameful).

It was another weird contradiction, however, that in placing the emphasis on sex and its prohibition, it had the opposite effect of making it more compelling.

'I wasn't meant to have sexual thoughts but then I'd wear a top that was a little too tight and my family would make it such a big deal. It would make me ashamed to have those body parts,' Samira told me. 'I wanted to tell them, "It's happening to me and you're making me feel so bad about it." I became really tomboyish and wore baggy clothes because of how uncomfortable they made me feel. As though I'd done something so wrong for being feminine.'

It was a sentiment echoed by many of the Middle Eastern women I spoke to.

'When I was younger, my grandparents would always be really weird around us about sex,' Sondos told me. 'If I was wearing a vest top and I bent down and my back was showing, my grandmother would say, "Cover yourself, your uncles are in the room!" At the time I thought it was a respect thing but I was also amazed. "Are you trying to tell me my uncles are going to look at me in a sexual way?"

'It made me feel really uncomfortable even around my uncles, let alone other men,' she continued. 'My mum would never let us stay at our friends' houses if they had older brothers . . . as if they were just looking at me like a piece of meat.'

With hindsight, I realise I often felt uncomfortable too. As I grew older it played out in all sorts of ways. It felt strange to have a male personal trainer or a male doctor – let alone how I felt in the company of boys who actually liked me! In being taught to be so conscious and aware of ourselves and our bodies, we are sexualised from a very young age, taught to believe that the prospect of sex was forever ominously looming. Simultaneously, we are taught to feel bad about it, and to shoulder the burden.

'I remember going to the doctors when I was fourteen with my mum because of really bad period pains,' Samira told me. 'The GP suggested the contraceptive pill and my mum stopped her in her tracks as soon as she started asking questions such as, "Do you have a boyfriend at the moment? Are you sexually active?" My mum stepped in and said, "We don't do boyfriends."'

My mother's reaction was often the same when it came to sex, although it wasn't a subject she had tried to broach with me yet. By the time she did try to bring it up, the following year, I had already lost my virginity.

While my parents never believed in the unspoken rule that the sexes should be kept apart – and I always had many male friends while growing up in Egypt – in London it was different, and being in an all-girls' school made the opposite sex seem mysterious and out of reach. One of my best friends at the time – the ringleader of the Mean Girls, Regina – had come back from the summer holidays having met a boy we'll call Satan. He had close-cropped hair that he had dyed red and a stocky build. He was originally from Morocco and was a few years older than us. She liked another guy, who she had obsessed about for much of the previous year, but was flattered by Satan's attention.

He started to call me on the phone late at night to ask for advice on how to approach Regina. I'd give him some insights and then he would ask me about my day. Reporting back to her at school in the mornings, she would always roll her eyes and cringe. At some point, I started to look forward to his calls.

One night, he got drunk and called me and told me he couldn't stop thinking about me and that he was really starting to like me. Then he hung up. It was a masterclass in how to make a young, naive, lonely and confused girl fall in love with you. He might not really have even been drunk, only pretending for the guise of 'vulnerability' and honesty.

He tuned every string and hit every note. I didn't know at the time, but he was pretty much an expert at this. He had certainly done his 10,000 hours, and I know now that he was grooming me.

There were a million red flags that the twenty-nine-year-old me who is writing this would have spotted, but the fifteen-year-old Alya was oblivious. It had never occurred to her that people could be so malicious or self-serving, nor that they would even want to be. She didn't understand what she was feeling or that it was OK to feel it. She really wanted to believe everything he said, so she did.

The next few weeks and months are a bit of a blur, more a thudding in my heart and a sinking in my stomach than any clear memories. The phone calls grew more frequent and the questions became more probing. He told me he was no longer interested in Regina, no longer speaking to her; he only wanted me. When the things Regina told me contradicted that, Satan would say she was lying. I believed him, my heart allowing me to conclude that Regina must be some sort of compulsive liar, desiring only to mess with my mind.

He'd leave me long voicemails that I'd play back over and over to myself, fawning at the way he would call me 'baby' and tell me how much he cared about me. He convinced me not to tell anyone about our conversations or about 'us'. He said people always talked and always ruined things and that this was so special to him that he didn't want that to happen. I believed him and kept it to myself, even when I really needed someone to talk to. I believed him even when the red flags were smacking me in the face.

I had concluded that everyone in the world was against me and my potential happiness – the potential snippets of happiness that I thought Satan represented – and I tried to guard the secret of our relationship as closely as I could. Regina had started to check my phone for messages from him, causing me to delete them en route to school every morning, all the while pained to be losing his words. She would still bring him up, their story still seemingly evolving. Whenever I'd call him in tears to ask if the things she said were true – that they were speaking to each other and seeing each other and that he was still expressing interest in her – he'd say she was lying, and I would believe him.

I couldn't tell my other friends in London, as they were all Regina's minions, nor my friends in Cairo, who I knew wouldn't approve. Nor my parents – obviously. He became the thing that both hurt and healed me, and the most important part of my life.

He would meet me before I walked into school and then at a nearby Tube station after school. He'd call me every night, hanging up every so often (to call other girls, I later discovered), before calling me back, talking to me about all sorts of things until I fell asleep. I'd write him love letters (which he read out loud to other girls, I also discovered) and fell so hard, so fast that very quickly nothing mattered to me other than him.

It became increasingly difficult to hide our relationship and I turned into even more of a liar as a result. My parents were at peak strictness and the Mean Girls had started to suspect something was going on between Satan and me, and had taken to following me home from school, calling my house phone to try to find out where I was, and making snide remarks in the school hallways. I was constantly on full alert, panicking every time my phone rang because it might be someone else that I would inevitably have to lie to. I was lying to everyone around me and to myself, and the truth was becoming increasingly subjective.

One night Satan called and told me that he wanted to show me how much he loved me and would I consider letting him? I can't remember how I decided, but I have memories of walking alone in the park, bracing myself against the English wind and listening to his voicemails, wanting to feel the love he was talking about. I remember telling him I was scared and that I had never even seen a penis in real life and could we not take it slow – maybe go in order of base, or something? I remember him bringing it up every time we spoke for weeks after.

The next scene sees me at his house, him pleading in my ear. I said no and he said yes, and maybe I stopped saying no or maybe I kissed him back or maybe he managed to convince me finally, but then he was inside me. I hadn't even seen his penis.

We went out for a cigarette and then we came back and did it again and when I left his house that evening, I remember his dad, who was sitting in the living room, saying 'take it easy' in passing, and being convinced he knew what we had done and that was why he had said that, and I felt the shame pooling in my knickers.

I remember standing on the platform of the Underground on my way home, taking my phone out of my bag, before realising I had no one to call to talk to about what was meant to be a momentous occasion. I had no one I *could* call. My virginity was supposed to be the most 'precious' thing about me, or so I had heard, and I hadn't taken good care of it at all.

In truth, it's interesting and sad that one of the great ironies of a sexually repressed household and culture is that it can so often encourage the opposite. I had learnt that sex was wrong – all sex. What then marked out sex that was *actually* wrong? How could I differentiate between sex with Satan – the liar, and undeserving of sharing in what was meant to be a special thing with me – and sex in general?

In a home where no topic is forbidden, where girls learn the boundaries of their bodies and become empowered enough to call out when something feels wrong, they can make good choices. If I had learnt early on that sex and desire are natural and healthy, and not wrong in and of themselves, I might have been capable of more, of making better and different choices. If boys and girls, and men and women are going to be having sex – which they are – surely it would be better to talk about it, to examine why it can be complicated when you're younger, to support you so that you feel that your opinions are valid – and in this way make informed, conscious decisions?

It's a big job, and one that schools could certainly be doing more to help with. While schools in the Middle East don't have sex education as a topic, even schools in the West do a pretty awful job of it. I don't remember learning anything other than perhaps how to put a condom on a banana.

Sex education in schools in the UK is to become compulsory as of 2020, as part of a new impetus on health education and mental health in schools. The new draft of guidance was updated in 2018 for the first time since 2000 (which, as one writer put it, was 'an era when the Spice Girls were equality icons').[79] Lessons will reportedly include teaching about same-sex relationships, consent and how to stay safe online.[80] Time will tell how these plans pan out. Certainly, what would be helpful is an education on some of the things that actually plague adolescence and life thereafter. How do you form a relationship? What does a healthy one look like? When is the right time to have sex? What does consent look like? What does it mean to desire and be desired?

Shaming girls into avoiding sex doesn't work. The point is not to *not have sex ever*, the point is to lose your virginity (and have sex in general) when you're ready, when it's right, when you want to, with someone who cares about you and will take you and your feelings into consideration – in a safe place, in a safe way, using protection.

The only thing that trying to shame girls into not having sex does is ensure that they won't be able to talk about those things, that they won't be able to feel like it's OK to raise those sorts of questions. If everything is supposedly wrong, it makes it harder to know when you're ready and to know what's right. I do wonder if I would have even found myself in such a situation had my ideas around sex not been framed by shame.

Now that every Arab mum's nightmare had come true, I needed to lie more and more. The deceit sat like a stone in my stomach. I'd lie to my parents and to my friends about where I was going and I'd find myself at Satan's house, where we'd inevitably end up in bed – me always hoping that this time, at least, I'd feel the love he had been talking about, rather than the minute-long pump and collapse.

That I couldn't speak to anyone meant I existed in a world that only included me and him. But it had an impact on far more than just the fact that the whole thing was incredibly unhealthy. It ultimately meant that I had no one I could turn to when I needed help.

The condom slipped off one time and I freaked out. He made jokes about baby names. By the time I finished school and found a clinic the next day, they were all too busy or closed. Frantic for the morning-after pill, I begged a random woman on the street to go into the pharmacy and buy it for me, pushing the money into her hand. They had refused to sell it to me because I was underage. I remember wishing then that I could have just spoken to my mum and asked for *her* help rather than this stranger in the street, but it just wasn't a conversation I could even begin to have with her. The woman went into the pharmacy and returned, handing it over to me – in my school uniform – with a look of half-pity, half-disgust. I took the pill and hoped I wouldn't have to explain away any of the side effects over dinner with my parents that evening.

I remember feeling so grateful that I could afford the morning-after pill, that I could access it relatively safely and in time. But what if I hadn't? Would I have ended up pregnant and potentially had to do something drastic because of it, as several of my friends had had to do? Sneaking away for secret abortions while their parents were away, depending on childish boyfriends or their equally underage friends to help them in case of emergency.

My phone would ring incessantly. It was always one of the Mean Girls or my parents trying to find out where I was. I would lie to them and Satan would lie to me. It started to become harder to believe his lies – but still I managed, for a while longer. I began to notice that the box of condoms would often be far emptier than it should have been, but he always had a story to hand. I didn't yet know that he was using up boxes of condoms on more girls than I could possibly have remembered the names of, that he was taking virginities like they were a prize. I guess they were, in a way. Just as we were taught to prize and guard them, boys are taught to prize taking them.

It all came out eventually, despite my best efforts not to see the truth. Regina called me from Satan's house phone and it confirmed what she had been telling me, what I had been in denial about all along: he had been lying the whole time. She was his girlfriend too, as were countless other girls he had similarly managed to mislead.

As is so often the case, the women attacked and blamed each other, and left the man unscathed. Regina carried on dating Satan, who would often come and pick her up from school. The Mean Girls – who didn't believe that I hadn't known Regina was his girlfriend all along (to be fair, I wouldn't have believed me either) – all instantly sided with her and took great pleasure in making sure I knew Satan was hers, not mine; had never been mine. They'd scream at me in the school hallways, hurl balls at me in PE and talk about me in front of me, calling me a 'whore' and a 'slut' – all words I'd started calling myself too. Teachers sat me down and told me I shouldn't have sex with another girl's boyfriend. And then that night my house phone rang. I could hear my mum pick it up in the other room. Ashen-faced, she entered my room minutes later. 'That was Regina's mum,' she told me, her voice rising in pitch with every word. 'She said you were having sex with Regina's boyfriend.'

There was literally nothing worse that could have happened to me at that moment in time until: 'Put your shoes on.'

'Where are we going?' I asked her.

'To the hospital,' she said. 'To check.'

I could hardly believe what she was saying to me. I still can't. Sure, in some societies and cultures in the Middle East and its diaspora that does happen, but I didn't expect *my* mum – in *London*, in her fucking Juicy Couture tracksuit – to be joining in on the insanity.

I managed to dissuade her, to convince her that it wasn't true. Putting months of practice to good use, I lied like my life depended on it. She wouldn't have killed me, of course, but at the time it felt like she might have attempted it. That's how scared I was, and how angry and distraught she was to have received this 'terrible' news.

Some girls do, obviously, get murdered. Five thousand women every year are the victims of the horrific crime of 'honour killing',[81] their lives the heavy price to pay for their 'transgressions'. The fear can sometimes lead women to resort to surgery to 'restore' their hymens in an effort to give the illusion of virginity. In an article in the *New York Times*,[82] a twenty-three-year-old French student from Morocco was interviewed after having hymenoplasty. 'In my culture, not to be a virgin is to be dirt,' she said. 'Right now, virginity is more important to me than life.'

Luckily for me, that was as bad as it got. But it felt *really* bad at the time. She believed me, or pretended to believe me, and promised to keep it from my dad. It just became my life. I succumbed to Satan every so often then swore to myself that I'd do better. I made other friends, inside of school and elsewhere, and (mostly) learnt how to tune the Mean Girls out.

I must have managed to at least partially convince my mum of my 'purity', because months after that phone call, and at least a year since I had first done it, she sat me down in the living room to have 'the chat'. There were literally zero useful takeaways from that conversation. I can sum it up in a sentence actually: 'Don't have sex until you're married or he'll think you're a whore and never love you.'

It's a very damaging mentality that has vibrated through many of my thought processes and into many of my life experiences – as we'll further explore in the next chapter – but it's also indicative of the mentality so often pervasive in the Middle East, one that completely removes women from the equation. Where was any mention of my desires or my feelings in that conversation? Indeed, women are often considered passive recipients, devoid of such needs. Sex, when talked about, is only discussed in connection with marriage and reproduction.

The more extreme end of this spectrum sees this belief remove a woman's autonomy and any emphasis on her sexual pleasure entirely, resulting in female genital mutilation, where a woman's clitoris (whole or in part, depending on the specific customs practised) is removed.

'If I were to tell my mum I was no longer a virgin, she just wouldn't believe it,' Samira told me. 'She'd probably say, "Who did this to you? Who took this precious thing away from you?" She wouldn't believe that it was something I had chosen to do . . . It would almost be like I told her I'd been raped.'

'My mum probably thinks I'm still a virgin,' Dunya told me. 'I would never talk to her about that at all; whatever she wants to think is up to her.'

What my mum told me is sadly not dissimilar to what many of the Middle Eastern women I spoke to said their mums had told them – if they had said anything overtly at all rather than mere scaremongering. Yet surely, as women, they must know that the things they preach aren't true? Why pass on those same complexes? And still we so often do.

On a mission to get to the bottom of many of these questions, I asked my mum what on earth she had been thinking when she had given me that advice, almost fifteen years ago. She could hardly believe it herself, she told me. She had been petrified that I would end up in a situation where I had sex under 'horrible circumstances', that I would do things I would regret.

'But that's what happened, anyway,' I told her. 'The only difference was that I didn't have you, or anyone, I could talk to about it.'

She knows that hers wasn't the best way to approach it – she knew at the time too – but she just hadn't known how else to have the conversation or how to reconcile the thought of her daughter having sex. In truth, it's very difficult not to absorb the messages surrounding sex, not to end up believing the invisible jury. She was just telling me what her mum had told her, what she had also believed to be true. What she still believes at some level.

It came down to judgement – my own. 'I wouldn't have wanted you to be a virgin until today,' she said when I asked. 'I would have felt sorry and worried about you. Now I can trust the way you think and I know you won't go and get yourself pregnant or whatever . . . Before, when you were young, there was no control. It's not about "for marriage", it's just that you were young and I didn't know if I could trust your judgement.'

But it's not the lack of conversation or the banning of something that protects people from the supposed lure of sex, or from making bad decisions, it's consciousness and understanding. It's an understanding of your worth, of your value as a human being. It's a facilitating of good judgement; an open conversation to aid coming to those conclusions.

'If my daughter does choose to have sex before marriage, then I need her to be making the right decisions,' said Ola, a thirty-one-year-old Libyan who was raised in London and was weeks away from giving birth to her first child, a daughter, when we spoke. 'I need her to know what sex is, what these parts of her body can do; I don't want it to just be "3aib, 3aib" because, if something does happen, I don't want her to think that she's done something wrong. I want her to be able to tell the difference between what's actually 3aib and what isn't. Not just the biology behind it, but the emotion.'

It was only years later that I began to untangle the different messages I had absorbed about sex. I'm still trying to, I think. For a long time having or even wanting to have sex was shameful, but I couldn't decipher why. As always, sex took up most of my headspace at a time in my life when I didn't feel able to have it.

Sex is about a lot more than just a penis and a vagina. Across cultures – but in conservative cultures like the Middle East especially – it's important to get rid of the shame that's clouding the topic and start having some real, open conversations.

Because the shame contributes to some really destructive notions. It allows the dominant messages to reign unchecked – not least allowing boys to think of girls as conquests, and hindering both from making decisions rooted in good judgement, in unbiased, unbrainwashed understanding. Simply being able to have an open conversation, free of hysteria, can make a big difference.

Chapter 6
When You're Not Supposed to Like Sex

A 'cock-block' is slang for an action – intentional or not – that prevents someone from having sex. It's normally used when describing someone else, often a third wheel, who is inadvertently cock-blocking. I've spent the vast majority of my life cock-blocking myself. It was only relatively recently that I came to this conclusion. In fact, it was this realisation that first made me want to write this book. That initially made me take note of the invisible jury.

As I grew older, I began to realise that outside the confines of a long-term, committed relationship – something I had spent much of my adolescence in – I found it impossible to satisfy my sexual desires. It wasn't something that tied into the version of myself I had in my head. It didn't make sense to me why I felt that way.

I wish I could claim I was exaggerating when I say there have been times (many times, actually) when I have literally *cried* because I was so desperate to have sex and yet was unable to act on it while single, seemingly paralysed by the conflict raging inside me. In nightclubs, in taxis heading home alone, in my bed at night, I've sobbed because I couldn't understand what the fuck was wrong with me. I lived in a country and in a culture where all I needed to do – to scratch my itch, so to speak – would be to swipe right on Tinder a bunch of times, or to bat my eyelashes at that guy who had been checking me out at the bar. I wanted to be able to be as free and sexually liberated as my peers, but I *couldn't*.

It turns out that shame and guilt are pretty powerful cock-blocks, as were the standards to which I held myself – standards that were stifling and impossible to adhere to. Although I had already had sex, I was still paralysed by the code that governs women's desires and behaviour. This is the case all over the world but more so in Arab culture, where guilt associated with sex is drummed into women from childhood, and sex is portrayed first and foremost as something dirty. Cue all sorts of shame and guilt if – like me (and literally every other normal functioning resident of planet Earth) – you should feel any sexual urges or, God forbid, act on them.

For a long time, I didn't realise that I had been immobilised by these messages, but it became far more obvious the older I became. This was something that came up time and again with many of the Middle Eastern women I spoke to.

'I remember as a child, it wasn't even that sex "is something for people who marry", it was just a really bad thing altogether,' Daniah told me. 'I just had this vision of it being dirty; even if you were married, it had to be very secretive. I remember my older cousins even being a bit embarrassed to say they were pregnant, because people would know that they had had sex.'

It is forever awkward. Even after marriage in the Middle East and its diaspora, women are held to double standards – expected to be virgins before marriage, and chaste even after. For men, as the Arab proverb goes, 'only the[ir] pocket . . . can bring him shame'. For Arab men, shame is associated with poverty or with the actions of 'their women'. Women, on the other hand, are a walking embodiment of shame, held to impossible standards.

As Nawal El Saadawi wrote, even in the case of prostitution in Egypt, where it's outlawed, if a man is caught having sex with a prostitute he is not put in jail but is instead used as a witness against her, whereas the woman is sentenced to a term of imprisonment.

Many of what are considered the most offensive swear words are testament to the fact that honour lies squarely on the shoulders of women: the worst insult you could give someone in the Middle East is 'kos omak', which means 'your mother's vagina', or 'kos okhtak', which means 'your sister's vagina'. Modesty and honour are all tied up between a woman's legs, specifically those of your mother and sister.

From the most extreme actions (FGM and 'honour' killings) to the most seemingly banal (slut-shaming), the message around sex for women is clear.

Many of these ideologies are inherent to 'purity culture', a term author Mona El Tahawy[83] first came across while she was in the United States, 'where it is used to describe the religious right's rhetoric that stresses virginity and modesty as the way for women to attain "purity".'

'I find it appropriate,' she wrote, 'as a way to describe the pressures women in the Middle East and Africa are subjected to, and it reminds us how much the global right wing has in common.'

In reality, proponents of purity culture are, to varying degrees, inherent in most countries and most cultures around the world, with particular impetus placed on women: their clothes, how much make-up they're wearing, even if they're walking in the street alone. All are factors that are taken into account when assessing a woman's 'pure' quotient. The dire consequences of this are apparent in many horrific cases around the world, such as when an Indian court blamed a 'promiscuous' rape survivor. She was scolded for drinking beer, smoking, taking drugs and keeping condoms in her room.[84] It also happens in the West – a 'she asked for it' argument often applied if the woman was considered to be wearing 'slutty' clothes or found with any trace of alcohol in her system.

In the Middle East, the pressures to be 'pure' are so all-encompassing that even the actual man you're sleeping with can turn against you.

'Many young men openly admitted to me that they would never consider having a serious relationship with an Arabic girl they met at a club or party,' wrote Ramy M. K. Aly.[85] 'Others insisted that they would not consider any female they had had sex with as a potential marriage partner,' he continued.

It's sadly an extension of the 'Masry' mentality and is something I've seen played out, for instance when a friend's older sister was dumped by her fiancé after she lost her virginity to him because – wait for it – she was no longer a virgin.

'The least that will be said of her is that she is a girl without honour and without morals,' wrote Nawal El Saadawi.[86] 'No man will marry her, even the man with whom she is in love. He will explain to her that he cannot trust a girl who allows herself to love a man before marrying him, even if he is himself that man.'

It's the same thing my mum had told me when she sat me down for potentially the worst conversation I've ever had in my life. It's an idea that runs deep and leaves its mark. Even I sometimes still have the thought that a man might think less of me, despite the fact that I now wholeheartedly agree with artist Kaija Sabbah that 'if you consider a woman less pure after you've touched her, maybe you should take a look at your hands'.

In the Arab world and its diaspora, it can almost seem like there's no alternative to being a virgin until marriage. So what happens when you're not? How best to proceed with your sexual life in a culture that has told you, for your whole life, that you shouldn't be sexual?

How come – and this was the part I really struggled with for a long time – if I didn't actually think I was doing anything wrong (because consciously, I didn't) I was still having these feelings of guilt and shame? Why, as I got older, did they start to play out in far more obvious ways?

After finally managing to exorcise Satan from my life, I started dating a Kuwaiti who we can call Smoky. He was my escape from the Mean Girls (who were still bullying me at school), from my parents (who were still fighting) and from my never-ending adolescent rage. I spent pretty much all my time with Smoky, cooking dinner and playing 'house', and I often stayed over at his, telling my parents I was at one of my girlfriends' houses. I was a seventeen-year-old 'good' Arab girl, playing at being a 'good' Arab wife.

Sex under those circumstances didn't feel wrong or shameful. I didn't feel guilty, but I still couldn't tell my parents, obviously, which was confusing: if you're not doing anything wrong, why should you have to lie? Yet so big was my need and/or desire to hide it from my parents that when I had taken myself to the clinic to put myself on the pill, I provided a friend's home address in case the doctor ever deemed it necessary to send anything to my house.

Smoky and I broke up when I was nineteen, just weeks after I had moved out of my parents' house and into a flat with a childhood friend of mine. After I finally got over the heartbreak that was the dissolution of the life I thought I wanted, I began to struggle with the idea of sex. I wanted sex, but I didn't want to throw myself into a new relationship just so I could get some. For the first time I was forced to consider why, who with and under what circumstances I could sleep with someone.

I cried a lot about it. One time a taxi driver in Lebanon bore witness to my tears, when I drunkenly sobbed to my friends something along the lines of 'I used to have sex all the time!' and 'I'm too hot to be this horny!', at the time feeling like I would never, ever have sex again.

While having sex within the confines of a long-term, monogamous relationship felt fine, what to do when not in one was a problem. It is a sentiment echoed by a number of the Middle Eastern women I have spoken to.

Samira told me how, after she lost her virginity and subsequently broke up with her first serious boyfriend, she too had faced similar frustration. She told me how, having opened the 'flood-gates of desire', she struggled massively and for years kept herself away from entering into any sort of relationship with men for fear of increasing her 'body count' (a low number of sexual partners regarded as second best to being a virgin).

It's something I worried and simultaneously tried not to give a shit about. I was beside myself, trying to fight the discomfort that would arise in me every time I would get near a boy so I could just do it already. I hated that there was a voice inside my head that seemed to be telling me things that were contrary to how I consciously wanted to live my life.

'I definitely felt guilt and shame too,' agreed Shahd, a twenty-six-year-old Iraqi Londoner. 'I think it's partly that we're women, but also our culture as well, because it's just like . . . in our brain. I've got friends that will sleep around but I just can't do it,' she continued. 'It's not [anything to do with] morals because my friends have morals [too], obviously, so it's not that at all . . . I have no idea what's stopping me.'

My problems were temporarily assuaged when, two years later, I started dating a guy who we'll call Courtney. Shortly after we first met, I travelled to Tanzania for a couple of months on my gap year, to teach English. I racked up a disgustingly high phone bill while we got to know each other via a flurry of messages, and by the time I got back to London, we were both sprung and fell into bed happily. Sex within a relationship had always felt comfortable and I was happy to once again be able to enjoy a sex life.

But I was – and still am – very uncomfortable with public displays of affection. In Egypt and in many Arab countries, kissing in the street is illegal and, while I'm definitely not a prude in the sheets, I do find it strange to do what feels like losing control of myself in public. As though it's something I should be embarrassed by.

'I notice I hold back in my sex life,' Lamis told me. 'I'm trying to work through it,' she continued, grimacing. 'We're not supposed to like or want sex. It's really fucked up.'

Many of my Arab guy friends have complained to me about this too, telling me that – even though *they've* moved past closed-minded principles of women – the women they were sleeping with often just couldn't let themselves go. But I do wonder why they were surprised that the very same women who had been taught to consider sex as dirty were suddenly – like magic – supposed to know how to view it as anything other than that.

It's certainly a weird tightrope you're expected to walk. If you are ignorant about sex, they say you're frigid and that you don't know what you're doing. If you're not ignorant, or if you show that you enjoy it, it can often be 'Where did you learn that from?'

What's more, it's been drilled into us – and by 'us', I mean the world in its entirety – that women are subservient to men, everywhere including, and maybe especially, in the bedroom. It's been drilled into us that sex is something done *by* men *to* women. Or just like . . . a favour women perform for men. It's not really ever portrayed or suggested that women could be engaging in sexual activity for their own sake, for their own pleasure (although this is gradually changing now, with mainstream TV shows such as *Girls* and *Insecure* portraying real, nuanced female lives).

As writer Suzannah Weiss puts it in an article for *Bustle*,[87] 'In both the bedroom and other areas of life, women get the message that they exist to please men.' The double standard around oral sex is potentially the best example: in a study, both men and women think giving oral sex to a woman is a 'bigger deal, more difficult, and more distasteful than giving it to a man'.[88] Another study found that men are also far more likely to have received oral sex during their last sexual encounter than women.[89] All this, coupled with the fact that sex is usually considered over once the guy has had an orgasm (whether or not the woman has also had one), and it's a pretty sad picture.

In the West, it was not all that long ago (in the Victorian era, in fact) that any woman showing signs of expressing her sexuality was labelled 'hysterical' and even sent to a psychiatric hospital.[90] It's taking a #claimyourorgasm movement to start the conversation around the world.

'Women in Europe and America may not be exposed to surgical removal of the clitoris,' wrote Nawal El Saadawi.[91] 'Nevertheless, they are victims of cultural and psychological clitoridectomy. "Lift the chains off my body, put the chains on my mind."'

'Sigmund Freud was perhaps the most famous of all those men who taught psychological and physiological circumcision of women,' she continued. 'He described the clitoris as a male organ and sexual activity related to the clitoris as an infantile phase.'

Even today, women considered to be actively pursuing sex in any way – or even just being too suggestive in what they're wearing – are called 'sluts' or 'easy' and are often told that men won't want to pursue serious relationships with them because of it. But, as Weiss argues in another piece, titled 'What we teach women when we tell them not to be easy',[92] 'calling a woman "easy" for engaging in sexual activity with a man assumes that he's the one who wanted it and she merely gave in'. Not only does that have some seriously disastrous consequences for the notion of consent, but, as Weiss posits, it also means we tend to believe that 'men are more sexual' and that 'any sexual activity on a woman's part is somehow a compromise, or at best, an exchange for something else, like love or financial stability'.

This has an impact on all sorts of things, including our understanding that we deserve pleasure too, and that we can and should ask for what it is we want and like. It also plays a big role in the level of shame we attach to sex, and explains why it is so often portrayed as something that a woman is giving up and a man is gaining. Even when it's something she wants too.

It's something Suhrah, a thirty-year-old Iraqi who was born and raised in London, elaborated on. She told me that if ever she sleeps with a guy who isn't her boyfriend, she always inevitably ends up feeling like she's done something wrong. 'It's this guilt that says, "OK, I've had fun and it's been great but they've basically just got what they wanted",' she said. 'Even if it's what I wanted too . . . It's a bittersweet feeling.'

The thing is, when we try to dissuade women from having sex in an effort to protect them from being objectified – which rings particularly true in Middle Eastern society – it's actually doing the opposite. 'The assumption that sex is inherently objectifying to women is objectifying in and of itself,' argues Weiss.[93] 'Women have their own sexual needs. They can be subjects, not objects, in their sexual encounters.' Indeed. It's normal to be a sexual human being, and to try to divide women into the equally demeaning categories of 'whore' or 'Madonna' is reductive. Women are nuanced human beings.

None of these were thoughts I held when Courtney and I broke up after five years together, when I was twenty-six years old. Emerging from the heartbreak, I found myself equally as awkward and just as sexually repressed as I had been before I met him, maybe even more so.

It just didn't make sense. It wasn't even that I felt judged by my parents anymore. They knew Courtney had been staying over at my house and he had even come on holiday with my dad and some family friends a few times and stayed in the same room as me. I had even broached the subject of birth control with them.

I was living an independent life. I felt far more empowered in who I was and what I wanted than I ever had been before, and I was writing an increasing number of feminist articles for women's magazines around the world. I was making things happen for myself in all areas of my life. But here, I just couldn't reconcile my desires with my reality.

As Mona Eltahawy put it: 'despite all that I had achieved so far, despite all the fight and all the feminism, I was not free. I could not do with my body what I wanted without feeling the weight of guilt, culture, religion and "fornication".'[94]

It felt like everyone in the world – or in London, at least – was having casual sex, enjoying their youth, their bodies and their freedom. Everyone except for me. It wasn't so much that I wanted to sleep with anyone and everyone that came into my line of vision, I just didn't want to have semi-panic attacks (as I was prone to) because I was so conflicted about what I wanted to do and how I thought I should behave, or because shame denounced my feelings of desire time and again.

For me, being sexually liberated means having the option and the freedom to choose to do whatever it is you want to do; whatever you feel comfortable with. To act out your desires in a responsible and respectable way. Not, as I had found myself, limited by the invisible jury and their subsequent influence on me.

'I was really put off guys and the thought of sex in general just disgusted me for a long time,' Sondos told me. 'It got to the point where watching a sex scene in a film just made me feel so uncomfortable; my heart would sink to my stomach . . .

'But I began to feel like I was cock-blocking my life by not being open,' she continued. 'My defences became physical to the point where I would shake.'

I felt like that sometimes too, and I really didn't want to any longer. And so I stubbornly decided to try to stretch my comfort zone to something perhaps a little better suited to me. I signed up to all the dating apps and pretty much banged my head against the wall in frustration. Fuck love, I wanted sex, and I was going to damn well make sure I got over this shame so I could get some. I had to. Life was too short. Why waste what could potentially be some of the best years of my life limited by the opinions of an invisible jury?

So, in my efforts to be a 'normal' twenty-seven-year-old woman on the dating scene in London, I went on a date with a guy I had known for a few months through mutual friends. We got drunk and I went back to his house, trying to convince myself to have sex with him while also trying to fight off the voice in my head that was calling me a slut and telling me he'd think of me as one if I were to sleep with him.

In the morning, as I was leaving his house, I heard the words 'do you think less of me now?' come out of my mouth. They slipped out before I could catch them, and his face as he answered suggested that if he *were* to think less of me it would have been due to that comment, not whether or not we had slept together.

It felt like the final straw. I'm not very good at just letting things be; there's *always* a way, I like to believe. One of my best friends had recently discovered a hypnotherapist and had been to see her to get over her fear of dogs. It had worked so well for her that she had ended up with her own dog, so I thought I'd try hypnotherapy in the hope that it would alleviate some of my anxiety and frustration, and help dispel some of the unhealthy ideas that had been ingrained in me around sex.

After an initial chat with the hypnotherapist, in which I expressed my issues and what I was hoping to achieve through our session, I lay back on her sofa, closed my eyes and gave myself over to her voice.

Hypnotherapy is nothing like what you see in the movies; I was present the whole time and can remember much of the conversation, but it felt like I was in such a deep state of relaxation that my defences were down and so I was really able to express what I felt and to pinpoint some of the circumstances that had formed those thought processes. As per her instructions, I summoned up an image of my younger self and, tears streaming down my face, proceeded to console her, telling her all the things I now know to be true: that sex is not dirty and wrong and shameful. I saw her exhale in relief.

Leaving the hypnotherapist's office after that first session, I already felt like a huge weight had been lifted from my shoulders and I immediately felt more confident and less awkward around men.

But it's always easier to get out of your comfort zone when you're literally out of your comfort zone, and when I went to the US for a couple of months – for precisely the reason of pushing myself further out of my comfort zone (in more ways than just this one) – I was able to begin to put into practice a healthier mindset around sex and sexual relationships.

There, Mr Chill entered my life. I sort of knew him from London, where we moved in many of the same circles, and we connected after discovering that we were both in the same city. A quick meal confirmed that we had very good chemistry and he was unwaveringly comfortable with himself. That, in turn, made me feel infinitely more comfortable too.

Days later, I invited him over to the Airbnb where I was staying (the fact I actually let him into my house was already a huge milestone for me, as ridiculous as that sounds) and we put on a movie. Credits rolling, he leant over to kiss me, bringing up all sorts of feelings that both terrified and excited me at the same time.

Is this what freedom feels like?! I let myself go and then we fell asleep, side by side but not touching, and the next morning he kissed me and left me stretched out in my bed sheets, smiling to myself; my own personal revolution.

I group-texted every single one of my friends: 'I HAD SEX!!!!!' and received a torrent of applause and hands-to-the-sky emojis; every single one of my friends had had to listen to me complain and cry and curse my lack of sex.

He sent me a respectful and friendly text later that day, putting our dalliance into writing. It's been over a year and we still have sleepovers, in between busy work and travel schedules. We talk openly and honestly and we have sex. Great sex. There are no strings or expectations or 'why didn't you call me's?'

Until that point, I didn't know any of this was possible. I'd always thought that, while men may be able to just have sex, women would always automatically catch feelings. I guess I had bought into all the misinformation around sex and emotions, and I was ecstatic to discover that there were alternative scenarios.

In the months afterwards, I picked up a book called *What Do Women Want? Adventures in the Science of Female Desire* by Daniel Bergner,[95] which debunked many of the modern stereotypes around female sexuality and many of the untruths, such as: 'that women's sex drives are lower than men's; that they're aroused by love, not sex; and that they're naturally fitted to be sexual objects, not agents.' Bergner wrote how these ideologies have been ingrained in the psyches of men and women for centuries. In the Middle Ages it was 'lust-drunk witches' who left men 'smooth, devoid of their genitals'; in the last century it was 'Freud's theory that women have "a weaker sexual instinct" than men'. And today, because these days I guess we want scientific research to back up some of these ridiculous claims, it's 'modern psychology that says that "women are rigged by their genes to seek the comfort of relation-ships"'. Across cultures, Bergner writes, 'with scientific or God-given confidence, girls and women are told how they should feel'.

Embarking on my 'relationship' with Mr Chill made me realise that sex and intimacy comes in all different forms. That there are lots of different ways of being intimate with someone, of having sex, and that that can be a whole, beautiful, amazing thing in itself too.

I think I got a bit spoiled by him actually, by the way we were both able to create and curate the relationship to suit us, to actually be *friends* with benefits. Our ability to be so respectful towards each other was not something I was even close to mimicking with anyone else in the months after.

We spoke about it once, discussing how there was never any drama and how there was always such good energy between us. 'It takes two people who are very secure in themselves and in what they want,' he said. More than that, I think, it takes two people who are not dicks, who are genuinely good people. Two people who have the same definition of common decency and respect. I met a couple of dickheads on my quest for sexual freedom.

Because it took me a while to really understand that there was no 'right' way, no one way to be sexually liberated. I had always thought that sex was the hardest thing in the world to have. In my months and years of celibacy, I would often marvel at the way the space between two people could just disappear. I couldn't remember how it happened, how two people who were at one point strangers could end up naked and in bed together, limbs and bodies entwined.

So, as the pressure came off, I got a bit giddy with this new-found power and control I had over myself and my body, and subsequently over men's bodies, too. But the power was also a little confusing. The 'could' overtook many things – including sometimes the 'should' – and there were a couple of times the power of 'could' dizzied me, tricked me into thinking I wanted to, when in reality I was just overexcited that I *could*.

Sex is the easy part, I quickly learnt. The hard part is finding someone actually *worthy* of sharing that with you – that moment, those feelings, your body. Not to mention that it's messy, the whole hooking up and dating and 'just chatting' and ghosting and breadcrumbing and thirst-trapping. Sex can often make it even more complicated.

Just like with most things these days, sex can be viewed as another commodity. We have come to expect instant gratification in all areas of our lives – sex and intimacy included – regardless of the fact that, when it comes to human beings, it's never that simple.

A documentary on Netflix called *Liberated: The New Sexual Revolution* attests that, far from the free-love sexual revolution of the 1960s, today's sexual revolution has severed the connection between sex and emotion entirely.[96] In the documentary, a female college student from Florida says the bar for the behaviour of a date or hook-up is so low that, if a man texts her the next morning, he's considered a rare 'great guy' – despite that being, by most people's standards, common courtesy.

A psychologist quoted in the same documentary said: 'A hook-up is "whatever" because that's how you're successful at it. If you're "whatever" about it you can walk away and say, "I don't care if I ever see that person again, I don't care about the experience either." The message we're receiving is that ambivalence is the best attitude to have about sex.'

It's true. And I think what's really sad is that women are buying into these rules too. We're playing by the same rules that were set long before we joined the game – rules that are based on incorrect notions: that men want sex, that women need to be coerced into having it, that we're having it probably in exchange for something else, which is love, and that men therefore need to be dicks so that women don't fall for them.

In rebelling against the abundant negative stereotypes associated with my gender – that we are desperate for love, crazy, needy, obsessed and obsessive – I sometimes tried to prove how very much 'like a boy' I could behave. In doing so, I sometimes hurt people and I sometimes got hurt too, because, as I learnt, people will start to believe you.

It's sad. And dangerous. And it takes all the fun and beauty out of it. All the human connection and decency. Surely that's not what we want – to be sexually liberated in order to be able to join in that? Not me, anyway.

It doesn't have to end in romance, it doesn't have to end in marriage, it doesn't even need to be much more than just a fling or even casual sex. But it should always come with decency and respect and a shared enjoyment in whatever it is, for however fleeting it is. Because that's the whole point: it's supposed to be an enjoyable human connection; an expression of love, of a mutual fulfilling of desire, for however long, in whatever form it takes for those moments.

What I've learnt is that ultimately, as long as you're respecting yourself, respecting the people around you and the situations you consciously place yourself in, life is way too short to abide by standards other people have set for you. Crying in nightclubs because you want to have sex but can't because of shame and guilt is not a viable way to enjoy life as an adult.

Having respect for yourself and your body doesn't mean refraining from having sex. It means being attuned to your wants and needs and acting on them with consciousness, with enthusiastic enjoyment and without shame. It means engaging with people who respect you, and respect themselves, too.

In truth, women want and enjoy sex. And that should be a *good* thing, for everyone involved.

Chapter 7
When You're Supposed to Be
With an Arab

Did I mention Courtney is black? It's potentially not something I would have thought to immediately bring up, were it not for the fact that for the entirety of the five years we were together, the colour of his skin was the first thing most people saw.

It was the first thing my mum said, when I showed her a picture of him, weeks after we had started dating. 'You know he's black, right?' Her reaction didn't really bother me at first, it was early days and I had yet to realise that that reaction, and the subsequent conversation, was something I was going to come up against – a lot.

I've always been into hip-hop (minus my year in Egypt where I found myself being an Avril Lavigne fan). I had a particular weakness for the rapper Lil Wayne. When I say weakness, I mean I used to write him letters while he was in jail and I got a necklace custom-made to say 'Mrs Weezy'.

I finished my university years no closer to knowing what it was I wanted to do (or who I was, for that matter) but – partly thanks to Weezy – fully immersed in west London's hip-hop scene. A whole new world opened up to me, and introduced me to Courtney.

I used to say hip-hop saved me. I loved the confidence and the bravado in the lyrics. They had helped me time and again with my growing pains; the self-possession and assertiveness of my favourite rappers suffusing themselves into me via the speakers. But falling in love with hip-hop gave me far more than just confidence; it brought me Courtney, new like-minded friends and, soon after, a purpose in life when I discovered what I wanted to do with my career and I ended up interviewing many a rapper in my early days as a journalist. Courtney was a rapper by profession too.

Prior to discovering west London's hip-hop scene, I had spent many of my nights out suffering through the high-end nightclubs that my friends used to frequent and where the bill would often be in the thousands – a point of pride and competition with the neighbouring tables. Much of the night consisted of ordering magnum bottles, which would be sent to the table complete with sparklers and a change in music to herald their arrival.

I had hated the booming techno music, hated the sparklers and the fuss and the posturing all around me. But I didn't know there might be a place I would feel more comfortable, more in my own element, until a friend of mine started interning for a hip-hop DJ and invited a few of us out to the nights he was DJing.

Emerging from the hip-hop clubs, skin glistening and sticky with the exertion of losing myself to the beat, felt like heaven every time. I would dance for hours with my friends. There was no pretence or posturing, at least none that I saw or allowed myself to feel. We would often go out wearing trainers, there only for the music and each other's company.

It was in that scene that I started to find myself, among a group of girls I had known for years but was coming to know better now under the flashing lights. It was there that I began to meet and interact with different people, from different walks of life, aspiring to and aiming for different things; far removed from the private school and Middle Eastern bubbles I had, thus far, spent most of my life in.

It was there that I met Courtney, months after my university graduation. I was on the stage rapping along word for word to Lil Wayne. He let me finish and then approached me, finding a way through the awkwardness and the barriers I had constructed around myself, until one day soon after I found that I had fallen for him.

Growing up, my dad had often told me he didn't mind who I dated, didn't mind who I ended up with, as long as he was a good person and treated me well. Regardless of nationality or religion, he always told me it would never bother him. And it didn't. But what I hadn't realised at the time was how much of an anomaly that made him. Or how the systems and structures that were in play in the Middle East – and specifically in Cairo as it related to me – would make his personal opinion (although I am grateful every day for it) less pertinent, in a way.

As I came to learn, in Arab culture women are supposed to end up with a certain kind of person. Many women are expected to marry someone from the same country and, if not, then at least an Arab and most certainly of the same religion (regardless of whether or not it's a religion the family themselves actually practise). In my social circles in Egypt, many marry into families that have long been intertwined with their own, bloodlines and allegiances easily traced.

The inclination to marry 'within one's own race' is one that is by no means limited to Middle Easterners. Across all countries and all cultures, the vast majority of people marry into the same racial, ethnic or cultural-linguistic group. The number of white British people in interracial relationships is 4 per cent. People from Bangladeshi, Pakistani and Indian heritage are also least likely to form a relationship with someone from a different ethnic background. This, says the Office for National Statistics, is because of 'cultural, racial and religious differences'.[97]

That said, research has found that the rate of interracial relationships is higher than it's ever been (and steadily rising). The UK has the highest rate of interracial relationships in the world: ten times the European average. The 2011 Census found that 2.3 million people

– that's almost one in ten people in England and Wales – were cohabiting or married in an inter-ethnic relationship.[98] It's important to note that this statistic doesn't include younger people or those who are dating and not living together.

'My dad has always said, "I don't mind who you end up with as long as you're happy", but at the same time I know that's not entirely true,' Lamis told me. 'He always says it's not about money, it's not about where they've come from, as long as they have that will and that drive. He always says that is so much more important than ending up with a rich Arab man who is spoilt and had everything given to him,' she continued. 'But in a sense, that's already categorising the sort of man that I should be with. Someone who's driven and hard-working.'

Indeed, along with the rest of the prerequisites, the ability for a potential husband to be able to 'provide' and who comes from a 'good family' came up time and again with many of the Middle Eastern women I spoke to.

But since Smoky – who had checked off each and every one of those prerequisites – I hadn't even looked at another Arab man. I think a lot of it was me subconsciously acting out against the preordained life I knew was written for me. With an Arab guy, as I had experienced with Smoky, it was so easy to fall into the same patterns. That said, I don't think falling in love has anything to do with rationalised logic, not even with hindsight.

Thanks in large part to my discovery of the west London hip-hop scene, by the time I met Courtney I had grown worlds apart from the Middle Eastern friends, circles and stigmas I had known growing up, and had found a new life among London's young creatives. I was meeting people from all different nationalities and all different religions, who identified as and with all sorts of different things. They were far more reflective of the reality of London and of the real world, I soon realised. And yet, at the same time they weren't, in that the creative scene is no doubt one of the most progressive segments of any society anywhere.

It may have been naive and ignorant of me, but I was surprised to discover that there were still some people out there who made negative assumptions based on the colour of a person's skin. What initially surprised me most was the reaction from my friends in Egypt. People I had always considered as 'open-minded' as me. Some of them asked me outright, 'but you're not actually going to *marry* him, are you?' Others just gossiped behind my back.

As expected, perhaps, the reaction was all the more passionate from the older generation, although some of them did have the reserve to wait until we had broken up before they told me so. One of my parents' friends approached me soon after I had stopped crying from the break-up to share her heartfelt confession. 'I was so disappointed in myself to discover I was racist,' she told me. 'I had never known I was, until I found myself shocked that you were dating a black man, and hoping that you would break up.'

There were many things I subsequently learnt about how common racism is in the Arab world. I learnt that 'abd', a word used for Africans and dark-skinned people, actually means 'slave' and is still used as an insult. I learnt that many Arab countries had played a big role in the slave trade – and in some ways still do.[99] I learnt that not just racism but also colourism (the belief that the lighter the skin tone, the better) was very real and deeply entrenched. I learnt that – even though she loved Courtney, and even though we had been together for years – my mum would still point out single, Arab men she considered more worthy. I learnt that I could feel deep shame and disgust at these ideologies, but still love the people who had bought into them.

Of course, sadly it's not just Arabs who engage in racism and racial profiling, nor even just black humans who are subject to it. Racism is a pervasive part of reality around the world, every day. From the treatment of the Windrush generation (who migrated as children and have spent decades in Britain) being classified as illegal immigrants and facing deportation to countries of which they have no memory,[100] to London nightclubs charging black women double the entry fees,[101] to events far more insidious such as the treatment of the Stephen Lawrence murder, which unearthed many a racist attitude among the British police force and citizens,[102] there are far too many examples that highlight the racism still inherent in much of the Western world. There are plenty of incredible books – like Reni Eddo-Lodge's *Why I'm No Longer Talking to White People About Race* – that give this issue the space and credence it deserves, which I can't do here.

I was only privy to a tiny proportion of what is an everyday reality for black humans around the world, and it was only ignorant comments that I had to deal with. Unlike other stories I've heard, I never faced any outright pressure from my family or any external sources to end things with Courtney.

He was bringing out the best in me; making me more motivated, more able to dare to dream, more connected to the real world. Spending time with him made me a much better person in all sorts of ways. Anyone who loved me could see that and was thankful for it.

We lived blissfully for a few years. We were young. We'd order food from Pizza Hut and stream movies, holing up in my flat for days. We travelled across continents. We made plans and we attended events together, supporting each other in our respective endeavours diligently and passionately. We were best friends and we used to say we could read each other's minds. It felt like that a lot of the time.

But he never came to Egypt with me, although I would have really wanted him to. The bawab was one of the predominant reasons why he couldn't come. 'What would he think!?' my mum shrieked at me when I asked her for the hundredth time if he could come to Cairo with me. 'Not only are you not married but he's BLACK!' she said, as if that explained it.

'I've got an Egyptian passport and in my British one it says I have an Egyptian dad – they write it at the back,' Rahma told me when

I asked her why she hadn't yet taken her half-Jamaican boyfriend of seven years to Egypt with her. 'I asked my cousin who works at a hotel in Cairo and she told me it's fine as long as I don't speak Arabic and I use my British passport, but my name is Arabic so I am scared to take him,' she continued. 'It's for that reason that I haven't yet. And it's really sad because Egypt is a big part of my life and of me and I really want to share it with him.'

Rahma told me she was scared of her dad's reaction, and ultimately of what people would say. In reality, beyond race, the difficulty in taking a boyfriend 'back home' was a common sentiment that arose time and again with many of the Middle Eastern women I spoke to. Courtney's skin colour was not the predominant factor here, his gender was, as was the lack of a ring on my finger.

Many of the women I spoke to explained how – even if their boyfriend was also Arab and Muslim, and even if their parents were OK with them sleeping or travelling with their boyfriends while abroad – they were still hyper-vigilant of letting that 'laxness' be observed by any extended family or friends 'back home'. To have become accepting of these things was perceived as having become Westernised and thus ruined, in a way.

To my dad's credit, he never cared about what other people thought. The first time I took Courtney on holiday with him and some of our family friends from Egypt, I asked him if he was concerned about what they would think of us staying in a room together. He instantly responded that if any of his friends had a problem with what I did, or what he had given his blessing to under his roof, then they shouldn't be his friends, nor should they join us on holiday.

But he still objected to me taking Courtney to Egypt. 'Why rub it in their faces?' he said when I recently asked him what his objection had been and if he would likely object again in future if the occasion were to arise. 'If it's such a big deal for them, just leave it,' he continued. 'It's not necessarily giving in, it's just being considerate. Especially if it's just for one week or whatever. Just make a bit of effort not to ruffle feathers and go back to your life.'

Having to compartmentalise one's life in that way is strange, though – and unpleasant. But my dad was on board with our relationship and, to me, that was the only thing that mattered. We were young, and we were both British, I reasoned. People's opinions in Egypt – let alone what the fucking bawab thought – had nothing to do with me. The similarities between us were far bigger and far more important than our differences, I believed. Still believe. None of these factors were, on the surface, why we broke up.

$$\text{\Huge \char"2AC}$$

Courtney called me while I was writing this chapter, almost exactly three years after we had parted ways. He told me that his ears had been burning. We had a long, honest catch-up and I asked him for his thoughts.

'You said the odds were against us,' he told me.

'Did I really?' I asked, surprised.

'You told me I would have to convert if we were ever to get married,' he said. 'I remember being taken aback by that.'

I hadn't remembered being so aware of it at the time, although as soon as he said it, I did recall something along those lines. Certainly, it had begun to dawn on me when I realised our relationship was real and solid. This was despite the fact that I lived in London and was not a practising Muslim. I remembered how heavy it had felt.

Because, even though my parents wouldn't ultimately object if I were to marry someone who was not a Muslim (I mean, the assumption that two people must share the same religion to really understand each other is seriously flawed), the law in the Middle East would be an obstacle or at least the thing I would most need to consider. Even without strong religious conviction from either family, marrying someone of a different religion – particularly if you're a Muslim woman – is a very difficult, if not impossible, feat.

Nemat, a thirty-five-year-old Muslim Egyptian who was raised in America but moved back to Egypt for her studies and subsequent job, told me about the troubles she was facing with her Christian Egyptian boyfriend. 'When we first got together, we spoke about him converting – marrying someone who was not Muslim was acceptable in my family but they would have to convert – and he had said he'd do it when the time came,' she told me. 'After a couple of years, he went to his family and asked for their blessing and his parents said *absolutely not*. His mum literally stayed up for three months reading the Bible,' she continued. 'It was very hard on our relationship because there was something that was so clearly an obstacle that was not from either of us – it was sort of imposed from my family and not allowed from his – but we're both close to our families, so neither of us wants to tell them to fuck off.'

In Egypt, and in many Middle Eastern countries, the law states that if two religions intermix, the marriage is not valid,[103] leaving Nemat, and many like her, at an impasse.

One of the reasons for this is the children the couple may eventually have: in Islamic law, children automatically take the father's religion, which means that Muslim women cannot marry a non-Muslim man because the children would therefore not be Muslim. The only way around this, essentially, is for a non-Muslim man to convert. Muslim men can, however, marry a Christian woman without either of them being forced to convert.

The conversion is often just a formality so the couple can obtain a marriage certificate, but to change your religion for someone else can be a big ask. Without a marriage certificate in countries like Egypt, however, you can't do much. It is illegal to live with someone of the opposite sex if you're not married, you can't really have children out of wedlock and there is no alternative to marriage.

In Lebanon and in many Arab countries, current laws discriminate against women who are married to foreigners, denying citizenship to the children and their spouses. According to Human Rights Watch, this will affect almost every aspect of their lives, including legal residency and access to work, education, social services and healthcare, and leaves some children at risk of statelessness.[104]

Arguably, if I were to fall in love with someone who wasn't Muslim and get married or have children with him and then we were to continue living in the UK, the effects of the laws in the Middle East would have less of an impact on me. But it would impact the relationship that my future children and I would be able to have with Egypt – a country and a part of my life that is very important to me.

Without my potential husband converting, our marriage certificate would not be recognised in Egypt or in other Middle Eastern countries. This would mean that, unless I chose to pretend I was a foreigner when visiting with my husband, we would not even be able to share a hotel room.

It would also impact my children in that they would not be recognised as legitimate and therefore not be able to obtain Egyptian birth certificates, which they would need for everything from Arabic school to their ability to inherit from my family and me.

Of course, if those were to be the circumstances of my life (likely, because I don't allow my feelings or my choices to be governed by things like religion), I would have to find a way to deal with them. But it's frustrating all the same, frustrating that it's even an obstacle.

For some, the religion itself *is* an important factor, away from the law. 'I want to be with someone who shares the same religion as me,' Samira told me. 'When I realised the guy I was seeing was Christian, I started thinking ahead: would he convert for me? But if I love someone, why would I want to change them? But then what about our kids?

'The conversations became really intense and it ruined a lot of the relationship,' she continued. 'They would drift away from us and delve right into religion itself; it was like we were battling. Religion is supposed to be about bringing people together and there was no love here . . . And then I started thinking, a lot of the Muslim guys I know don't live a very Muslim life and his way of living was a lot closer to Islam than many of these men . . . On paper other people are Muslim but nothing about them is halal, so I started to wonder: am I just doing it so I can tell people he's Muslim?'

For Arab women who live abroad, choosing a partner is a lot more complicated than just falling in love with someone. Just like your behaviour, it is an announcement of who you are, of which side you are choosing, of what sort of life you're opting to have. It's a minefield. This is further exacerbated by the sorts of expectations an Arab man (and his family) might themselves have for what a good Arab wife looks like.

'I do say to my mum sometimes that I wish I was a practising hijabi girl,' Dunya told me. 'Sometimes I ask: "Who am I? Who am I linked to?"

'If I meet a guy who is Arab – some don't drink or don't like girls who drink or have tattoos – but then I think: I do! So, who should I go with? Should I go with an English guy? But then I want my culture, I want someone who is Arab,' she continued. 'I often think if I wasn't like that, if I was more "Arab", there's more chance that I would already be married.'

Every life choice seems to bring with it so many consequences. What's more, many of the Middle Eastern women I spoke to said that the older they became, the more they thought they might want to date an Arab man – if only for that feeling of 'home' and continuity it gave them.

'We're in such a multicultural society that I could meet a Greek guy and fall in love with him, or a Pakistani and fall in love with him, but the older I get the more I realise that in the back of my mind, when I meet guys, I want them to be Arab,' Suhrah told me. 'That's just what I want. There are certain things that are missing otherwise: banter, understanding, cultural stuff like mum jokes, things like that that other people just won't get.'

'Eid and eating together as a family is something that is really beautiful about the culture, and those are things I'd want to do with my family,' Rahma added. 'Religion-wise I'd like them to understand it, but I wouldn't want them to feel obligated because I don't practise. I would want them to know all aspects, like: *insha'Allah* [God willing] and *alhamdulillah* [thank God]. We use both terms a lot in Arabic and we're very thankful,' she continued. 'It's a beautiful thing that we don't have enough of in Western culture.'

There are many aspects of Arab culture – like those Rahma mentioned – that I love, and after Courtney and I broke up and I embarked on the episode from the previous chapter, I began to really think about what it was that I wanted from my life. The things I found myself attracted to started to differ, as I began to think about the direction in which I wanted my life to move and what I wanted it to look like. I started to realise that, although I had never been interested before in copying the template of the life I had seen played out thousands of times around me, I didn't want something that was totally foreign either.

And then I met him. Or, re-met him. We had had a crush on each other when I lived in Cairo, but nothing had ever happened between us and time had moved on as it had. We kept in touch on social media, but we had different friendship groups in Egypt, so I never really saw him.

And then just as I had begun to conclude that it was time to try something different, he told me he was coming to London on a work trip. My mum laughed when I told her, after excitedly jumping up and down in glee. She said I was making things happen so I could write about them in this book, an endeavour I had recently embarked on. Maybe she's right. But for so long I had been caught in circular thinking – imagining that the things I had always wanted were the things I still wanted. I was curious to see how much my wants had changed and grown with the rest of me.

With hindsight, I realise I liked him before I even saw him. Somehow, I had bought into all the things I was *supposed* to want or have, and I surprised myself in doing so. Minutes into our first drink I felt at home; I didn't need to explain anything. He just knew. His mum was not Egyptian and he had lived abroad for a few years and he was all the things I loved about Egyptians, but also so many other things, from his exposure to another life.

Foolish, to think I could look into the abyss and not fall in.

He'd break into Arabic or tell a joke, pausing to ask if I was able to follow. He'd call me 'habibti', which means 'my love' in Arabic, and all sorts of other things that I had never cared about before. Stupid shit I had never thought mattered.

'I was with a Pakistani guy for four years and I didn't even think about it, then after we broke up I was with an Arab guy and very quickly, after a few Arab jokes and some banter, I thought, "Wow, we're vibing, this is vibing right now",' Suhrah told me when I shared with her my feelings and how fast I appeared to be falling for this guy.

It was definitely how at home he made me feel; all the things I didn't need to explain or even think about because he just got it. But it was more than just that. He was hard-working and ambitious and adventurous and so damn charming. He made me realise that those were things I cared about, that I wanted.

Between London and Cairo, we filled in the gaps of our lives; each pleasantly surprised time and again at the way the other's mind worked, at the choices we made and were making, at who the other person was. I was enjoying flexing my ability to act on my desires and getting to know him – getting to know myself more in the process.

He told me he was coming to Europe for work and to go and visit him, so I went. It was my own personal revolution. He told me he had booked for us to go skydiving, and everything in me railed against the idea but then I did it – partly to impress him and also partly to see myself in this new way, as someone who is capable of jumping out of a plane. But also someone comfortable enough in herself and her desires to act on them.

We kissed goodbye and then I picked up my bag and went to the airport. And then he essentially proceeded to ghost me. It didn't sit right with me for months. It just didn't make sense.

It might have ended at that had I not written him into an early draft of this book. 'This relationship needs some attention,' wrote my editor in response to the messy inconclusion. 'Why do you think this happened, considering you both seemed to so enjoy each other's company?' she probed.

It had been the question plaguing me. So three months after we jumped out of the plane, after he had turned into someone other than the person I thought I knew, I called him. I blamed it on the book, left my ego and my feelings out of it. 'I need an ending,' I said. 'What happened?'

He thanked me for calling and explained how, because we had slept together, he had assumed I would now have exceedingly high expectations of him and essentially want to marry as soon as possible. He had consequently distanced himself from the situation. Despite my best efforts, his doing so played into my long-held fear that he would lose interest in me after the fact. We had both acted and reacted accordingly.

Ironic that despite always having prided ourselves on the fact that we were different and unconstrained by stereotype, and despite the fact that I was literally writing a whole book about these expectations – we had ultimately built our own narratives based heavily on preconceptions of gender, tradition and culture. We had played right into them.

In truth, it took me a while longer to realise that the familiarity our shared history had afforded had allowed me to craft my own version of events. I had liked him before I ever even saw him, which I see now was not an unbiased place to start. This, coupled with my desire to play it cool and to disprove the assumptions he had of me, made me ignore the fact that I had needs (and that requiring someone to meet those needs was not, in fact, a weakness). As I settled into an acceptance of this I found that what I had wanted was not nearly as lavish as I had feared it would be, or as he had made it out to seem.

As a result of the pressures to wed that we'll further explore in the next chapter, this fear of commitment (emotional and otherwise) is apparently a common occurrence in Egypt, and I have no doubt in many other Arab countries too. While in London, my friends and I (as well as young men and women elsewhere in the West) are increasingly free to enjoy each other's company and just see where things go without a ravenous desire to use pronouns like boyfriend, fiancé or husband, in the Middle East, pressures prevail.

'My cousins in Egypt are now telling me that they don't even get into relationships anymore because they're so scared of the pressure and the expectation to get married,' Selina said. 'They don't even want to have the idea floating around that because they're seeing each other or are in a relationship, they are bound to get married.'

But what a waste to not even allow yourself to get to know someone before jumping to conclusions and ultimately ruining potential growth and experience and shared enjoyment because of it.

As I'm increasingly realising, relationships of all kinds are hard work. It takes all sorts of things to make a life with someone. It's hard enough making a life on your own. Meshing and merging your life with another requires compromise – not to mention courage! And that's regardless of whether you're from the same culture or not.

While, on the surface, it might certainly feel convenient to date or marry an Arab, in an inclusive and diverse society like London can we really choose who we fall in love with? No. And nor should we wish to. As F. Scott Fitzgerald said, 'There are all kinds of love in this world, but never the same love twice.' And that's amazing. In reality, you never know what you'll learn, where you'll go, what you'll do. I think people always come into your life for a reason, and usually you're left all the better for knowing them. Because these connections help you grow.

For hybrids like me, the things we think we want in a partner make up a complicated checklist. We are more than just Middle Eastern, we are also Westerners, and often a very specific and unique concoction of both. As an Egyptian friend of mine who has grown up in London put it: 'We want the best of all worlds. We want people from all different upbringings and all different sorts of outlooks but then we also want a bit of the old too, the thing we're familiar with . . . I think you'd be very lucky to find all those things.'

I think she might be right. But I also think that the things you want – or the things you think you want – change all the time. Also, I think people can change your mind. As my friend put it, 'The things I used to look for, I don't look for anymore. I thought I had figured out my non-negotiables a long time ago, but then when put into practice, I negotiated on many of those things.'

I think you can make all sorts of decisions, but life will force you to reassess them, every time. There is a particular art to making a life – one you enjoy living, that you're living on purpose – whether that's alone or with somebody else, and whether that potential someone else shares your culture or not. It's going to be a challenge, of that there is little doubt. A challenge that is full of growing pains.

Chapter 8
When You're Supposed
to Get Married ASAP

My grandfather told me I was too young to write this book. While I don't think he's right, I do accept that some of my thoughts may be subject to change. Especially when it comes to marriage. It's especially here that I am still trying to work out what I've been *conditioned* to want and expect and what it is I really want. Which parts of my personality and beliefs have been built in opposition to that conditioning?

I recently took to my Instagram stories where, in response to something that had happened in pop culture, I passionately expressed the opinions I hold as truth: that women are not the property of men, that they are allowed to post whatever images they want and behave in whichever way they deem best, that their actions do not need to be sanctioned by 'their' men.

And then I posted another video, saying my mum was no doubt going to call me any second, criticising me for expressing those opinions on a public forum, and saying that because I had, I would now find it more difficult to 'find' someone who would want to marry me. The implication being that this 'someone' would be Arab and that they would therefore take offence to my strong opinions. This ignores, of course, the assumption that I would even *want* to be with someone who would judge me negatively for having strong opinions in the first place.

'Yeah, but why do we only have to marry Arab men? And why do we have to pretend to believe in certain things that we don't, just so we can get a man?' one of my Middle Eastern followers responded. Why indeed.

To her credit, my mum didn't call me or say that – on this occasion, but she has numerous times prior, and has recently taken to telling me that I'm too tough, too strong-willed, that I'm going to need to make some compromises or no one is ever going to love me. But I don't believe you should have to. I don't believe you should have to be subservient to be loved. I don't believe that you have to have two versions of yourself or that it is even viable to maintain such a fake front for long.

While my dad always told me to wait as long as I could before getting married, again he was the anomaly in a sea of voices that became louder and more persistent the older I became.

Marriage is a widely accepted social norm the world over but in many cultures, such as in the Middle Eastern culture, it's ingrained from a young age that marriage is the inevitable rite of passage to enter adulthood and that you should aspire to get a ring on your finger as soon as possible.

It's for these reasons that many of the other 'conditions' seem to stem: the need to look good and to behave respectably, essentially to be a 'good Arab girl'. This will ensure that you are marketable, marriageable material. It's for this reason, ultimately, that you are supposed to be this ideal version of a woman: because that's what will get you hitched to a 'good' Arab man, one who can take care of you and replicate the life your parents had, and the one their parents had before them.

Boys, meanwhile, are allowed to make mistakes, chase girls in the street because they're 'dressed a certain way', and sleep around as much as they like. That doesn't hinder their marriage prospects; in fact, it might even enhance them. As El Saadawi argues, they're taught how to project their personality and how to prepare for a typical Arab man's life of 'strength, responsibility and authority'.[105]

The good, respectable behaviour of women isn't suddenly unnecessary once they marry, of course; women are then expected to be good, respectable wives. A friend of mine who recently got married and lives a relatively independent life – in that she goes out with her friends and sometimes travels without her husband – was told by her mum to stop doing so as it might alienate him.

It was something Sondos had also brought up: 'Growing up, when I'd ask my mum if I could do something, she'd say, "This is haram", but when I would ask my dad the same question he'd say, "When you're married, you can do what you want." So, in my mind, "haram" meant "before marriage", not actually "forbidden",' she explained. 'As I got older, I realised that what he was actually saying was, "When you're married you can ask your husband if you can do these things and we'll see what *he* says."' Indeed, many women swap the rules of their father for those of their husband.

Samira told me: 'I get into fights with my cousin's husband all the time because he bosses her around so much and I don't let him. She's almost scared of him. He says things like, "This is not a request, this is an order."' She told me of an occasion where she and her cousin were on their way out the door for dinner with friends when her cousin's husband demanded his wife cook him dinner. 'What will I eat?' he had said. To Samira's incredulity, her cousin took off her jacket and made him dinner. It was her duty, after all.

'The pressure to be a good Arab wife depends on who you marry,' Shahenda, a thirty-six-year-old Iraqi who was born and raised in London, told me. 'I had it massively – to the point where nothing I did was enough or deserved gratitude. I slaved for my children and my home and the culinary needs of my husband, with never a sign of recognition or a thank you,' she continued. 'Women need to teach their sons that this is not a woman's job, that it is done from our hearts and with love, and it is to be cherished and appreciated.'

'My ex-husband's side of the family definitely expected me to be a certain kind of wife,' Hiba, a thirty-one-year-old Libyan who was born and raised in London, told me. 'One evening we were all together for Eid and my husband came in and someone commented that his shirt was creased. His mum asked me why I hadn't ironed it and was really insulted and shocked when I laughed and said I didn't iron his clothes.'

'It wasn't companionship or team work,' she continued. 'It was like: "These are my obligations and these are your obligations." For a long time, I adhered, to a certain extent, because of pressure from society and the fear of losing my husband and being divorced.'

In truth, men can get away with most things. While by law in many Arab countries, men are allowed to marry up to four women, that's not really something people actually do in my circles. That said, men having affairs is widely expected and accepted.

'When I first found out my husband was cheating on me, my mum and my conservative friends told me I needed to check myself, to see what I did wrong,' Halima, a forty-year-old Egyptian, told me. 'My mum said I'm too rough with him, that I don't talk to him nicely . . . Not that she thought what he did was OK, but that it was somehow my fault he did it in the first place,' she continued. 'It's so weird. He's the one who cheated, but a lot of people were pointing fingers at me.'

'I think because Arab men are so often the providers there's a level of expectation of what the woman is supposed to contribute,' Hiba explained. 'If your man is cheating on you people might wonder if it's because you're overweight, for example, and that you haven't been keeping your side of the deal, so no wonder he's going to cheat on you.'

Certainly, part of the role of being a good, respectable wife is keeping up 'your side of the deal', and putting up with these transgressions. Divorce is often regarded as immoral, and sustaining a marriage a lifelong project – one that falls to the woman.

'When I told my parents I wanted to leave my husband, they sort of fell out with me,' Dunya told me. 'My mum kept telling me that the grass wasn't greener [on the other side] and that real life isn't all fairy tales. She told me I was making a mistake by walking away from security and that I should just shut up and put up.'

When it comes to divorce in the Arab world, three forces come into play: religion, sharia law, and culture. Divorce laws across the region are unequal for men and women, with women discriminated against in child custody and guardianship decisions. In Egypt, for example, laws state that women can only retain custody of their sons until the age of seven and daughters until they turn nine, after which the children must live with their fathers. In Jordan, mothers must also be deemed as trustworthy and 'able to perform their duties' and are not allowed to remarry.[106]

The stigma around divorce lays thickest at the feet of women. In a survey of 2,007 respondents across the Arab world, divorced women were found to be labelled as unwanted or pitied and were usually blamed for having failed to keep their former husbands happy.[107] But as divorce rates across the region increase and times change, many women are increasingly challenging the stigma. In Saudi Arabia, parties to celebrate divorces have become relatively common.[108]

Perhaps partly in opposition to the ending that had supposedly already been written for me, I have long railed against the assumption that I must get married. I was never the girl who fantasised about marriage and children. It sounded like a jail sentence to me, and I never understood why people would wish to rush to the altar. Despite what Beyoncé preached, I never believed he had to put a ring on it in order to prove that he liked it.

It is when I am single that I feel most comfortable with myself. I've worked hard to build a life I love and enjoy the freedom to explore my own wants and needs, and this seems to work best when I am not in a relationship. While I do enjoy dating, it's never been with the end goal of marriage as a necessity. I haven't felt ready for a relationship in quite a few years, let alone one that's supposed to last until I die. Most of my closest friends in London are single. We meet up and talk about all sorts of things: careers, interests, travels, aspirations, friendships, boys. I take up as much space in the bed as I like.

I'm far from an anomaly. In the UK, the average bride is thirty-five by the time she walks down the aisle, according to the Office for National Statistics.[109] For the first time in history, less than half the women in England and Wales are married, with two in three women under thirty reportedly single.[110] Similarly, in the US, the percentage of married Americans fell from 72 per cent in 1960 to 45 per cent in 2017.[111] As Kate Bolick, author of *Spinster*, attests:[112] 'Today, single women are regularly hailed as society's fastest-growing demographic, wielding enormous power.'

But whenever I go to Cairo, I increasingly want to scream. In the Middle East the pressure to wed, and at a young age, is rife and in opposition to fast-changing attitudes in the West. So deeply entrenched are the ideas that on one of my recent visits to Egypt someone actually said to me 'Don't you want your dad to be proud of you?' when I told them that I was single and that marriage wasn't on the cards at the moment. As if everything I had achieved in my life – as if all the effort I had put in to become the person I am – was not good enough without a ring on my finger.

Of my friends who are currently married, the vast majority are Middle Eastern. According to UNICEF, one out of five girls in the MENA region are married before they reach the age of eighteen,[113] although statistics suggest that Middle Eastern women are gradually marrying at a later age.[114] Certainly, no one I know got married quite that young, but in their early to mid-twenties that's still decisively earlier than my friends in the UK or elsewhere in the world.

The lure of freedom can for many be a driving factor. 'I ran away and eloped when I was twenty-two,' Amani, a thirty-five-year-old

Egyptian, tells me. 'I divorced a year later; it was a horrible decision,' she continues. 'The fucking irony! Had sex not been a big deal in my head – had it not been "haram" and all the other messy things – I may never have gone down that road.'

For many women, getting married is traditionally the only way out of the family home, the only way they can have sex and generally live more liberated lives. For some, it's the only path to independence.

While I'm obviously very happy that my married friends have found partners with whom they wish to share their lives – and most, if not all, seem to have made worthy selections – with each wedding comes a tide of ever-loudening voices saying 'okbelik'. The expression essentially means 'God willing, you're next', and is traditionally said to single men and women at engagement parties, weddings and baby showers. It's meant to be encouraging, I guess, but the weight of the word comes with its own burdens, namely the expectation that to live a good life you have to be married and the subsequent question of why you are not yet. I hate it.

'I try not to attend any weddings because of my family's and others' reactions, which really make me feel uncomfortable,' Souha, a twenty-eight-year-old Tunisian, told me. 'For them, marriage is like a race. The first one who gets married is the winner.'

'My younger sister is getting married and it's a big deal that I'm older and still not married,' Sondos told me. 'When she got engaged, the first thing my grandmother said to me is, "Don't worry, someone is going to come for you." She went to Umrah [pilgrimage to Mecca], and told me afterwards, "I prayed for a husband for you."

'I flipped and asked her, "Why would you pray for something like that when you can pray for me to have good health or to be successful?" If it's Eid or something, every single time my grandmother will say, "*okbel el 3arees el sana el geya*" [God willing a husband comes for you next year],' a spin on 'okbelik', where the prayer is for the marriage to occur imminently as opposed to just sometime in the future.

These kinds of comments are customary, and the judgement and competition that ensues from society and the invisible jury can at times be very insidious.

'My cousin was getting married and another was engaged and I went to Egypt with my family for the wedding. It was as if I was a leper because I was older and not even engaged,' Selina told me. 'I was treated as if I was a bad omen to the happy couples. The hen party was really awkward and I sensed that people either felt sorry for me or they thought I was jealous.'

I've long joked about wanting to create a badge that says 'Don't Okbelik Me' to pin on my dress for when I attend these events, so annoyed do I get at the number of people who will kiss me hello and then dump the saying at my feet. Time and again a tight smile crosses my face as I attempt not to be rude to my elders and behave instead like a good Arab girl.

'I used to feel the same, but I've turned it around,' Mariam, a thirty-year-old Libyan who was born and raised in London, told me. 'When it's coming from someone who I know loves me and wants the best for me, I know they mean: "I wish you happiness and love."'

Of course, most of the time such comments are not meant to cause harm or offence and are purely good wishes, but it's the underlying implication that if you're single or unmarried, it is not through choice, but circumstance. The deep-rooted assumption that love and happiness are inextricably linked, and the stereotypes embedded within such sayings, are infuriating.

When I took to my Instagram stories to ask my Middle Eastern followers if they too felt the same pressure to marry, over 80 per cent of those who responded said yes.

'Definitely twenty-three onwards I started to get pressured,' Shams told me.

'My mum used to compare me a lot to my female cousins in Egypt,' Samira added. 'She'd always point out the ones who were getting married.'

Much of the significance of marriage seems to revolve around the wedding itself. This really struck me when I spoke to Anwar, a twenty-five-year-old woman from Oman who identifies as gay. Arab society today is riddled with the kind of anti-gay prejudices that were more common in Britain half a century ago, and persecution is commonplace. While rules and penalties around the region vary, homosexuality is punishable by death in Iran, Saudi Arabia and Yemen, among others. In countries like Egypt, gay men can be charged with 'debauchery' and forced to undergo anal examinations to determine whether they are 'habituated' to anal sex.[115] Prominent figures such as the Muslim clerics and the Coptic Pope in Egypt condemn homosexuality in no uncertain terms, the latter once declaring that 'so-called human rights' for gay people were 'unthinkable'.

While it is also illegal to be a lesbian in the Middle East, there is less evidence of official persecution than in the case of gay men. But the stigmas surrounding homosexuality run deep and travel far. While same-sex marriage is increasingly being legalised around the world (more than two dozen countries have enacted national laws allowing gays and lesbians to marry[116]), even if you live outside the MENA region there can still be a big stigma attached.

When Anwar came out, it was the fact that she couldn't have a traditional wedding that most upset her mum. 'My older sister is gay too; you'd think having a sibling who is also gay would make it easier, but in Arab families it makes it so much harder because if one of you is written off, then all the pressure is on the other,' she explained. 'I come from a privileged background and that adds so much pressure to have a huge, flamboyant wedding to some rich Arab guy. It's like they have to prove to the rest of the family that they've done a good job.'

Certainly, Arab weddings are often lavish affairs with guest lists in the high hundreds – so extravagant they sometimes even make the news worldwide. In 2011, the Institute for International Research in Dubai estimated that the cost of a typical Emirati wedding is about

Dh300,000 (£63,406).[117] As an article in *Arab News* put it: 'Weddings in Saudi are costly, and many associate that with the need for families to show off they are better and richer than the rest; the bigger your wedding is, the better.'[118]

That isn't just the case in Saudi. As the article continued, 'Others succumb to peer pressure from their families, whether it be the groom's or the bride's, to satisfy societal expectations.'

A mother of five was quoted as saying: 'I can assure you, at least in my case, it wasn't to impress anybody. The point of celebrating lavishly was to show how happy I am for my daughter and to send her off lovingly. There are also societal aspects to keep in mind, of sharing that joy with others who have included me in their celebrations before.'

The need to reciprocate prior hospitality is often top of the list of concerns when drafting an invite list. The number of annual wedding invitations, then, can often be counted in the hundreds.

Across the region and its diaspora, Arab parents only seem to consider their daughter is safe with a secure future once she has a husband. Husbands are considered a protection.

'For my mum, settled means married,' Samira told me. 'Even though I don't really need anything and I've got my own money – I could move out tomorrow – I'm not considered an adult until I'm married. Not my brother, though; my brother can live on his own.

'My brother asked me, "Do you even want to get married?" And I said, "Yeah, obviously", but really, I don't know if I do actually,' she continued. 'I found myself saying to him that I wanted to get married because I want to have kids. It made me realise that if it wasn't for the religious and cultural side of things, I would have had a child already out of wedlock, because that's ultimately what I want. I'm not fussed about a wedding or saying "my husband" . . . I'm not against it! But

I'm not convinced this is how it has to be. If it wasn't for my parents, I would happily be raising a kid on my own. But it just can't happen. My mum's response would be, "What respectable woman would want to do this?"'

Indeed, while in the UK and elsewhere, couples of all sexual orientations are increasingly cohabiting, getting married, entering into polygamous relationships or living and thriving alone, adopting or inseminating or having children naturally if they so wish, in Arab culture – due to societal pressures from the invisible jury, as well as limitations from the law in the Middle East itself – none of this is feasible, at least not without some conflict.

'When I was twenty-five I came out to my mum on WhatsApp,' Zainab, a thirty-year-old half-Yemeni, half-Pakistani woman who lives in London and identifies as bisexual, told me. 'I was tired of living a double life but I was very scared of their reaction. Since I was eight, I knew I was very much inclined towards women, I just didn't know what it meant. I thought maybe I had been born in the wrong sex, that maybe I'm a boy because I'm attracted to girls.'

As Anwar explained, it's especially difficult in Arab culture 'because it's not the same sort of homophobia you might experience in England; in Arab countries it goes against the Quran – and Islam is the law.

'My mum knows that in the Quran it says that being gay is wrong,' she told me, 'but she has a really big heart so I think she's conflicted a lot of the time by how *she* really feels and what religion tells her. My grandma and aunts wouldn't want to know. It's only my cousins who know I'm gay . . . Growing up, I found it really hard because I thought there was something wrong with me,' she concluded.

So strong is the pressure to fall in love and marry an Arab man, Anwar told me, that for a long time – for years, in fact – she tried.

'I thought I have a duty to marry a guy and be with a guy, so I dated my best friend for about four years,' she told me. 'It was fine for the first couple of years, but when we started to experiment physically I realised I just couldn't do it. It was hell.'

'It was hard work constantly fighting with my mum, trying to make them understand,' Zainab told me. 'Now that I'm thirty she kind of lets me be, but now and again she tells me she doesn't accept it and she doesn't agree with it, but I'm grown now, and "what you do is between you and your God".'

These days, while both women live mostly independent lives to varying degrees, they still introduce their girlfriends to their parents as their 'friend', and considerations for the future are beginning to weigh heavy.

'I will marry a woman one day and I want to have kids. That hasn't changed because of my sexuality,' Anwar told me. 'I really worry – when I eventually do have kids – how they will be treated in Oman, because obviously I'm going to want my family around me, but I have to accept that it's going to be difficult when I get married . . . They have the most elaborate baby showers out there and you have so many family members around you and it makes me sad, and worried,' she said. 'I've got a girlfriend now and her family is amazing. Sometimes she'll joke about what kind of wedding we're going to have and how her family will be there and I'll think, "None of my family will be there." Which is shit.'

In truth, life options can often feel limited, if not by the law then by the invisible jury and by the totally natural need for approval from our families and societies. Of course, it's often out of care that families place these pressures on their children – out of love, out of the assumption that that's what is required to be safe and happy – but that's part of the problem: the assumption that abiding by tradition, cocooned in your culture, is what is required to be safe and happy. It plays into the absurd notion that women are helpless without a husband.

Regardless of other achievements or accolades, women in the Arab world are expected to first fill the roles of wives and mothers before all others. As we'll explore in more detail in the next chapter, other life experiences, such as work and career, are often considered secondary achievements or not at all.

'It was always very important in my family to get a college degree and have a career, but I feel that – as much as they believe in my being ambitious – at the end of the day, even if you have it all, they think something is missing if you're not married,' Aisha, a thirty-year-old Kuwaiti who moved to Ireland to go to medical school, told me. 'My mum now tells me, "I wish I didn't encourage you to go to med school, I'd rather see you married with children."'

Without marriage, the rest of it doesn't matter – that is the message Arab women the world over receive. My mum parrots this same mentality, even responding 'Great! And then you can find a husband to take care of you' when I first shared with her the news of my book deal.

I know she's proud of me, I know she doesn't mean it really, but also she kind of does. All her friends' children are getting married and having kids and, for her, that's what's supposed to be the next step. But I don't think it bothers her the way it used to.

While I'm sure she hasn't given up on the thought of me finding a 'good Arab husband', she now places more importance on me being a happy, healthy, whole person rather than simply a 'respectable, married daughter'. What's more, as she's gotten older and seen more varied life experiences, as well as more divorces (including her own), I think she's come to see that getting married isn't always the happy fairy-tale ending she had been taught to believe. That maybe, then, getting married wouldn't automatically secure that future for me.

There are plenty of ways a woman can secure her own future: being confident, financially independent and well educated are just some suggestions. In reality, they are perhaps the only *real* suggestions.

Language is, as always, revealing. The word for a single woman in Arabic is 'ahnes', meaning a branch that withers and becomes useless. The English language is no better for describing unwed women: Wikipedia attests that 'spinsters' have a reputation for 'sexual and emotional frigidity, lesbianism, ugliness, frumpiness, depression, astringent moral virtue, and overly-pious religious devotion'. The word 'bachelor' summons up more preferable images. The message is often the same across cultures. The narrative a singular one.

Around the world, the media portrays similar ideologies and ideals: that marriage is an imperative, the only correct way to do adulthood. Perhaps even more heinously, societies everywhere portray women as the ones most desperate to pursue this route, with men only wanting to escape from the ball and chain.

Studies looking into Arab print magazines for women found that they overwhelmingly depict women as wives and mothers. They tend to focus on 'traditional preoccupations' such as fashion, cooking, cosmetics and home affairs. Only one had a political section.[119] This narrow depiction has traditionally been the case in Western media too. But, increasingly, a number of women-centric publications have been doing wonders to broaden the range of interests and topics addressed – because, naturally, women can like fashion and also be interested in politics, can (and should) have other interests other than just how to get and keep a man.

Assuming that a woman is straight and *does* want to marry, in Arab culture it often seems like we should be content to pick a man as we would a chocolate bar from a vending-machine shelf. Marriage should not be another item on the checklist to adulthood, but that is often the mentality.

An Arabic proverb that sums up the ideology is: 'Better a man's shadow than that of a wall', the idea being that it's better to have a man to cast a shadow in your home than no shadow at all. Except . . . surely not just *any* fucking shadow.

I asked my Instagram followers if they had any phrases that riled them the same way 'okbelik' bothered me. Rana's response was funny and very telling: '*Yallah, sheddi 7elik*, which is "Come on, pull your socks up!" But how?! What do they expect us to do?' she fumed. 'They always make it seem like it's your fault you haven't found the right guy.

Like it's your fault for not settling. Like you have no right to want your future partner to have certain qualities.'

Indeed, it's the same mentality that tells me to adjust my views and hold back my opinions, so I can 'get the man'. And that, while this man might not be the prize, he is still a man and that in itself is all the qualification that is required. The alternative – being single for the rest of my life – is supposed to be too horrific to even consider.

'People are settling like it's normal, but I'm one of those people who will never settle,' Shams told me. 'I have conversations with people at work, in Kuwait, where I live and they think I'm nuts. I told them about a very wealthy family friend of mine who my parents were trying to set me up with,' she continued. 'I found him the world's most boring human, but my colleague said to me, "Are you an idiot? He's a millionaire, he's great on paper, just marry him and you can live your own life." But really . . . why would I do that?!'

As sociologist Maha Karkabi-Sabbah said in an interview,[120] 'In order to marry, women will compromise on such things [in a partner] as age, social status [and] educational level.

'Studies show that educated women in Western countries are less inclined to compromise, and sometimes opt to stay single if they do not find the right partner. For [Middle Eastern women], the social pressure overcomes women's personal choice.'

The thing is, marriage is hard. Divorce rates attest to this. Forty-two per cent of all marriages in the UK end in divorce,[121] while divorce rates in the Middle East are particularly high and spiking. Jordan's divorce rate is among the highest in the world,[122] while the divorce rate in Egypt has risen by 83 per cent over the last twenty years.[123] Acquaintances of my age in Egypt have already married and divorced. Some have even remarried. If that's not evidence that marriage is not something to be entered into lightly, I don't know what is.

𝕏

Not only are we taught that marriage is an imperative, we are also taught other unhealthy mindsets. Predominant among these is that we are only half accomplished without a husband, incomplete until we have a man and a ring on our finger. Greek mythology has long spewed the idea that we are divided, doomed to search the earth for our other halves, our soulmates. It's a damaging ideology that places undue impetus on being half of a whole.

In reaction to these ideas, I've always struggled with having feelings for someone without considering them a weakness, without feeling like I was losing some of myself along the way. While in Arab culture the focus is on marriage – with love often thought to be something that grows with time and respect – in the West, romanticism is one of society's driving forces. In that respect, much of the content I've grown up consuming – from TV shows, to movies, books and beyond – promotes happily-ever-after as if it's the rule rather than the exception. It also insists that love needs to be all-consuming, that ideally love should be the thing that guides and instructs you, that you should sacrifice yourself for it. But that's not love, that's insanity! As an article in *VICE* put it,[124] stories like *Fifty Shades of Grey* – one of the most commercially popular books and films of recent years – further conflate the idea that love and obsession are one and the same.

'They're part of a long history of movie couples perpetuating the idea that a satisfying relationship means being completely consumed with each other,' the article continues. 'In *The Notebook*, Noah writes Allie a letter every single day for an entire year. I mean . . . if you're going to write every day, at least consider working on yourself by journaling.

'In *Fatal Attraction*, Alex attempts suicide just to keep Dan in her life. *Bonnie and Clyde* celebrates lovers who literally killed for each other. And perhaps the OGs of all-consuming passion were Romeo and Juliet, who were more foolishly emo than necessary.'

These messages have an effect on our perceptions of love and marriage. A 2014 study analysed the extent to which movies and TV shows were influencing the love lives of 625 college students (392 of whom were female). They found that more exposure to romantic movies led to a greater tendency to over-idealise love, to believe that it can overcome all obstacles and that true love will nearly always be perfect.[125]

Fairy tales teach us that perfect, blissful love is a birthright. Perhaps it's for this reason that one of my favourite books is Alain de Botton's profoundly unromantic, romantic novel *Essays in Love*, in which he follows protagonists falling in love, falling out of love, and then each falling in love with new people. The narrative arc of the story didn't end with a supposed happily-ever-after, or at the heartbreak. There was more, as there almost always is.

It took me a long time to unlearn that, a lot of obsession confused for love, but I came to realise that the longest relationship you'll ever have is the one you have with yourself, that you had therefore damned well make it a good one! Falling in love with myself has been a long and hard and often beautiful process. I have yet to figure out how to reconcile that with loving another person romantically. That kind of love has, to me, for a long time also meant weakness.

As women we are taught to place importance on another person, be that our husbands, our fathers, our mothers, or our extended circles. We are taught to be caregivers instead of giving that love to ourselves. We're taught to hold our tongues and, in doing so, to suppress our own instincts and desires lest we offend or cease to be 'loveable'. We're taught to aspire to be desired, influencing everything from the way we dress to how we converse, whether we consciously realise it or not. We're taught to view ourselves through the eyes of others instead of assessing our own sense of worth.

Instead of being encouraged and shown how to build and nurture all our relationships – including and especially those with ourselves – or how to develop interests and hobbies and embark on fulfilling careers, we are taught to place men on pedestals, and to base our self-esteem and our contribution to society on whether or not we are able to find a husband. Other than how unhealthy and damaging that is in itself, if we don't approach love on an equal footing with men, then women are forever at a disadvantage; we are automatically the weaker, needier sex. We are the ones who want and men are the ones who give. This affects everything, from the very first moment. Every single word, touch and suggestion is clouded by inequality.

As Kate Bolick put it,[126] 'women have never been so free. We enjoy more educational and vocational opportunities than any women . . . For the first time in history, we don't need marriage for social status or economic security. We can make our own lives, with or without a husband' – despite what our Middle Eastern families may try to tell us.

Haifa said: 'A lot of girls get married just to tick it off their list. But a lot of us are not getting married, because . . . we're cool, we're enjoying our lives. I don't want to be single for ever, it's not about that. I would love to meet someone but I can't fake it. I don't believe that as long as he's rich or ticks off a checkbox he's the one,' she continued. 'I've seen too much to pretend to be happy. I need to be genuinely happy with someone because my life is already good! It needs to be an improvement.'

The thing is, getting married or falling in love is not the key to happiness or independence. It's not the key at all, at least not to that door.

I was put off romantic love for a long time because of these ideologies, because of the pressure, because of the assumptions – many young women and men are. But as I increasingly see healthy examples of wedded life around me, I realise it's not getting married that's the problem per se, or being in love; it's the impetus around it and the suggestion that it's the only important thing, that a woman's worth is intrinsically and inherently bound up in her marital status.

In my opinion, true happiness and independence are achieved when we are true to ourselves, not once we prefix our names with *Mrs*. That is what I aspire to. And if I then meet a man who is also happy and independent, then whatever happens between us is a bonus to my life; he will not be the sun around which I pivot.

It's the only way, I think, to make a whole, real, engaging life with another: two complete individuals who come together of their own volition, bearing fruit; jam they've spent years perfecting. Two perfected varieties of jam on your morning toast, instead of two mediocre ones haphazardly stirred together in the hope they stick.

And if not? I'll have happiness and independence anyway. I'll be whole anyway. I'll still have my own jam, and it will be perfect.

Chapter 9
When Your Dreams Are Limited

For most of my life I have been in the habit of putting pen to paper in an effort to figure out what I was thinking. Along the way, I made that my career. But I think of it as a fluke, sometimes, discovering my ambition.

I wasn't always this person. The one who wakes up at 7 a.m. every day and crafts her own to-do lists and assiduously executes each task. The one who, to put it bluntly, makes shit happen for herself.

Before I met Courtney when I was twenty-one, I had never thought about what I might do with my life, although I was already starting to panic that I hadn't figured it out yet, and I guess that does indicate the seeds of ambition. It just wasn't a topic of conversation in my house, what I might want to do when I was older. While my parents showered me and my brother with as much love and attention as they could at the time, there wasn't much left over to enquire about things like that. It was just one day at a time. Let's just make it to the next day without setting the house on fire.

At school, I wasn't one of the particularly clever ones. Between getting bullied, the tension that was ongoing in the house, moving back and forth between Cairo and London and all the uncertainty that comes with that – as well as the normal growing pains – excelling academically was pretty much the least of my priorities.

And while it's common for children in the West to get part-time jobs from their teens – many if not all of my British friends had weekend jobs – Arab parents are not always fond of the idea, especially if you're a girl. My dad was always against it, arguing that I shouldn't waste my time working for extra money I didn't need when I could be engaged in more worthwhile endeavours. Very generous of him, and I am very grateful, except for the fact that I *didn't* spend my time on more worthwhile endeavours.

In reality, the advantages of my having a job while still studying would have gone far beyond the extra bucks, would have no doubt taught me valuable life skills, and might have instilled in me a work ethic from an early age. Perhaps it would have even helped give some indication as to the sorts of things I enjoyed and didn't enjoy doing, helping pave a path to a future career.

'My dad never used to let us work either,' Lamis told me. 'He'd always say, "Oh, I don't worry about the girls because you'll just get married and have kids." If I'd tell him that I wanted to work anyway he'd say it was irrelevant what I did because it wasn't like I was going to really contribute financially, anyway.'

In Arab culture, having a career is regarded as a low priority for women. If I'm hard-pressed I can think of perhaps two Middle Eastern women in my circle who would be financially independent without the support of a father or husband.

Even my mum, despite being university-educated, quit the job she had briefly held after graduating once she married my dad. None of our female family friends ever really worked either, not in London nor in Egypt, although this is gradually changing among my friends.

In a poll I carried out on an Instagram story (to which 137 people responded), 35 per cent of the Middle Eastern women who responded said that their mums were also unemployed. The number was actually lower than I had thought it would be, but it more or less rings true with other statistics, which have found that the unemployment rate for women in the MENA region is often as high as 40 per cent.[127] Of the Middle Eastern women who responded to my Instagram poll, 65 per cent said that their families had put more pressure on them to get married than they had on embarking on or excelling at their careers.

The invisible jury is everywhere and socio-cultural norms and traditional gender roles in Arab culture play a big role in issues such as the perceptions of working women and the sorts of jobs Arab women are expected to take on, if indeed they should work at all. Fields like engineering or medicine were often brought up as 'respectable', 'worthwhile' careers by many of the Middle Eastern women I spoke to. Some suggested that this might be because they are precisely the sorts of job that might make them more marriageable.

'With Egyptian parents, during school it was all about my grades so I could get a career,' said Mandy. 'This would, in their eyes, in turn get me a good husband. They wanted me to be a doctor or a lawyer or an engineer (in that order). Having graduated and now gotten employed, there's pressure to get married.'

'I think there's a very narrow definition of the sort of job considered to be respectable,' Sarah agreed. 'I remember when I worked in fashion, I would come home and my dad would say things like: "What are you even doing, are you just wasting your time?"'

As a result of economic necessity, in Egypt today, figures estimate that women are breadwinners for over 3 million families, representing 14 per cent of the total number of families.[128] But of the fifteen countries with the lowest rates of women participating in their labour force, thirteen are in the MENA region. Only 24 per cent of women in Arab countries work outside the home and not a single Arab country ranks in the top 100 positions on the World Economic Forum's global gender gap report.[129] Not one has a legal quota for the percentage of women it must include on corporate boards, and Saudi Arabia only recently passed a law stating that women are allowed to study and work without a man's permission.[130]

Entering the workforce in itself can be a struggle in a patriarchal region governed by such strong socio-cultural norms. As an article in PRI put it, in the Middle East, 'faced with the choice of a man and a woman with equal skills, an employer will often give the job to the man, particularly if the man has a family. If a woman is hired, and a man in the same place is doing the same job, chances are, he'll be paid more – often, much more.'[131] Plenty of other factors exist to create an inhospitable business environment for women.

While I was in Cairo and at my grandfather's house for lunch, I broached the subject of why my late grandmother – his wife, who was a phenomenal designer and seamstress – was never allowed to pursue her talents professionally. He looked at me like I was crazy and, to paraphrase, said something very much like: 'Why should she? I'm the man, I'm her husband and she should never have to work.' In almost the same breath he said: 'Women are not equal to men.' My face must have given my thoughts away because he rushed to clarify his position, arguing that women are actually *better* than men are; more precious, and so should not have to undertake such earthly endeavours. My grandmother had never even been to the bank on her own, he explained; it was his duty as a man and a husband to look after her in all of these ways and more.

It sounds better – and less offensive – coming out of his well-meaning mouth than how this plays out in practice. In truth, it's this sort of ideology that removes autonomy from women, that renders them helpless and in need of a man just to survive. It is this sort of ideology that places undue pressure and expectation on women to inhabit the role of delicate, defenceless maidens rather than take up the challenge to express themselves as autonomous, capable, equal human beings.

In a study of views in Egypt, Lebanon, Morocco and Palestine, results found that male attitudes towards the role of women in the workplace and at home, as well as their participation in public life, were 'stereotypically sexist'.[132] Nearly 10,000 people between the ages of eighteen and fifty-nine were questioned and a majority of men were found to support a number of 'traditional and inequitable attitudes towards women, including a belief that they are not fit to be leaders, should not work outside the home, and that it is more important to educate boys than girls'.[133]

In Egypt, only 31 per cent of Egyptian men thought married women should have the same rights to work outside the home as their husbands, while more than 90 per cent of men agreed with the statement that 'a man should have the final word on decisions made in the home'.[134]

Even once successful, women are still challenged on the degree their careers can impact the family home and are often shamed if they're believed to be spending too much time away from their families, even if it's just a business trip. These career women are still often asked, 'Why do you do this to yourself?' or told to consider taking up more 'female' endeavours. I've even heard stories of women telling other women that 'men don't like it when their wives out-earn them'!

'Egyptian and Arab society still considers that women have been created to play the role of mothers and wives, whose function in life is to serve at home and bring up the children,' wrote Nawal El Saadawi.[135] Much of what she argued in her book *The Hidden Face of Eve*, published in 1977, still rings true today. 'A woman is permitted to leave her home every day and go to an office, a school, a hospital or a factory on the condition that she returns after her day of work to shoulder the responsibilities related to her husband and children, which are considered more important than anything else she may have done,' she wrote.

Across the world and across all cultures, women still carry the brunt of these responsibilities; what is often referred to as 'emotional labour'. Even Socrates, often hailed as the first moral philosopher of the West, believed that 'Man was created for noble pursuits, for knowledge and

the pleasures of the mind, whereas women were created for sex, reproduction and the preservation of the human species.'[136]

More recently, a *Harvard Business Review* article referred to some
of the words associated with ambitious women, implying that they
are selfish, self-aggrandising or that they manipulate others for their
own ends.[137] Other than the fact that those associations would never
be attached to an ambitious man, these are traits considered not particularly becoming for women – anywhere in the world, let alone in
traditionally patriarchal societies like the Middle East, where women
are supposed to be agreeable, meek and docile.

Dating Courtney opened up a portal that led into a whole new world.
One in which people my age – women especially – knew what they
wanted to do with their lives. The people I was meeting through him
were often very driven and extremely hard-working. Courtney was relatively well established in his career as a music artist, and I would accom-
pany him on the seemingly endless number of events he was invited to.
Between store launches, his friends' shows and his increasingly sold-out
gigs, every night we were surrounded by some of London's up-and-
coming creative talents. I revelled in their company.

Up until that point, none of the people I usually hung out with had
much clue as to what they would be doing from one day to the next.
Before I met Courtney, my friends and I smoked weed and went club-
bing a lot, often having to drag tired minds and feet to our university
classes, more following the motions than moving in any sort of direction. Meeting people who had dreams they were actively pursuing – and
so often making a reality – inspired me in all sort of ways.

I had just finished an undergraduate degree in Sociology and
Psychology, and I remember being acutely embarrassed by my vague and
wishy-washy answers to the inevitable 'so what do you do?' questions.

I have always been a writer, but it was never really something I thought I could turn into a career, until one day – early in our relationship and in the midst of my post-university gap-year existential crisis – I wrote Courtney a poem and he surprised me by saying, 'You're actually pretty good at this; why don't you give writing a go?' It felt like a revelation but, at the same time, inevitable. Writing had always been, for me, a way of thinking through my fingertips.

When I first found my ambition, first discovered what I wanted to channel my energies into, I jumped in head first, working overtime to make up for what suddenly felt like aimless and wasted years when . . . *obviously* this is what I should have been working towards the whole time.

I began an internship at an online music publication, where I would attend gigs and interview artists, as well as put together listings of all the events happening in London that month.

My network quickly grew, thanks, in part, to all the events I attended with Courtney. It was just before Instagram, in the early days of social media, but making connections online was something I had been doing for years; growing up, I frequented numerous chat rooms and had anonymous blogs through which I forged friendships with people all over the world. It was only natural, then, that I was an active user of Twitter, and cemented many of the real-world connections I was making with an exchange of follows and messages.

I embarked on a Masters in Journalism, which I threw myself into, alongside writing for a number of publications and my own blog – a compilation of mostly album reviews and interviews with music artists, both UK and abroad, as well as dipping my toe into expressing my opinion on things that were happening in my life or in the world around me.

Those years allowed me to practise expressing my opinion, allowed me to hone my ability to use my words to say what I wanted them to say, and to learn to resist the fear of negative feedback. I read everything with a passion I hadn't felt since I had needed to use books as an escape from the world around me. I'd spend hours poring over magazines and newspapers, taking notes on the sorts of features that tended to get picked up; thinking of offshoots of ideas, stories I felt perhaps I could contribute to, that perhaps I could tell.

I sent hundreds of emails and tweets – to editors, to PRs and to fellow journalists I admired, often asking the latter for just an hour to pick their brains. I kept an eye out for opportunities on social media and put myself forward every time, even if and when I doubted myself in the back of my mind. I did unpaid internships and went on unpaid press trips, and my network and my confidence grew and I began to learn how to work smarter instead of just harder.

I crafted spreadsheets of editors' emails and ideas for features, and I'd spend hours every day distilling my ideas into pitches and ushering them out into the ether. The rejections would pile up in my inbox but some said yes.

As my work and my interests evolved, the things I was writing about continued to grow and change too. I became more interested in human connections than ever before; how and why we live our lives the way we do and how we think and feel about them. I realised that those were the stories I had been telling all along, and I felt an increasing compulsion to tell more of them. No matter what I wrote, there was always someone who said 'me too'. It made me even braver.

I didn't have a plan. I still don't. It's always been about forward motion. About thinking through my fingers because I have no choice but to do so. My work has been the joy of my life and has done so much for my personal development, helping me to become the best version of myself I can be. I can't imagine what I would do instead; the work is fulfilling and deliciously consuming.

In my travels and through my writing, I have connected with a network of incredible working women (and men) who inspire me to try to do and be better every single day. In my social circle growing up, women who worked hard and were fulfilled by things other than their families were largely absent.

The reason for this is partly that the women didn't particularly need to work as their husbands tended to have careers that were financially lucrative. Of course, most families do need two incomes. But working isn't just about money, it is also about contributing to something more substantial than the family income. It is about one's self-worth. It's not that there's anything wrong with being fulfilled by your family, but I can't deny it's wonderful to have a choice and to have something you do for yourself.

For me and many of the Middle Eastern women I spoke to, seeing our mums not working actually encouraged us to strive harder to make a different sort of life for ourselves.

Shahd, a twenty-five-year-old who was born in Syria and currently resides in France, told me: 'I was raised by a single, hard-working pharmacist mum, so having learnt so much from the struggles that my mum had to deal with, I have always believed that it is important I have a career and be financially independent.'

In a 2017 interview with the *Telegraph*, Shadia Bseiso, the first Arab woman from the Middle East to join the WWE, the world's biggest wrestling promotion, credited the 2012 London Olympics (in which Saudi Arabia sent two female athletes to compete) with inspiring her to start wrestling. She explained how it was the first time she had seen Arab women competing at a professional level and that it had made her wonder if she would have taken up sports earlier had she seen such examples growing up.[138]

I often wonder the same. If I had seen more kick-ass working women I could relate to growing up – in the media, at home, in the world I inhabited – would I have found the deep-seated ambition and work ethic that was inside me all along any earlier? Certainly, socio-cultural norms make being a visible Middle Eastern woman particularly difficult, meaning that there weren't really any Middle Eastern women I could see in the media while I was growing up.

Many kids in the West now say they want to be a blogger or YouTuber,[139] but in the Middle East, this is still not really a 'thing'. The culture is one that does not look favourably upon people who make themselves too visible. This idea has a lot in common with the old-fashioned view that entering the entertainment industry was very unsophisticated, especially if you were from a particular family. What's more, being a Middle Eastern woman in the public eye comes with its own set of challenges. In addition to the invisible jury, now the whole world sits in judgement.

Citing the example of American journalist Noor Tagouri, who is originally from Libya and appeared in *Playboy* magazine in her hijab for their 'Renegades' edition, Samira told me her mum had had *so* much to say. 'She told me, "She's supposed to be a diamond, why would she lower herself?" I tried to tell her that she hadn't even taken her clothes off and that she was challenging ideas . . . encouraging progress, but her response was, "Progress to what? To *Playboy* magazine?"'

Haifa brought up the example of supermodels Bella and Gigi Hadid, who have Palestinian origins and subsequently get chastised for almost every single thing they do. 'Like, "Oh, you wear bikinis and you call yourselves Muslim . . ."'

It can be a struggle to find the balance. Even in my work, as much as I try to be as honest as possible – and I'm very lucky to have a supportive family who allow me to live (and subsequently write) about my life in the way I deem best – I've often felt myself self-censoring or shying away from writing about topics that I imagine might cause offence to my extended family. (Although I guess this book brings an end to that!)

I have even received messages on social media asking me why I wear bikinis, and during Ramadan one year I was asked why I wasn't fasting. It's hard to be proud of your identity and culture *and* be the full version of yourself at the same time, when it's pointed out, time and again, how incompatible this ideal is. (Perhaps that's why for a long time I shied away from writing about identity politics.) But it's for precisely these reasons that a greater variety of role models is needed. The more open we are about our lives and our views, the less people might judge and the more comfortable they might feel to live their own lives in ways that differ from the consensus. The world is, after all, changed by examples.

There are an increasing number of Middle Eastern-born females making names for themselves, Huda Kattan foremost among them. The thirty-something Iraqi-born, US-raised, Dubai-based founder of Huda Beauty has over 35 million followers on Instagram at the time of writing, and is hailed as one of the most influential beauty bloggers in the world.[140]

In recent years, the prevalence of aspirational working women of Middle Eastern origin across the board is improving. The Deputy Governor of the Bank of England is Egyptian-born Nemat Shafik, the CEO of Swatch is Lebanese Nayla Hayek, and the Minister of Education in France is Moroccan Najat Vallaud-Belkacem. All of them featured prominently in *Forbes'* World's 10 Most Powerful Arab Women list in 2017,[141] alongside Amal Clooney, a successful human rights lawyer whose achievements have little to do with her marriage to George Clooney.

While MENA countries rank in the bottom 20 per cent of the female entrepreneurship index, the progress of the region's female entrepreneurs is reportedly on a par with their counterparts in Europe and America. Thirty-three per cent of women-run enterprises in the UAE are said to generate revenue in excess of $100,000. This is in comparison to just 13 per cent in the developed US market.[142] While only 10 per cent of all internet entrepreneurs are women, the percentage of female internet entrepreneurs in MENA countries is 23 per cent.[143] In the Gulf, it's 35 per cent.[144]

Social media and technology have facilitated and invented new career prospects for men and women around the world, and for women in Arab countries this is all the more prevalent. This is due, in part, to the fact that technology allows entrepreneurs to work from home, making it easier to get around the socio-cultural norms and lack of accessibility for women in countries such as Saudi Arabia.

The thing is, working allows women financial independence, which is imperative in order to achieve true equality and empowerment. Being financially independent gives us the freedom to make choices about our lives. It gives women the credibility to participate in the making of important decisions, both for themselves and for their whole family. It provides an autonomy and an independence that result in a far more equal footing between husband and wife. When a woman is contributing to the household, she has far more say in how that money is spent.

'To sit around and do nothing is my nightmare,' Lamis told me. 'Sure, it's nice to feel supported and comfortable – and I mean no disrespect to women who choose that way of life – but they're solely dependent on either their fathers or their husbands. It's not just about the money and the financial independence, it's also the sense of achievement.'

But it is important to underline that being financially independent provides the confidence and ability to walk away if the marriage fails. I have seen and heard far too many stories of women unable to leave failed marriages because they have no other option. Being financially independent affords *choice*. In India, where it has been reported that 70 per cent of women face some form of domestic abuse,[145] restricting access to financial resources is an often-used tactic[146] to keep women in the home.

The social benefits of improving women's status in the workforce are not to be underestimated either; women's under-representation in business feeds through to under-representation in politics, as money often equals influence. This in turn is reflected in the laws we make as a country, often to the detriment of women's lives. What's more, the positive impact women in the workforce have on the economy of a country itself has been well chronicled. A 2004 World Bank study estimated that 'if women in the Middle East were to work at the same rates as their peers in other parts of the world, the average household income would rise by as much as 25 per cent – enough to push many families out of poverty'.[147]

Undeniably, the glaring issue of inequality still needs to be addressed the world over – in the workplace and beyond. While women are increasingly entering the workforce all around the world – and excelling – women continue to face discrimination.[148] According to the World Economic Forum,[149] 'women are still paid less, female bosses are still in the minority, and motherhood still carries the risk of total career derailment'. In the UK, there is an 18 per cent gap between men's and women's salaries, with British women effectively working for free for the first sixty-seven days of the year.[150] But you can't add to the conversation of inequality or contribute to making any changes if you're not even at the table.

It's important for there to be role models to inspire women all over the world, but perhaps particularly for young Middle Eastern girls, who have long needed a different version of life to aspire to. To grow up having access to female success stories is the best motivation to succeed yourself. It is always easier to imagine breaking through the glass ceiling if someone has smashed through before – and thrived.

My argument is not about choosing work over family or marriage over independence. It is about the importance of autonomy, of having room to dream, of *choice* – *real* choice, not just the route you take when you think there is no alternative.

Chapter 10
When You Are 'Technically Muslim'

This is the chapter I've been most afraid to write. It's further evidence of why it's important to do so, but I've never felt the desire to tiptoe around a subject more than this one.

I'm 'technically Muslim' – as in, my birth certificate states Muslim because my parents are both technically Muslim and my grandparents technically Muslim too. That's how it works in Islam. You take your father's religion, even if it's not one he actively practises.

As you might have gathered by now, my parents are not religious in the least, and religion was never a big part of our lives. Sure, my mum used to recite the fatiha with my brother and me before we went to sleep at night when we were younger, and I still recite it in my head every single time I get on an aeroplane, but that's really where it ends.

My maternal grandmother was probably the most religious person in my family. She used to wear a verse from the Quran around her neck, along with a pendant of the Virgin Mary.

I never gave it much thought growing up, other than perhaps during the year I lived in Egypt when I got yelled at for eating during Ramadan. I never really needed to consider religion. We didn't celebrate Eid or Christmas, we ate and drank whatever we wanted, we learnt our values elsewhere – attributes like loyalty and the importance of having good judgement and being a good person, as my father had hoped we would.

I believe in God. I've just always had my own relationship with Him and I speak to Him in my head. Sometimes, I go to church, where I'll recite the fatiha followed by the Lord's Prayer. It doesn't bother me which language I use or whether I call Him God or Allah – it's the same God. There is only one. The main difference is that Islam considers Christ as God's closest and most beloved prophet as opposed to His son. Both prayers end in 'Amen', albeit with different pronunciation.

The events of 9/11 set the world on a new course, and who and what I identify with is increasingly something I've needed to consider since. When the Twin Towers fell, I was too young to really understand the magnitude or the sheer tragedy of the situation, or why I came home from school that day to find my parents with tears streaming down their faces, heads buried in their hands in front of the TV, distraught for the lives lost.

'I remember specifically after 9/11 my mum said to us, "If someone asks if you're Muslim, don't say you are",' Selina told me. 'Before that, I was too young or I wasn't even asked . . . it didn't even make a difference. It was like a switch. It was horrible.'

As an 'invisible immigrant' and certainly an 'invisible Muslim', I've never been subject to the vitriol that has become emblematic of Islamophobia, and neither has my family, but the stereotypes and prejudice persist. I've somehow become a technical ambassador.

Now, in London or elsewhere in the West, whenever I say I'm from Egypt, people automatically assume that I'm Muslim. And that if I am Muslim, I must also be an anomaly as I do not subscribe to the strict code of behaviour that is especially visible for females.

People who aren't Muslim are often shocked to see that I don't adhere to this code. However, it is the practising Muslims who can at times be even more shocked, and it's this group I feel judged by and who made me scared to write this chapter, and even this book. They are the cause of my imposter syndrome: I'm constantly waiting to be called out for being a 'bad Muslim'. Even if it's not a label I identify with. Certainly, far more pious Muslims than me are often called out by other Muslims for a seemingly never-ending list of things, such as in the case of blogger Dina Tokio, who recently stopped wearing her hijab and was vilified for that choice, subjected to an onslaught of hate, abuse and even death threats.

With the rise of fundamentalism and increasingly restrictive interpretations and stereotypes of what it means to be a Muslim, both from inside and outside the religion, unpacking what is 'true' is increasingly difficult, and religion in general is a topic I have long tried to avoid becoming embroiled in. It can be tricky terrain to manoeuvre when we view ourselves as Muslim by identity but don't practise. As some academics have termed it, I am culturally Muslim, and there are many of us.

'Religion is a vertical relationship between you and whatever you believe in; it's personal,' said Duha. 'What is religion at the end of the day? It's not something you have to advertise or preach. Religion doesn't make good or bad people, it's the way they live that makes them good or bad people.'

I agree. And while I've never really suffered with any guilt in regards to God's judgement per se – believing, as I do, that He's forgiving and doesn't necessarily care about lifestyle choices like how much or if I drink, as long as I'm a good person – I've still been made to feel that, somehow, that's not good enough when it comes to what is supposed to be 'my' religion.

'I say I'm Muslim but not practising when someone asks me,' Dunya told me. 'It's because of the assumptions they would have [otherwise]. I'd have to say "not practising" just to make them feel I'm a more Westernised or open-minded person. Because I am.'

'You feel like you have to say something after; you can't just say, "I'm Muslim", because then the inevitable questions follow, such as, "How come you're drinking?"' Haifa agreed. 'I don't think drinking is such a big deal but I still really believe in my religion.'

It got me thinking, so I contacted a young British imam and asked him if he would consider me Muslim, despite the fact that I do things like drink and eat pork and have sex before marriage, all of which are haram in Islam. He told me that no one should be the judge of anyone other than themselves.

'The Quran states that God is the almighty, wiser and better than all, and that no one can judge us other than Him,' he said, adding that – while of course there are certain requirements, such as praying five times a day – how much or how little of one's religion one subscribes to is between the individual and God. When I told my parents of the imam's words, they – separately – laughed and said I was lucky that I had spoken to a young, moderate imam. There are certainly others who would have responded differently. But I feel like that's almost part of the problem.

As Khaled Beydoun, author of *American Islamophobia*, tweeted:[151] 'Reject the "moderate" Muslim label. Qualifying Islam with "moderate" implies that the religion is inherently extreme or violent. It's an inherently Islamophobic label. We don't add "moderate" to Christianity, Hinduism, or other faiths. Islam shouldn't be distinct.'

He's right. But along the way something has made people – my 'technically Muslim' parents included – feel the need to use it. Something happened that has made me, and many like me, feel like an imposter in what is 'technically' our religion.

Taking to my Instagram stories, I asked my Middle Eastern followers if they felt the same pressure to be a certain kind of Muslim in order to freely claim being a Muslim at all. The results were interesting and made me realise that much of my imposter syndrome was probably due to the fact that I had grown up in London. The majority of people who responded 'no' were either men (perhaps because they are subject to fewer of the assumed restrictions, both behaviourally and visibly – not being 'expected' to wear a head covering or to dress 'modestly', for example) or were women who had been raised in Middle Eastern countries, where the majority religion is Islam. Most of the people who responded 'yes' were Middle Eastern women who had grown up in countries where they were a religious minority, like me. It made me realise that our imposter syndrome was likely due to our minority status. We were used to being asked questions such as 'where are you from?' and 'are you Muslim?' more frequently. Also, we had grown up surrounded by Westernised and orientalised media depictions of Islam and what it entails, as opposed to the reality of the religion and the many shades of adherence or non-adherence.

I have had many interesting debates with people since, including why these days – while this was most certainly not the case in the past – no other religion seems to be subject to such a narrow definition and such rigid expectations. Certainly, it's much less of a thing for other religions to feel the need to add the prefix 'technically' because they didn't go to church or celebrate Easter or they had sex before marriage. Does practice equal belief, I am forced to ask?

Another interesting question: if you 'just' believe in God, and are not bound by differing practices, then what makes you a Muslim vs a Christian vs a Jew, for example? An even more interesting question is: who cares? I mean, does it really matter?

As the Lebanese-born French author Amin Mahlouf so eloquently put it in *On Identity*,[152] 'I . . . do not feel entitled to say what is and what is not consonant with Islam.

'Of course, I have my own hopes and preferences and point of view, I am frequently even tempted to say that this or that kind of extreme behaviour – planting bombs, banning music, legalising female circumcision – is inconsistent with my interpretation of Islam. But my interpretation of Islam is of no importance.' He continued: 'There will always be different and even contradictory interpretations . . . The same authorities may be cited to tolerate or to condemn slavery, to venerate icons or to burn them, to ban wine or to allow it . . . Over the centuries, all human societies have managed to find religious quotations that seem to justify their current practices.'

To paraphrase Ali Rizvi's argument in *The Atheist Muslim*,[153] we don't get our morality from religious texts, rather we use our *existing* morality to interpret them. Indeed, religion – for me at least – is not a question to be answered, only one that can be pondered, if the desire to do so even arises. The answer, if one can even be reached, is likely to differ massively from one person to another and, even then, perhaps still be subject to change just as frequently as one can change their own mind.

The thing is: while the notion of a 'Christian world' throws up a variety of images, these days the idea of a 'Muslim world' often brings to mind narrow generalisations and stereotyping. That's a problem because it means those negative generalisations are incorrectly and sweepingly applied to a massive percentage of the global population. As an article in *Time* magazine put it,[154] 'labeling all North Africans and Middle Easterners pious Muslims is akin to assuming that everyone who lives in America, or Europe, is devoutly Christian'. You wouldn't. For starters, not all Arabs are Muslim. Christians are estimated to represent between 15 and 20 per cent of the Arab population. Also, not all Muslims are Arab; in fact, fewer than 15 per cent of the global Muslim population is Arab. The countries with the biggest Muslim populations are Indonesia and Pakistan.[155]

Beyond that, there are further breakdowns to be made around how the religion is practised and lives are lived. As Professor Aaron Hughes argues,[156] like '[the way] Catholicism, for example, is practised in rural Italy differs from the way this is done in, say, New York', Islam too is very different around the world. 'Language, culture, tradition, the political and social contexts, and even food is different in [Italy and New York].' Each of these things and more has a specific impact on a region's people and how they live, believe and practise or don't practise.

There are 1.8 billion Muslims[157] across the world and no two are the same. We come in all different forms and we believe or don't believe, and practise or don't practise to different extents and in different ways. Even in Saudi Arabia, which is often referred to as the 'home of Islam', 19 per cent – which equates to almost 6 million people – think of themselves as 'not a religious person'. In Italy, that figure is 15 per cent.[158] In truth, when you're just born into a religion, checking off 'Muslim' from a drop-down menu doesn't always mean much.

Hughes goes on to explain how in Islam, differences are further pronounced by the fact that it is a 'religion predicated on law (sharia), variations in the interpretation of [which] have contributed to regional differences'. In Islam there are various schools of thought with 'distinct interpretations of Islamic law. Some of their interpretations are more conservative than others.' He continues: 'Most fundamentalist movements in Islam, including Islamic State, have emanated from . . . ultra-conservative elements . . . The goal of many of these groups . . . is to return to what they imagine to be the pure or pristine version of Islam . . . They often have strict interpretations, strict dress codes and separation of the sexes.'[159]

Some groups like Isis and the Taliban have had massive influence on the political landscapes of Syria and Pakistan, fuelled by religious conviction. In some cases, strong religious convictions can cause the downfall of a country and its people.

The ideologies, values and behaviour of the ultra-conservative seem to be spreading. While the rules and enforcement of these ideologies – as well as the degrees to which they are restrictive and backwards – varies, in some countries they are enforced by law. Women in Saudi Arabia, for example, must be veiled in public. This is enforced by the morality police. They are also not allowed to mix with members of the opposite sex who are not of their family.[160] In many Arab countries, it's illegal to kiss in public,[161] while some fine people for eating publicly during Ramadan.[162] Even Morocco, despite its long-standing reputation for tolerance, is becoming increasingly draconian. A recent example is the case of two women who were faced with the very real possibility of two years in jail because they were wearing miniskirts and accused of 'public indecency'.[163]

'Certain Muslims take it to extremes. That's who I blame the most,' Haifa told me, echoing the thoughts of many. 'Some of them are just so extreme they ruin Islam for everyone else,' she added.

'I've got some cousins that wear the full thing [the full face covering], which is something we hate in my family,' Rahma told me. 'One of my cousins has a beard to "show how devout he is". My dad told him, "I can do all of that [believe in God and be a good person] and not need to look like you – what are you trying to prove?"'

Increasingly, restrictive ideologies are alienating to Muslims and non-Muslims alike. In truth, the clue is in the name: they are extremist ideals. While the rise of secular Muslims is no doubt partly due to the rise of secularism the world over[164] – and the subsequent rise of spirituality – it may also partly be in an effort to create distance from the more extreme definitions of Islam.

As author of *Muslim Girl*, Amani Al-Khatabeh wrote after the hijab policing aimed at Dina Tokio and other visible hijabis: 'Muslims are making Islamic worship even more intolerable for women, especially during a hostile day and age in which they are already tremendously suffering, behind the scenes, for holding on to their faith.' She continued: 'The lack of community support in addition to the collective emphasis on the way they dress over their humanity has turned many away from representing themselves as Muslim women altogether.'[165]

More broadly, Mustafa Akyol argued in the *New York Times* that 'Authoritarianism, violence, bigotry and patriarchy in the name of Islam are alienating people in almost every Muslim-majority nation.' He went on to cite a Twitter campaign titled #ExMuslimBecause, which lists plenty of reasons such as the 'despotism of the Saudi religion police, the attacks on secular bloggers in Bangladesh and the demonisation of gay people in Malaysia'.[166]

'If Islamic authoritarianism persists,' continued Akyol, 'it is likely to produce mass secularization in Muslim societies. Islam may still count as the fastest-growing religion in the world, thanks to high birth-rates, but it will lose some of its best and brightest.'[167]

In the US, a recent survey found that 23 per cent of those raised as Muslim no longer identify with that faith.[168] In France, less than a third of Muslims are 'practising'. And while going to the mosque is not, of course, an indication of how religious you are, only around 23 per cent of those surveyed said they go to the mosque on Fridays, and only 40 per cent said they went more than once a year.[169] In general, younger generations are found to believe less in God or to feel the need to subscribe to a particular faith. We are also a lot more liberal. The Muslim population – the majority of whom are very young (34 per cent of the global Muslim population in 2010 was under the age of fifteen[170]) – also appears to be following these trends.

In Egypt, other than media institutions and music celebrities, seven of the ten most-followed Twitter accounts are those of liberal commentators like Bassem Youssef.[171] In Saudi Arabia, six out of the ten most-watched YouTube channels are satirical shows produced by rebellious youth groups.[172] There's also been a surge in atheism via dedicated Facebook pages, with tens of thousands of followers, as well as gay-rights groups, which would have been unthinkable not so long ago, considering the flagrant homophobia often pervasive in the region.[173]

Terrorist acts committed in the name of the religion have been harmful to the image of Islam and to the vast majority of peace-loving, spiritual and sincere Muslims the world over. Indeed, distancing oneself from one's religion can also sadly sometimes be due to a perceived need for protection. Post-9/11, many people took steps to create this distance, such as anglicising their names. For example, a boy in my class whose name was Mohammed returned to school after the summer break as Mike.

When questioned on television about whether Islam promotes violence, historian Reza Aslan offered a succinct response: 'Islam doesn't promote violence or peace. Islam is just a religion and like every religion in the world it depends on what you bring to it. If you're a violent person, your Islam, your Judaism, your Christianity, your Hinduism is going to be violent.' He continued: 'There are marauding Buddhist monks in Myanmar slaughtering women and children. Does Buddhism promote violence? Of course not. People are violent or peaceful and that depends on their politics, their social world, the ways that they see their communities.'[174]

Sadly, throughout history people have done the most inhumane things in the name of religion, from the Crusades to the Spanish Inquisition. Fanaticism and the extremist ideals that sometimes arise out of religion are nothing new.

As Amin Mahlouf says, 'The introduction into the world of a society that respects liberty in its various forms has been gradual and incomplete, and in the context of history as a whole, extremely tardy . . . The impetus toward liberty has often come from people who stood quite apart from religious thinking.'

The stereotyping of Muslims as potential terrorists has profound effects on the lives of law-abiding Muslims. As a result of increasing Islamophobia, Muslims have been shot and killed in their living rooms[175] and inside[176] and outside mosques.[177] They have been kicked off aeroplanes for speaking Arabic,[178] set on fire,[179] and received death threats just for being Muslim.[180] From 2001 to 2015, there were 2,545 anti-Islamic incidents in the US, according to the FBI – a surge of 67 per cent.[181] In the UK, Islamophobia has increased hugely, with a 500 per cent surge in Manchester following the Manchester Arena attack[182] and Islamophobic hate crimes doubling across the UK between 2016 and 2017.[183] Donald Trump, the president of the United States at the time of writing, has partly succeeded in instating a travel ban from Muslim-majority countries,[184] while the UK voted to leave the European Union due in large part to a deep-seated unease around immigrants.[185]

Even 'invisible' immigrants like me have felt the effects, whether that's simply by being called on to distance ourselves from terrorists or be deemed their sympathisers, or in the really heartbreaking wake-up call that, although we may feel British, many still consider us 'other'.

The media has had a big role to play in the fearmongering. 'Much of the British press incites hatred against minorities, not in fringe mosques or on street corners, but to millions of people,' wrote journalist Owen

Jones in an article for the *Guardian*.[186] Among numerous examples, he cited a headline that screamed: 'Muslims tell British: Go to hell'. What's more, research has found that 90 per cent of news media about Muslims and Islam is negative[187] and that over the past twenty-five years the *New York Times* portrayed Islam and Muslims more negatively than they did cancer and cocaine.[188]

'There's no accurate or varied representation of Muslims in the media; it's just what Britain First [the British fascist political organisation, formed by members of the British National Party, which campaigns primarily against multiculturalism and what they see as the Islamisation of the UK] wants you to believe,' Shahd told me. 'I've noticed the outside world gets really uncomfortable now when they see Muslims. If they see a lady who's fully covered, they won't sit next to her [on the bus] or they'll get off. I've even felt people react like that towards me because of my skin colour.'

So pervasive are the negative attitudes, so prevalent the images of terrorist bombers and their attacks, that even I'm scared, even I feel uncomfortable when I see people who fit the images that are portrayed in the media, even though I should know better. A few years ago, while boarding a flight to London from Cairo on Egypt Air, I was terrified because while approaching the gate I had noticed that my flight was filled with men who fit the media stereotype of what a terrorist looks like. I became convinced that they were going to blow up the plane. I called my dad in tears and asked him if he thought I should miss it. Far from saying I was being silly, he asked me for my flight details and to describe what I saw around me. When I told him there were dozens of men, he laughed and said that if they were really planning on blowing up planes, they would have at least spread out so as not to waste all their lives on just one plane. I spent the entirety of the boarding process, and then the journey itself, alternating between praying and seeking solidarity and understanding in the eyes of the few white, Western people on the flight. Very often, but never more so than right then, did I feel more like one of them than I did the stereotype of an Arab.

When I landed safely in London, I felt sad and horrified that I had succumbed to racist thinking towards those who are technically my own people. It made me realise that if even I – a 'technically Muslim' person who was familiar with the customs and the culture – could be so easily manipulated, what chance does someone who has never been exposed to anyone that looked different to themselves have? How could they *not* be scared?

'I watch a lot of TV so I feel like I know what terrorists are supposed to look like, and there have been so many times I've been on the train and I've panicked,' Sondos told me. 'I feel awful every time. The media has definitely perpetuated all these things. People are doing it to me, but then I'm doing it to other people.'

Responsible reporting would go a long way to easing the negative and reductive stereotypes. As Jones argued in the *Guardian*: 'too many of those working in the . . . press act as hatemongers who play with matches then express horror as the flames reach ever higher . . . With the far right globally in the ascendancy – from Italy to Brazil – the role of the media must be urgently debated.'[189] In truth, there is a dearth of minorities in newsrooms and across all media the world over, suggesting that more emphasis needs to be placed on diversity and on commissioning more nuanced and representative stories. There are undoubtedly more than enough different examples to go around.

As Ali Rizvi put it in *The Atheist Muslim*,[190] 'There are more American Muslims having beers at bars after work, dancing at clubs on a Saturday night, regularly spending the night at their girlfriend's or boyfriend's place, or having non-halal steaks and fast food than there are who actually pray five times a day . . . Rarely in this discourse do we hear about these American Muslims, who exist in plain sight.'

Pop culture has graciously started to depict some of the challenges and issues of being 'culturally Muslim'. An episode of *Master of None* featured a scene in which Aziz Ansari's character, Dev Shah, indulges extravagantly in the consumption of pork behind his family's back. A recent article on media conglomerate VICE also addressed the topic of pretending to fast during Ramadan. It feels as though rejecting some aspects of the religion is entering a wider and more public debate, which helps tackle both my imposter syndrome and some of the more reductive stereotypes that contribute to Islamophobia and internal judgement and fracturing from within religious communities. As always, it is easier to be yourself if you can see yourself.

Zayn Malik, one of the most famous pop stars in music, has Muslim heritage. As does his girlfriend, supermodel Gigi Hadid, and singer Dua Lipa, actor Riz Ahmed, and Amal Clooney. Importantly, there is an increasing number of people in the public eye who don't conform to the narrow stereotypes of what it's supposed to mean to be a Muslim, and who are many things before they are their religion.

As comedian Kumail Nanjiani said of his movie *The Big Sick* in an interview, 'Everyone knows what a secular Jew looks like. Everyone knows what a lapsed Catholic looks like. That's all over pop culture. But there are very few Muslim characters who aren't terrorists, who aren't even going to a mosque, who are just people with complicated back stories who do normal things. Obviously, terrorism is an important subject to tackle. But we also need Muslim characters who, like, go to Six Flags and eat ice cream.'[191]

While some took offence at Nanjiani's words, arguing that Muslims can go to the mosque and then to Six Flags and eat ice cream afterwards, they are kind of missing the point. It's still only a narrow version of Islam represented in the media, a specific narrative that is consistently pushed by seemingly everyone.

Even while trying to be representative – and as good and important as that is – brands proudly pushing hijab-wearing models are still pandering to the same ideas: that to be a Muslim you need to be veiled. CoverGirl,[192] Nike[193] and L'Oréal[194] have all launched campaigns with hijabi women. As Qanta A. Ahmed puts it, while the West seems to have 'culturally appropriated [the veil] to be the Muslim symbol of womanhood . . . there is a litany of diverse practices of Muslim women in Muslim communities concerning the veil'. She explains how there are multiple ways of interpreting the Quran's passages in relation to the veil. Some read it as a physical partition, reserved to shield the Prophet Mohammad's wives from visitors. They argue that the Quran does not mandate hair or facial covering.[195]

While I don't particularly care to wade too far into this subject, as sticky and as nuanced as it is, I strongly believe that everyone should be free to come to their own interpretations without judging another for their choices. As with much else, the conversation is not a straightforward one.

As Rizvi wrote, 'In countries where Muslims are a minority, Islam is an identity. In countries where Muslims are a majority, Islam is a religion. This dichotomy has consequences for liberals on either side.

'For the liberal in North America, Islam is the faith of a small minority of Muslims who are often discriminated against and whose rights must be protected, as with any minority group. But for the liberal in a Muslim-majority country, Islam is a tool the government uses to justify censorship, oppression, and other *illiberal* values, like forcing women to wear the hijab, persecuting homosexuals, and publicly lashing bloggers.'

He wrote: 'The hijab – worn proudly by Muslim-American women who choose it as a symbol of their identity – is forced on women in many Muslim-majority countries by their governments, imams or husbands.'

In truth, it's complicated but one thing is for sure: there is no one way to practise religion and the narrow and reductive lens through which Islam is currently viewed is damaging both for those within the religion as well as those outside. 'Cultural Muslims' like me need not be scared or struggle with imposter syndrome. Our voices are valid, and things will only change and evolve if we take our seats at the table and use our voices to add to the debate.

'I used to always say I was "technically Muslim" until my dad – who is also not practising – heard me and then corrected me,' Maryam, a thirty-one-year-old half-Egyptian, half-Dutch woman who has lived in New York for the last ten years, told me. 'He told me to make sure I always say I'm Muslim so I can be part of the education – so I can help change what it's supposed to mean.'

I hear that. These days I make a conscious effort not to prefix my response with 'technically', although maybe next time I'm asked I'll try: 'It's none of your business.' To echo what Duha said earlier, religion is a vertical relationship between you and your God – how you choose to practise or not practise is no one else's business.

It was a point that came up again when I saw a tweet from Mona Eltahawy at the start of Ramadan in 2018. It read: 'I wish an easy and accepted fast to all who are observing. I also wish absolute freedom for those who choose not to. It is imperative: freedom of faith and freedom from faith.'[196] Eltahawy continued: 'in many Muslim majority countries [some of which have laws against public eating in Ramadan], it is a challenge to be a Muslim who doesn't fast and to be an atheist of Muslim descent . . . In countries where Muslims are a minority [and where Muslims are subjected to bigotry and demonisation], for those who choose to observe Ramadan, the challenge is to normalise the fast . . .

'I find that at times Muslims in both scenarios look at each other, perplexed,' she wrote. 'On the one hand fighting for the right to not fast and on the other, fighting for the right to fast . . . Freedom of faith and freedom from faith must be the goal everywhere.'

She summed up my thoughts perfectly, across all aspects of religion – and life. Freedom to and freedom not to. No one should judge another person for believing or sinning differently.

To paraphrase author Khaled Diab,[197] the only way to guarantee your own tolerance is to tolerate others; the road to hell is paved with pious intentions. Indeed, there can always be one more layer of piety you are supposed to reach: when will it be enough? And who is the judge? As the imam told me: as God says, you should judge yourself harshly and others not at all. Harshly in respect to your *own* moral compass, of course.

Chapter 11
When You Are (Not) a Feminist

I am not a feminist. I've said and written those words so many times, never quite understanding what it was I was saying, what it was I was vouching for by saying it. The word 'feminism' is riddled with many negative connotations: man-hater, angry, lonely and ugly top of the list. I bought into all of that for a long time too.

Growing up, I wasn't interested in anything remotely 'feminine'. From the media to gender-loaded words like 'crazy' and 'emotional', which are often used to describe women (and women alone), I had absorbed messages from the world around me that told me what women were supposed to be like, and I wanted out. You wouldn't have caught me dead in a dress, I loved playing football and I was (still am) a pro at video games. For a long time, I was proud of the fact I didn't wear much make-up or care very much about what I looked like. As if that actually proved anything about my character.

My discomfort, and inability to reconcile the acceptable face of what it was to be a woman with who I was and what I wanted for myself, made me take great pleasure in making a point of showing how unalike I was to the other girls. I always had many girlfriends (perhaps my subconscious way of telling myself I was being an idiot), but for a long time I believed my friends and I were the exception.

Men and women are socialised into gender from birth, taught restrictive and reductive ideas of what it means to be a girl or a boy, a man or a woman. Blue, cars and guns for boys; pink, Barbie and toy kitchen sets for girls. All around the world, children and adults are socialised to buying into these gender ideals via movies, ads, school textbooks and gender reinforcements from family and society.

While boys are taught to be assertive and masculine (which comes with its own problems and has led to what is currently being called a 'crisis of masculinity'[198]), girls are often socialised to think less of themselves from a young age,[199] and taught to believe that our purpose is predominantly to be attractive,[200] to be mothers and wives. Everywhere, femininity is associated with negative stereotypes, not least that we are passive, naive and – the one that jars the most – unstable.

As Amal Awad touched on in her book *Beyond Veiled Clichés*, across the Middle East these ideas are similarly ingrained. 'In the Arab world even school curricula suggest the ideal woman,' she writes. 'In Amman . . . recent changes to textbooks meant females were only depicted in hijab. Moreover, they are depicted in only a couple of professions, and as housewives or praying.' She went on to give the example of Fulla, 'the Muslim world's answer to Barbie'.

Describing Fulla's attributes, she writes: 'She is a plastic doll kitted out in modest clothing, with accessories such as veils, a prayer mat and prayer clothes. Fulla is the predictably modest, good Muslim woman – stick thin and pretty, inoffensively ambitious . . . She is no model/astronaut. She is a mother, or perhaps a teacher, life paths widely considered suitable for females in the Middle East. She represents the type of woman girls should aspire to be, an antidote to her scantily dressed Western counterpart.'[201]

It's a man's world, and the world reflects that back accordingly. Throughout history, textbooks and museums – mostly written, published and curated by men – eulogise thousands of members of the male gender, while women (if mentioned at all) are secondary or the exception. Even today, across all facets of society, men still hold the most power and most visibility. In the UK, across the biggest news sources including the *Guardian*, the *Daily Mail* and *Metro*, men account for a 75 per cent average of bylines on the front page.[202] In the US, men make up 80 per cent of the Senate[203] and 95 per cent of senior positions in the media industry.[204] Even on the internet, only 16 per cent of Wikipedia's profiles relate to women and their achievements, according to the Wikimedia Foundation.[205] Worldwide, women currently have only 60 per cent of the standing of men. In 2017, only 32 of the Fortune 500 CEOs were women. Women are only represented in about two out of ten political positions.[206] An estimate from 2017 suggests that women will have to wait 217 years before they earn as much as men and are equally represented in the workplace.[207]

The effects of this inequality are felt in the portrayal of women in the media and subsequently reflected in the world around us. Women are influenced by and viewed through the male gaze. We even view ourselves and each other through it too.

Where shall we begin? Perhaps with the fact that advertisements feature four times as many male characters as female characters,[208] or that in movies male characters receive twice as much screen time and speak twice as often as female characters.[209] Or that when female characters are portrayed they have unrealistic bodies[210] and behaviours and are defined by very narrow roles, either framed as a sex object or as a mother and often as bitchy or catty.[211] Or how research has found that only 3 per cent of advertising shows women as leaders, 2 per cent conveys them as intelligent and only 1 per cent portrays women as funny.[212] Or how, when Nicola Sturgeon and Theresa May met to discuss the future of their countries, the media chose instead to focus on which woman had better legs, coining the meeting 'legs-it' as opposed to Brexit.[213] I could go on.

Most disheartening is the reality that we don't even need to explicitly be told we can't be leaders, can't be successful, can't be smart or liberated, if the message is already embedded in the fabric of our society.

Researcher Kristin Mmari, who looked into gender stereotypes around the world, found that many had become entrenched before the age of ten, and that many are universal.[214] 'We were actually anticipating more differences than similarities,' she said. 'One of the big findings is that there are still very consistent forms of patriarchy around the world.'

Actress Geena Davis commissioned some studies to look into this after watching kids' movies with her daughter and realising that there were hardly any female characters. Results of the studies showed that only 17 per cent of crowd scenes featured any women at all, males outnumbered females three to one, and powerful roles like CEO were 'overwhelmingly' played by men. While this appears to be changing slowly, the ratio of male to female roles was found to still be the same as it was in 1946.[215]

In reality, for this to truly change, more women need to insert themselves into all levels of the industry. Yet, instead of bonding over this, women tend to internalise misogyny. It is a sad consequence of a societal view that causes women to shame, doubt and undervalue each other and ourselves. Actress Anne Hathaway, after she had finished filming *One Day*, admitted to trusting the director – a female – less than she would have a male director.[216] She's far from the only one: a 2013 study found that American women are more likely than men to express a preference not to be supervised by another woman while on the job.[217] When it comes to misogynistic hate speech on Twitter, research found that 52 per cent came from women, versus 48 per cent from men.[218] And just over half of white women also voted for Donald Trump,[219] a man who has openly made misogynistic comments.

As I grew older, I realised that I wasn't a rare exception to my gender, as much as I'd have liked to think that. There were countless incredible women out there. It didn't make me any less of a woman to be easy-going or strong or more focused on inner qualities than appearance – or whatever else I was wearing as a badge of honour. Being a woman and having any of those qualities were not mutually exclusive.

The socialisation goes both ways. Men are subject to the same socialisation, they absorb those same messages. And if we buy into them about ourselves, with all the evidence we have to the contrary, there's little hope that the majority of men won't subconsciously buy into at least some of them too.

In an experiment where participants were tasked with watching an entrepreneurial pitch video narrated by the voice of the entrepreneur, who was either a male or a female, 68 per cent of participants of both genders thought the venture was worthy of funding when it was a male voice, compared to only 32 per cent when pitched by a female voice.[220]

A prestigious Japanese medical school also recently came under fire after confessing to systematically rigging its entrance exams against women, apparently due to a concern that women would be more likely to quit the profession once they had children.[221]

Those are just a couple of examples of the ways in which women are disadvantaged by the stereotypes of gender. There are hundreds of other examples across all paths of life.

The first time I remember being made to feel acutely aware of my gender was in a nightclub in Miami, where I was on holiday with some of my girlfriends. We had joined our friend who was on a superstar rapper's payroll, at said rapper's table. By that stage I had interviewed some of the rapper's entourage for work, and my friends and I were intelligent, successful women. We had been invited to the club as friends, not 'eye candy'. But as soon as we walked in, that's what we were reduced to – because we were women. It was a heartbreaking wake-up call for me – big hip-hop fan that I am – to realise that when the rappers freely gave their views on women in their songs, they actually *meant* them. That was actually how they lived their lives.

One of the members of the entourage had struck up a conversation with me, but as the minutes ticked by I realised he couldn't remember my name – even though I had repeated it to him many times. When I eventually rolled my eyes and called him out, he said, 'Look B, you're a gorgeous girl but there are many of you. No, I don't remember your name, does it really matter?' while licking his lips and drawing me closer.

As I dodged his touch, I saw strippers drop to the floor behind him to pick up the dollar bills that had been hurled their way, and I in turn picked up my bag to exit the club, feeling devastated. I grabbed an Uber back to the hotel with one of my friends who had felt equally as harrowed and we talked about how it had felt to have been reduced to nothing more than a disposable vagina, just because we had one.

I remember thinking how, in the Middle East, these scenes may have played out very differently but they stemmed from the same underlying belief system. Arab women were traditionally hidden from view, ultimately so as not to incite the 'uncontrollable desires of men'. In doing so, this also turned women into not much more than disposable sex objects reduced to the sum of their body parts.

It is tricky to talk about the inequalities women in the Middle East face at the hands of men, because you're forever in fear of enhancing a stereotype – one that's already full of overwhelming generalisations. But it's important to do so, because the experiences of Middle Eastern women don't exist in a vacuum. In truth, they are the product of ideologies that are dominant the world over, and have been for thousands of years. Culturally ingrained sexism is definitely a problem that Arab societies endure – in abundance – but it's by no means a problem that is unique to the region.

There are many, many layers to the inequality, but an underlying commonality too. As Nawal El Saadawi put it, 'The oppression of women, the exploitation and social pressures to which they are exposed . . . constitute an integral part of the political, economic and cultural system, preponderant in most of the world . . . The situation and problems of women in contemporary human society are born of developments in history that made one class rule over another, and men dominate over women. They are the product of class and sex.'[222]

In countries where it's punishable by law for women to partake in everyday activities such as driving a car or going out in public without a male escort, the misogyny and sexism is no doubt played out in far more insidious and life-altering ways. Today, much of the Middle East fares poorly in terms of gender equality. In the 2017 annual Global Gender Gap Report – which ranked almost 150 countries on gender equality against a range of criteria including wage equality, number of women in parliament, and life expectancy for both sexes – among the ten worst countries for gender equality were Yemen, Syria, Saudi Arabia, Lebanon, Morocco and Jordan.[223]

The effects of a patriarchal reign are felt in the Middle East in all sorts of ways, from the preferential treatment of male children to divorce and inheritance laws (where men generally receive a larger share – sometimes double the share that women receive – and where distant male relatives can supersede wives, sisters and daughters[224]), as well as penal codes that allow rapists to avoid punishment if they marry their victims.[225] Egypt does not have non-discrimination laws in hiring and does not mandate equal pay. Women in Jordan only received the right to vote in 1974, and even today there are very few women working in ministerial positions. Women in Lebanon did not have any laws in place to protect them from domestic violence until 2014. Daughters in Morocco do not have inheritance rights, and there have been no female heads of state to date. Women in Saudi Arabia have only been allowed to vote and enrol in municipal elections since 2015. As of June 2018, they were permitted to drive for the first time.[226] What's more, many of these women are unable to protest or freely take to social media.

The 'brainwashing' of women in the Middle East, then – in terms of being fed a narrow idea of who and what their gender can be – is arguably even more insidious and deep-rooted than it may be elsewhere, in that it's being executed via religion, propriety and culture. As Arab women we are scrutinised on what we wear, who we associate with, our behaviour and plenty more besides. From a young age we are told

'Because you're a girl' as a fully reasoned argument in its entirety. The real challenge, then, is to wake up to these messages, both overt and subliminal, and to question the very basic assumptions about our gender. It's very hard, so deep have the seeds of inequality been planted. Many of the restrictions on our freedom are framed as protection, as care. Sometimes it can be difficult to grasp that they are far more than just an expression of care but are in fact just that: restrictions on our freedom. We often know the reality of it – we just don't *know* that we know. And that is the very definition of denial.

There is so much to object to that one becomes immune to the generalisations made. It can result in scenarios such as my grandfather thinking nothing of saying 'you are not equal' and meaning it 'in the best way'. Or in men always paying, and in women not needing to work. It means that as a woman you can be pampered, be looked after, be free from making strenuous decisions, if you so choose. But it also means that's what you become used to, that is the norm. You are expected to be looked after and you expect to be looked after too.

When I got into a debate about the difference in inheritance between men and women with my driver in Egypt (I seem to always have deep conversations with taxi drivers!), he explained that the reason this is the case is that women are married and are looked after by their husbands (and so don't need the money), whereas men are the providers for their families and so could use the extra help. It's a flawed logic that doesn't factor in a woman's autonomy in the least.

'Culture has taken its toll on women in a much harder way in this part of the world, but at the same time, it's about agency,' said Hadeel, one of the women Awad interviewed. 'This is the real issue. It's how women are perceived as minors . . . in everything. In marriage, in handling their affairs, in making independent decisions . . . It's about the lack of agency, and this perception is very dominant,' she continued. 'Sometimes it's done with the best of intentions, they want to protect women. But even in the systems, in courts . . . passports and civil documentation . . . civil status – you feel this.'[227]

In Arab culture, the misogyny is often cloaked in chivalry, adding another hurdle to the hundreds to be overcome (like a misplaced belief that any desire for change is a desire to Westernise) on the way to talking about feminism.

I woke up to the fact that I was a feminist slowly and then all at once – reaching the conclusion, as I did with much else, through my work. As I began to write for more and more women-centric publications, and subsequently read more of them too, I began to see the world through nuanced female eyes as opposed to the stereotypes that had formed the backdrop to much of my life. The popular quote 'If you're not angry, you're not paying attention' deeply resonated with me. I had started to pay more attention and, in doing so, I saw inequality everywhere. I began to understand that we are all products of societies that teach us that men are more important than women. I realised that I had always been a feminist, whether or not I had felt able or willing to claim it.

The definition of a feminist, stripped of the stereotypes, is: 'A person who believes in the social, political and economic equality of the sexes.' Yes, yes, I do. We all should. It affects everyone.

Throughout history, nearly every single society has struggled with sexism in some form, and often still does. In America, for example, women could not vote until 1920,[228] while today women often face harassment when trying to enter Planned Parenthood clinics,[229] and their access to basic reproductive healthcare is backsliding.[230] What's more, America is the only advanced economy that does not mandate paid maternity leave at a national level.[231] Every day, at least three women in the US are murdered by their boyfriend or husband.[232]

Although today, in theory, most European countries give women the same legal rights as men, this doesn't always play out in practice. One example is the persistent gender pay gap. 'Antiquated excuses abound as to why women are paid less,' writes Sahar Aziz.[233] 'Women are not as committed to their careers as men. Women "choose" to stay home to take care of children, thereby forfeiting a career. Women's salaries are supplemental sources of income to the man's primary breadwinner role.' She continues: 'These myths have been debunked in multiple studies; and yet continue to contribute to the deflation of women's salaries.'

Reports show that worldwide, women still bear the burden of household chores and caregiving responsibilities. In the UK, men spend on average sixteen hours per week on unpaid work, which includes adult care and child care, laundry and cleaning as well as the provision of transport (the latter the only area where men put in more unpaid work hours than women). Women spend twenty-six. The European Union average is worse, with women dedicating an average of twenty-six weekly hours to men's nine hours.[234]

For there to be real change, women need to insert themselves into all layers of society – a diverse, representative population of women – and gender stereotypes need to be eradicated. Indeed, gender is not a single category. For instance, while white, upper-class women were afforded the vote in the US in 1920, it was decades before black and Native American women were able to place their ballots in the box.[235]

Indeed, the difference between feminism and intersectional feminism is an important one to be made. While feminism advocates for equality of the sexes, intersectional feminism stresses the importance in factoring in how identities like race, ethnicity, class, religion and sexual orientation impact the way women experience oppression and discrimination. While the roots of the issues may be the same, they often manifest themselves differently.

Many blame the inequality so pervasive in the Middle East on religion, citing Islam as the cause of patriarchy and inequality in the region. That's not entirely the case. If it were, the laws and treatment of women would be the same across the region rather than differing as they do – widely, in some cases. Islam at its essence is not especially restrictive in its readings or requirements of women. As Leila Ahmed put it in *Women and Gender in Islam*,[236] 'There appear . . . to be two distinct voices within Islam, and two competing understandings of gender, one expressed in the pragmatic regulations for society, the other in the articulation of an ethical vision . . . The unmistakeable presence of an ethical egalitarianism explains why Muslim women frequently insist, often inexplicably to non-Muslims, that Islam is not sexist,' she continued. 'They hear and read in its sacred text, justly and legitimately, a different message from that heard by the makers and enforcers of orthodox, androcentric Islam.'

In truth, there are numerous ways in which Islam improved the situation for women, and some of these advancements were only made in the West years later, if at all. For example, Islam was the first religion to give women the right to inheritance, as well as full control of any money they inherit or earn, while female infanticide – a practice that was common in pre-Islamic Arabia, and still exists in some countries outside the region today – was prohibited. Women in the Middle East also don't take their husband's name when they marry.[237]

All of the religious books contain misogynistic elements. As Ahmed put it, 'The contributions of the . . . conquered societies to the formation of Islamic institutions and mores concerning women need to be taken into account, even with respect to mores that have come to be considered intrinsically Islamic.'

Throughout *Women and Gender in Islam*, Ahmed outlines the landscape that contributed to the environment in which Islam came to be. 'Politically dominant Christianity brought with it . . . the patriarchal ideas of its originary Judaism, and with these religious sanctions of women's social subordination and the endorsement of their essential secondariness,' she wrote. 'Through, for example, the biblical account of Eve's creation from Adam's rib.'

Judaism, Christianity and Islam originated hundreds of years ago, and the holy texts of all three reflect the times they were written in; each also reflects the others. The Torah, the Bible and the Quran all say that women are unclean during menstruation. The Bible specifically says that 'a woman should learn in quietness and full submission'.[238] The veil, which is often used as a catch-all symbol for the oppression of women in the Arab world, was in fact a product of Judaism long before Islam came into being. It was drawn from the Old Testament, Saadawi explained, where women were required to cover their head when praying to God, while men could remain bareheaded because they had been created in His image. The world has long been patriarchal, then; religion, if anything, has just served to cement it.

Religion and culture are often confused with one another. It was an aspect that came up time and again in conversations I had with Middle Eastern women for this book, with words like haram (which means religiously prohibited) and 3aib (which means shameful or culturally frowned upon) used interchangeably. Many of the inequalities affecting women in the Middle East and its diaspora arise as a result of the laws that have been interpreted from the Quran and put in place by men, and by the cultural practices that are seen as unshakeable foundations of society – practices that often place high restrictions on gender roles and relegate women to second-class citizens.

Holy texts have predominantly been both written and interpreted by men, who have been socialised by a patriarchal society. It is then men who create the laws, which are often shaped by these very texts, as well as who govern the societies in which those laws exist. It is this, argues Alaa Murabit in her TED Talk 'What My Religion Really Says About Women',[239] that is the crux of the problem. That women are absent from the table – in terms of interpreting these texts, in creating these laws, in being represented across all facets of society – is, she argues, a big part of what allows for these inequalities.

The Arab world has a long history of inspirational Arab feminists: the likes of Egyptian-born Nawal El Saadawi (who I've quoted many times throughout this book), Manal Al-Sharif (who was recently a figurehead for women's right to drive in Saudi Arabia[240]) and Nabawiyya Musa (who was the first Egyptian woman to have a high school education[241]). No doubt partly as a result of the efforts of these women and others like them, many things are changing. The broaching of inheritance reform is taking place in a number of Arab countries;[242] in Tunisia, Muslim women will be allowed to marry non-Muslim men;[243] and Lebanon is the latest country in the region to outlaw the practice of rapists being exonerated for their crime by marrying their victims.[244]

Of course, each attempt is met with its own difficulties. When Tunisia's president backed legislation to ensure equality of inheritance between men and women, some Muslim clerics took it as an attack on Islam. This underlies the difficulty in upending a centuries-old status quo, and of making change when, in the minds of many, 'change' so often seems to translate to 'Westernise'.

The Arab Spring – which began with protests in Tunisia in 2010 in response to oppressive regimes and a low standard of living, and quickly spread across the region – also impacted women's rights. As Bloomberg reporter Caroline Alexander put it, 'Women were on the frontlines of the Arab Spring and they fought to have a say in how their societies – which generally favoured men – were being reshaped.'[245]

But all across the Arab world, family honour often still outweighs individual rights, and marriage remains the most important facet of society and the entrance to adulthood. As author Leïla Slimani argues, 'there can be no gender equality without sexual freedom' – something that is very hard to picture in the Middle East. To paraphrase Slimani, you can't be considered an equal citizen if you don't have control of your body, if your body is everybody's business and if you can be imprisoned because of what happens or doesn't happen in between your legs.[246] In truth, it's scarily reminiscent of Margaret Atwood's *The Handmaid's Tale*.

The cultural expectations and the inherent inequality in the region weigh heavy. While I love being in Cairo, whenever I'm there I immediately revert to having the autonomy of a child. Suddenly, concerns like where I'm going, who I'm with, what I'm wearing and a multitude of other things are taken out of my hands. It even plays out in weird ways like how I behave with my parents' friends, who I often spend summers abroad with and where we behave as if *we're* friends too. When we're in Egypt together, the dynamic is markedly different and I strangely revert to wanting to call them 'Auntie' and 'Uncle' – which are customary terms of respect in many cultures, including in the Middle East.

It's as if the oxygen in the country itself dictates what is 'acceptable' and what is not.

Tradition and culture affect all aspects of our lives, but neither are set in stone. As Nigerian author Chimamanda Ngozi Adichie argued in her TED Talk 'We Should All Be Feminists',[247] culture doesn't make people, people make culture. We must, therefore, make it part of our culture to address the inequalities between men and women, instead of using culture as an excuse to ignore gender inequalities.

In the UK, being 'culturally appropriate' has numerous times been used as an excuse not to intervene in heinous practices like female genital mutilation or forced marriage, even when they occur on UK soil. According to estimates, there are 137,000 girls and women living with FGM, and even more at risk of FGM in England and Wales.[248] While it has been illegal in the UK since 1985,[249] there has not been a single successful prosecution.[250] The same can be said for forced marriages (not to be confused with *arranged* marriages), which became illegal in the UK in 2014, with only two convictions since, despite thousands of reports.[251] While of course there are many factors contributing to the low conviction rate, part of the problem is that people are often reluctant to get involved for fear of being accused of not respecting cultural practices. A recent report revealed that healthcare professionals and teachers often shy away from reporting cases of FGM, amid fears of being accused of racism.[252]

It is, understandably, a complex area. One nation does not necessarily wish to be accused of being patronising, offensive or culturally insensitive to another. Whether ignoring the Western influence on poverty and violence in Pakistan while championing Malala Yousafzai for standing up to the Taliban, or spreading an NSFW photo of Egyptian activist Aliaa Elmahdy (who was forced to flee Egypt and seek political asylum in Sweden after she posted photos of herself on her blog wearing only stockings and red shoes), it's not always easy to separate the issues or to know how best to contribute fruitfully to the conversation. Yet ultimately, it's about respecting people's rights without regarding all of their practices as above criticism. We should be able to call out barbaric practices. Not because they are culturally different, but because they are wrong; because they are rooted in sexist, damaging, dangerous ideologies. Neither religion nor culture is ever an acceptable reason to violate what should be an international human rights standard of equality and non-discrimination.

As Amin Mahlouf put it in *On Identity*,[253] 'Many ideas that have been commonly accepted for centuries are no longer admissible today, among them the "natural" ascendancy of men over women, the hierarchy between races, and even . . . apartheid and the various other kinds of segregation.

'Torture, too,' he continued, 'was for a long time regarded as a "normal" element in the execution of justice. For centuries, slavery seemed like a fact of life, and great minds of the past took care not to call it into question.

'Then new ideas gradually managed to establish themselves,' he wrote. 'That every man had rights that must be defined and respected; that women should have the same rights as men; that nature too deserved to be protected; that the whole human race has interests in common in more and more areas – the environment, peace, international exchanges, the battle against the great scourges of disease and natural disaster . . . And so on.'

Surely, just because something has always been done a certain way, it doesn't mean that that's the right way, or that this is reason enough to continue. It is not – as some argue – that feminism is a Western-born concept; it's that sometimes the issues and approaches required to combat inequality – as well as what that inequality even looks or feels like – varies according to cultural contexts. The fact that they are all predicated on a universal system of patriarchy is the constant. While women may face challenges, specifically in Muslim regions, criticising Islam or dismissing something as 'culture' or 'tradition' is an inadequate way to fight patriarchy and ultimately disrupts solidarity between women, whatever their religion or culture. We cannot push for the rights of some without working towards the rights of all, and we certainly can't do so by dismissing or judging any.

Overall, you could say that Arab women in the Middle East want what women around the world want: to be protected under the law, to have access to education and healthcare and to have reasonable expectations of safety. In order to achieve those things, 'superficial processes of modernisation', as Nawal El Saadawi classifies them, are not enough. Inequality exists in our minds first and foremost: in our biases and our prejudices, and that's what needs to be fixed first – everywhere. Otherwise, superficial emancipation will only lead to a different form of oppression. Citing sexual rights as an example, which are arguably practised in many Western societies (despite a persisting gender stigma), Saadawi argues that this has not led to the emancipation of women, but to an 'accentuated oppression, where women are transformed into commercialised bodies and a source of increasing capitalist profits'.[254]

Certainly, it is interesting that while, in the West, women are mostly told we are equal and can do anything men can do, we are simultaneously subject to wide-ranging degrading images – in porn, in advertisements, in music videos, in the images we sometimes post of ourselves on social media – that communicate the message that women are sexual objects first and foremost. We often contribute to the conversation ourselves, adding to the rhetoric. Of course, there are many disputing arguments to this, with the likes of Emily Ratajkowski (who rose to prominence after appearing topless in the music video for Robin Thicke's 'Blurred Lines') arguing that there is no conflict between posting naked photos of ourselves and being feminists; that owning our own bodies in this way is actually a feminist act in and of itself.

'I think a lot of people really feel that the idea of a woman being sexual or being sexualized is the opposite of feminism,' Ratajkowksi said in an interview with *Harper's Bazaar* Arabia. 'I feel like, in some ways, that conversation itself can be oppressive to women, because you're telling them how to dress and how to act, which is actually the opposite of feminism.'[255]

Ultimately the question is: is feminism a movement where one set of rules applies to all, or is it about the right to independent choice based on your personal opinion and the options available to you? Certainly, freedom and equality are bound to look different from person to person. Feminism should be more than just a slogan people wear on their T-shirts or a competition for who can be the *best* feminist – whatever that means. In the same way that I don't believe there's any one way to live, to love, to look, to think or feel, I don't believe there is any one right way to be a feminist, beyond the fundamental prerequisite for equal rights and opportunities.

We can have the most progressive laws, but if the culture and inherent beliefs we are taught from childhood – and that are reinforced throughout our lives – don't change, nothing will. While we may have evolved as humans, our ideas of gender have not so much. We need to change how we define masculinity and femininity, and to educate our children differently.

For me, feminism is about choice. It's about having the freedom to act on those choices, regardless of societal expectations and limits placed on gender. It means having the systems in place that allow you to make those choices – free from judgement or expectation or punishment. It means men and women are valued for their individual human attributes, whether those fit into the stereotypical gender roles or not. It means having equal rights and treatment for *everybody*.

As Jonah Gokova argued in 'Challenging men to reject gender stereotypes',[256] within patriarchy men too are having to 'project an image that is not naturally theirs'. Living the 'myth of male superiority', then, is hurting both men and women.

Chapter 12
When You Are Both and Neither

I always find it interesting how many words there are to describe a thing. The more there are, the more importance that thing is afforded in any given language.

I am both and neither. There are a multitude of ways to categorise it: global citizen, global cosmopolitan, third culture kid, cross-cultural kid. I could probably find more, but you get the point.

I feel very lucky to have grown up in London. It gave me an opportunity to feel part of a diverse, international community. The most recent census found that, of the 8.88 million people living in London, 37 per cent were born outside of the United Kingdom. Of these, approximately two-thirds were born outside of the European Union.[257] London is a beautiful blend of ethnicities; no doubt had I grown up somewhere less multicultural, it might have been harder to feel at home.

And while the rest of the UK might be less diverse, Britain has to varying degrees been a multicultural society for centuries. But the question: 'Where are you from?' has become increasingly emblematic of the state of affairs in the UK, and around the world too. While I certainly do feel both British and Egyptian, whether I'm in London or in Cairo, people always ask me where I'm from. As Afua Hirsch put it in *Brit(ish)*,[258] that question is the 'most persistent reminder of that sense of not belonging'.

Of course, it's not that there's anything wrong with being interested in people's heritages. I often find myself asking others where they are from, keen to map out the places and the events that brought us to the same place, at the same time. But, as Hirsch argues, it feels different when it's *a* question not *the* question. '*The* question is reserved for people who look different.' It's an assumption of foreignness, making you a perpetual foreigner even in the place you consider home.

'I immediately get annoyed when someone asks me,' Amina, a thirty-one-year-old Lebanese woman who was born and raised in London, told me. 'I always just say "here" and leave it at that. Sometimes people prod, "But where are you *really* from?"'

'People are always keen to gauge how foreign you really are,' Sarah agreed.

There are different things that give it away, that make people ask me *the* question: my accent – every single time – in both countries. In London, it's the way I look too. In Cairo, I think it's probably the way I carry myself and how I dress that gives me away, makes it obvious I'm not *really* Egyptian (whatever that means). Although my friends in Cairo often look and dress much like me, many people are quick to tell them they're not *really* Egyptian either. All of them went to international schools and often speak English better than they do Arabic. I recently met up with an Egyptian friend of mine while wearing a full matching tracksuit and he laughed at how British that was of me. Funny, what are considered the cultural qualifiers.

How I respond to the inevitable 'Where are you from?' depends on a few factors – primarily where I am when asked, as well as who's asking me. Usually, I say I'm from Egypt but that I've lived most of my life in London. Abroad, it's partly a caveat: I am more than what you think I am. But in Egypt, when I say I'm Egyptian, I feel the need to explain why my Arabic is broken and heavily accented with English. 'But I grew up in London' comes out in a rush of translation.

Courtney once told me that much of who he is – and how he lives his life, carries himself, talks and dresses – was in reaction to the world's stereotypes of who he was supposed to be as a black man. He said he considers himself a constant representation of black men, and thus – partly subconsciously, partly with purpose – tries to be the best possible example he can be.

It was only while writing this that I realised I also do this to a degree, but it's my blend of both cultures that I brandish. It plays out in all sorts of ways, such as a long-held refusal to abide by the status quo or to follow the path I felt was already carved out for me. But it also manifests itself in how I clutch my British passport to my chest prominently whenever boarding a flight to or from Cairo, or avoid Harrods like the plague lest I be confused as the sort of Arab who shops there, Lamborghini half-parked on the pavement. I feel a pressure to distance myself from those who are like me but *really not* like me. From the stereotype of the Arab. From the 'bad immigrant', the one who makes too much noise and doesn't follow the rules and stands on the left-hand side on the escalator. I try extra hard to prove 'we're not all like that'.

'If I see an Arab when I'm out, I don't speak Arabic,' Selina told me when I brought it up with her. 'I fan myself with my British passport in the airport when I go to Egypt,' she continued.

Half-Ghanaian, half-British broadcaster Afua Hirsch wrote in *Brit(ish)* about an experience that resonated with me. She described the time she found herself on a train with a Nigerian man who incessantly spoke loudly on the phone in a mix of Nigerian and English, angrily talking about some problems he was having with the police and a passport. 'The white businessman sitting opposite me is visibly uncomfortable,' she wrote. 'I want to look at him in sympathetic annoyance ... But siding obviously with the businessman whose table I'm sharing would make me complicit in his judgement ...

'This is the dilemma of the "Good Immigrant",' she continued. 'We must be good, we must be grateful – legally we are entitled to remain here unconditionally, but psychologically, in the perceptions of others, our right to be here is somehow conditional upon good behaviour, gratitude and adequate displays of the intention to assimilate . . . I am embarrassed by the behaviour of my Nigerian neighbour because he is breaking the rules.'[259]

The 'Good Immigrant' dynamic can be seen everywhere. As Hirsch put it in *Brit(ish)*, 'Winning Olympic medals for Great Britain makes you a Good Immigrant, putting athletes Mo Farah and Jessica Ennis-Hill very firmly in this category. So does becoming a Tory MP, raising money for charity, showing deference to the Royal Family, marrying a white British person, abstaining from drunken or excessive behaviour . . . or distancing oneself from Bad Immigrants, as I was so tempted to do on the train.'

The distinction between 'good immigrant' and 'bad immigrant' has dangerous consequences around the world, such as in the case of Trump electing to end the Deferred Action for Childhood Arrivals (DACA) programme, which protected young unauthorised immigrants from deportation and allowed them to work legally in the US, or in the recent Windrush scandal in the UK.

The much-publicised case of Shamima Begum, the teenager who travelled from east London to Syria to join Islamic State in 2015,[260] made me realise just how complicated and often toxic the good immigrant/bad immigrant rhetoric can be, as well as just how much immigrants like me can feel the need to distance ourselves from anything to do with 'bad immigrants'.

When Begum, who was nineteen at the time of writing, asked to be let back into the UK with her newborn son – her third child (after her first two had died in a war zone) – my initial reaction, like much of the population, was shock and disgust; not least because she didn't seem to be demonstrating much (if any) remorse. The home secretary Sajid Javid opted to revoke Begum's British citizenship rather than let her back into the UK to be tried and potentially prosecuted as a British citizen.[261] Javid argued that the fact Begum's parents were of Bangladeshi heritage meant she could apply for citizenship of that country, despite the fact Begum had never even been to Bangladesh. After Begum's citizenship was stripped, her family wrote to the home secretary to ask if he might reconsider as an 'act of mercy', and for assistance in bringing her baby to the UK. Begum's newborn son sadly passed away just days later, causing Conservative MP and former justice minister Phillip Lee to urge the government to 'reflect' on its 'moral responsibility' for the tragedy.[262]

The outrage surrounding Javid's decision to revoke Begum's citizenship made me realise that my thoughts (which up until then had been that yes, we should all aspire to be 'good immigrants' in the same way that we should all aspire to be good humans) were not so straightforward.

'You can be saddened by the Home Secretary's decision while also vehemently opposed to the ideology of extremists,' tweeted journalist Kieran Yates,[263] the first to make me realise that the two are not mutually exclusive. But it was a tweet from Buzzfeed's political reporter Hannah Al-Othman that made me really understand that, while obviously in an ideal world none of it would have even happened in the first place, this was ultimately a much bigger issue. She wrote: 'If I did a v horrible crime (which I have no intention of ever doing), I could theoretically be deported to Iraq – a country I have never been to, where I know nobody & don't speak the language. Depriving nationality is racist. It suggests some of us are less British than others.'[264]

That is ultimately what is at the heart of the debate. That a citizenship can only be revoked if you can be considered a national of another country (so as not to leave someone 'stateless', which is against international law) plays into the same rhetoric that says that dual citizens are less at home and belong less than those who are not.

As novelist Kamila Shamsie (whose book *Home Fire* tackled many of these issues) wrote in an article for the *Guardian*:[265] 'We first need to grasp that at no point in the process of becoming a British citizen does any piece of documentation signal to you that your citizenship is contingent, that the equality of all citizens is a myth.' To conclude, she told of a conversation she had had with a friend whose son was a dual national and thus potentially subject to deprivation orders. 'Tell him not to break any laws,' Shamsie had told her friend, trying to make a joke of it. 'Yeah,' her friend had responded, 'but how do I have a conversation with my son where I tell him that because he's Muslim and his mother's from Pakistan he has to be careful in ways that his friends don't have to?'

Certainly, this two-tiered system of justice, and the idea that citizenship is a privilege rather than a right (words uttered numerous times by Theresa May when she was home secretary),[266] contribute to that feeling of not being 100 per cent at home and, as Shamsie puts it, 'distinguish[es] between those who are "British British" and those who are British until the home secretary decides otherwise'.[267] This distinction and subsequent feeling of not being fully welcomed or at home is likely at least in part what allowed Begum, and others like her, to even be radicalised in the first place.

Rather than fostering a rhetoric of difference, governments should be doing all they can to aid the process of integration. Integration needs to be a two-way effort in terms of promoting an environment of less discrimination, racism and prejudice, as well as encouraging a mixture of ethnicities among housing and schooling, all of which would serve to increase understanding.

The most basic premise of being able to feel at home is the ability to speak the language. While it's said that 90 per cent of foreign nationals living in the UK speak English 'very well', Javid recently revealed that 770,000 people living in England speak no English, or very little, going on to describe his own experience as a 'six-year-old interpreter' for his Pakistani mother.[268]

While the question of whether learning English should be made compulsory for immigrants in the UK has been deemed a contentious subject, I think it's a no-brainer. *Obviously* people planning to live in the UK should be required to at least *try* to learn how to speak the language. No doubt it would make their lives far easier and far more enjoyable too. Javid said that his mother's decision to learn English fifteen years after arriving in the country had 'transformed her life', enabling her to work for the family business, make new friends and – years later – meant she was able to speak with his British wife and their children, her grandchildren. It's a game-changer and makes *everyone's* lives better.

To promote integration, perhaps we should look to Canada for an example, as an article by Nick Pearce in the *Telegraph* suggests.[269] Canada is often regarded as one of the world's most socially cohesive and advanced democracies. It has generous family reunification schemes, allowing immigrants to apply to bring their grandparents, as well as their partners and children, into the country. It also awards international students' credits to encourage them to stay and make their lives there.

Conversely, the UK is increasingly making all such steps more difficult for its citizens.[270] It's increasingly difficult for non-EU immigrants to bring their families over to the UK. Nor are students who study in the UK allowed to stay and work after completing their courses, despite years of living in the UK and making it their home. The fees to apply for citizenship – at over £1,000 – are among the highest in the world.[271] Perhaps, as Pearce suggests, migrants could be 'auto-enrolled' on a citizenship route. He argues this would help send the message that people who integrate and become part of British society will be rewarded with the rights, as well as the responsibilities, of British citizenship. It's certainly a better suggestion than the current situation of making it as hard and as expensive as possible, causing many to view and subsequently treat the UK like a pit stop.

Indeed, it's important to underline that it's not about compromising your cultural identity; rather, it's an acknowledgement that you can be both that *and* British. That being both can only ever be a strength.

As Amin Mahlouf wrote,[272] 'It's in this spirit of [reciprocity] that I would first say to one party: "The more you steep yourself in the culture of your host country the more you will be able to steep yourself in your own", and then, to the other party: "The more an immigrant feels that his own culture is respected, the more open he will be to the culture of the host country."'

Mahlouf went on to ask, 'What, in the culture of a host country, is the minimum equipment that everyone is supposed to possess and what may legitimately be challenged or rejected? . . . The same may be asked about the immigrant's own original culture. Which parts of it deserve to be transmitted like a valuable dowry to the country of adoption, and which – which habits? Which practices? – ought to be left behind at the door?' Certainly, these are valid questions that should be given ample consideration.

Brexit can be argued to have legitimised the racism found within pockets of British society, giving racists free rein to discriminate against any migrant, good or bad, European or not; evidence of a much larger rhetoric of exclusion. Voting 'Remain' in 2016 was the first time I had ever voted in an election. I had never felt like I understood politics or was able to wade in, so I kept out of it. But I couldn't with this election (or ever again). I felt strongly, as did much of my generation. Sixty-four per cent of registered young people – who are generally regarded as apathetic – voted in that referendum.[273] The majority voted Remain but, as has been publicised, the older generation swung the vote.[274]

Since the shock Brexit results, many – myself included – are far more politically engaged.[275]

As a consequence of living in a cosmopolitan bubble like London – and in a social-media echo chamber of my own making, perhaps – when I woke up to see the referendum's result, I felt floored. I really hadn't thought it could happen. London was a ghost town that day, the mood sombre – a mass funeral. My mood echoed the masses. Despite the fact I've had a British passport for half my life, it felt like I was no longer wanted here and I questioned whether I ever had been. But London is my home, far more than anything or anywhere else I'd ever known.

'Nothing has been the same since Brexit,' Selina told me. 'It's not because I've experienced anything personal, but even my friends back in Derby [where I grew up], some of them did vote to leave and it was because of immigration . . . It makes me hate the ignorance in this country. I've stopped reading comments even in the *Guardian* articles. I've never seen it that bad before. We've grown up knowing that this is an open and accepting country, and I felt for the first time that it wasn't. And then Matthew [my husband, who is originally from Italy] got told a couple of times recently to go back to his country.'

In the UK, in the years since the referendum, there have been thousands of instances of racial abuse and hate crimes, aimed not just at immigrants from EU nations but also at anyone who looks 'foreign' to racists, confirming this was part of a larger anti-immigrant unease.[276] The media has been reporting instances of visibly Muslim men and women being shouted at in the streets, and instructed to 'Get out! We voted leave', and a Sikh doctor was reportedly asked by a patient: 'Shouldn't you be on a plane back to Pakistan? We voted you out.'[277]

A survey found that many highly qualified EU nationals have been considering leaving the UK since Brexit, mainly because of a perception that British society has changed. Half of those surveyed said they felt less valued and welcomed in the UK since the EU referendum.[278] And many followed through on this: figures show that 122,000 Europeans left the UK in 2017.[279]

The thing is, both the UK and the rest of the world need immigration for its youth, dynamism and talent. The reality of immigration is far from the refugee crisis and the drain on the economy, as the far-right media and politicians tend to portray. A recent study showed that between 2000 and 2011, migrants contributed a total of £20 billion to the British economy. What's more, 60 per cent of new migrants are university graduates who enter the workforce and pay taxes, contributing 64 per cent more in taxes than they received in benefits.[280] In the US in 2010, immigrant-owned businesses generated more than $775 billion in revenue.[281]

Aside from the prosperity a healthy migration engenders, the cultural influence is also significant; cuisine, fashion, music, literature and much more add to the richness of a diverse society.

Interestingly, a 2018 study found that British voters feel more positively about immigrants than at any time since 2011. Results found that just 17 per cent of Britons thought immigrants had a negative impact on the economy, and just 23 per cent thought they undermined Britain's cultural life.[282] It is the lowest level since the question was first asked in 2011, with the study's researchers concluding that the EU referendum campaign may have served to cause immigrants to be valued in a way that was not in evidence before.

The thing is, we don't just blend into an environment, we contribute to its very shape, just by being there. What's more, our environments contribute to our shapes too. We live and grow and make decisions based on the worlds we inhabit, which in turn draws us further into those worlds. We are made up of where we live, and it is made up of us.

To paraphrase author Pico Iyer in his TED Talk 'Where is Home', what does the question 'Where are you from?' even mean? Does it mean what your blood is? Where you were born? Where you were educated? Where you pay your taxes? Where you wish to spend most of your time?

Because, for many people, the answer to each of these questions may well be different.[283]

There is a line in a book by Brian Andreas that I read many years ago, and that sticks with me. It reminds me of the power of words, of how much we can gauge about a culture and its people by the words they place importance on, the words they have to describe the things they find important. 'I read once that the ancient Egyptians had fifty words for sand and the Eskimos had a hundred words for snow,' Andreas wrote.[284] I find it telling that in Arabic, there is a single word for what it is to reside in a country other than one's own: 'ghorbah'. Loosely translated to English, it means 'estrangement'.

'The French have no word for home,' author Meg Fee posits.[285] 'They have words for "at my place" and "in my country" but not for "home" . . . and I can't help but think they are on to something.' After all, as Fee notes, home is often 'much larger than language allows for'.

'The older I get, the more connected I feel to my Arab friends but it's still not enough,' Dunya told me. 'I was saying to my mum the other day, I miss the culture. We aren't able to go to Iraq, the only place we're able to go to is Jordan because my family live there,' she explained. 'I don't feel at home in London; I feel a bit lost because of everything going on in my country. The first and last time I went was in 2002. As soon as we got our passports, we went straight to Iraq for ten days. It was just before the war and it was a dream.

'All my family lived in Iraq at the time, but over the years they've moved out and there is no more home,' she added. 'I say to my mum and dad, "Let's go to Lebanon or to another Arab country", or, "Let's try and make somewhere else home." I feel like the UK will never feel like home to me.'

The absence of choice can make settling in very difficult, but it was interesting that, despite the fact that I could easily go 'back home' to Egypt, I didn't feel entirely at home there either. A feeling of homelessness certainly pervaded many of my younger years. It still lingers on the days where I feel sad or down. In between sobs, I choke up the words, 'I wanna go home!' in London meaning Cairo, and in Cairo meaning London, both times meaning 'anywhere but here'. In truth, neither ever gives the desired solace.

In 2011, there were 220 million people living in countries not 'their own'. That figure has probably increased in the years since. And while a percentage of that number are sadly refugees, for those of us fortunate enough to move by choice and with ease, the opportunity to experience life in a country that is not your own, the chance to learn and take from two cultures, is a blessing that gives more than that feeling of 'estrangement' may take away.

The older I get and the stronger my sense of 'home' grows within me, the more I realise that it's people who make places feel like home, it's memories, it's familiarity – for example, when you've spent enough time in a city that you know which carriage to enter on the Tube so you can be closest to the exit when you get off, or what times to avoid the streets so you don't get stuck in traffic. It's laying your head back on your pillow at the end of a long day and feeling that flutter of relief in your chest. You can be 'home' and not feel at home, this I know too.

I think as we get older, what makes us feel at home changes. Home is often a time, much more than it is a place. The older I get, the better I am at making new places feel like home. You start to learn what it is that makes your soul happy and you seek that. I now realise – each time, with relief – that you can find those pieces everywhere.

'Growing up, the main question of my life was: "Where is home?" But I've realised now, that I can be at home in different places,' Selina told me. 'When I go to Egypt, a part of me does still belong there, [London] is more home, but then when I go to Italy I feel like there is where I want to call home. It doesn't really bother me anymore. Maybe when I was growing up, Egypt was more home because my extended family lived there and [England] was just the four of us . . . but I've got my own life now; I've made a life here aside from my parents and I feel like this is home.'

Egyptian journalist Rasha Rushdy penned a piece on raising her children as 'third culture kids', writing that her hopes for them are that rather than seeing themselves tied down to one place, one label or one box, they might instead see a potential new home in every city they discover: 'My hope is that they will have learned, early on, how to learn to observe and appreciate the community around them, and to seek to relate to others by trying to find common ground. I hope that their experiences will teach them that you will *always* find some common ground,' she continued. 'No matter how different you think you might be to another person . . . there will always be some element of sameness and universality in all human experience.'[286]

Indeed, belonging doesn't have all that much to do with where you were born, what language your parents use to speak to you, where you live or even what your opinions are; it's to do with forging connections based on what's in your head and what's in your heart. It's about seeking out the similarities rather than focusing on the differences. As such, there will always be common ground.

Maybe home is constantly a work in progress. Maybe, like Pico Iyer said, it's about 'constantly piecing bits together from many different places to make a stained-glass whole . . . like a project to which you're constantly adding improvements'.[287]

And maybe not being able to succinctly answer 'Where are you from?' is a liberation. As Iyer concluded in his TED Talk, our grandparents had everything assigned to them at birth, without much chance of stepping outside of that. Nowadays, 'at least some of us can choose our sense of home, create our sense of community, fashion our sense of self and, in doing so, step a little beyond some of the black and white divisions of our grandparents' age'.[288]

Beyond all the divisions – to be both and neither and more than that, besides.

A Conclusion, of Sorts

Writing this book has been a journey, one that took me far beyond just the process of sitting down every day and typing word after word on to these pages. I didn't really know what I was going to find when I embarked on it. I wasn't sure exactly what was going to come out. I had always written in order to decipher how I felt, how to make connections and find solutions – and I was hoping the same would be the case with *The Greater Freedom*. It was.

What I discovered is that there are literally millions of stories, and no two are the same, but there are common human elements that extend like invisible threads tying us together, whether we feel able to acknowledge them or not. I came to understand the true importance of telling these different stories, how having different examples can have an impact both on dispelling stereotypes and also on our ability to form and accept our own identities with all their nuances.

In writing this book, in researching and talking to other Middle Eastern women and digging deep, I learnt so much about myself, reached so many conclusions, and even an acceptance of sorts. When I was younger, I remember wanting to present new friends – new boys, in particular – with a disclaimer asserting, 'this is why I am the way I am'. I didn't really have an explanation then, though, only a need to express my discomfort, my difference (perceived or otherwise). I realise this book could be seen, in part anyway, as that disclaimer. But it's also a reflection of all the things I chose not to be.

In writing, I learnt that no matter how bad something feels at the time, with distance it's often possible to craft stories out of our traumas. It's possible to interrogate and decipher their lessons, in mere paragraphs, words and full stops.

To borrow from writer Diya Abdo in an essay she wrote for *Bad Girls of the Arab World*, I learnt that 'we can be good even if we're not perfect'. I learnt we can be perfect even if we are not 'the selves that others have constructed for us, expect of us, or want for us'. That we can be kinder on ourselves. 'How great the relief. How great the loss.'[289]

When Smoky and I broke up, my mum told me I was lucky. I didn't understand what she meant at the time, although I would soon come to. It wasn't that he was a bad guy or that I would necessarily have had a bad life with him, but splitting from him meant I had the opportunity to break away from tradition, to challenge expectations and to dismiss cultural assumptions. It gave me the chance to create my own life, become my own person, instead of blindly following the path that had been set out for me. My mum recognised that, even when I didn't.

I'm lucky I was able to move out of the house that same year, to have been born into a family that allowed and encouraged me to look further, work harder, keep growing. That I had been born with a brain and a heart that demanded I reach my own conclusions.

Much of who we are is reached by trial and error, by learning and unlearning different ways of thinking and being. No one is themselves from birth; we become who we are, and we keep becoming. It's worth considering, then, the argument outlined by Amin Mahlouf, that we each have two heritages: 'A "vertical" one that comes to us from our ancestors, our religious community and our popular traditions, and a "horizontal" one transmitted to us by our contemporaries and the age we live in.'[290] He suggests that the latter is the more influential of the two, and – thanks in part to cultural globalisation – that this becomes more influential with each passing day. Despite this, he argues, the heritage we most frequently align ourselves with is the vertical one. He suggests, instead, that we should think of ourselves as 'beings woven out of many-coloured threads, who share most of their points of reference, their ways of behaving and their beliefs with the vast community of their contemporaries'.

For sure, there are always far more things we as humans have as similarities than we do differences. And while the importance and influence of our vertical heritage can't be denied, 'it is necessary at this point in time to draw attention to the gulf that exists between what we are and what we think we are,' he writes. That is: beings woven out of experiences and viewpoints accrued from a multitude of life experiences and viewpoints rather than one thing passed down in our genes that is set in stone for all of eternity.

It is necessary, then, to consider – both for ourselves and for the children we have or will potentially one day have – what burdens and blessings we wish to pass on to the next generation. What is it we want to keep? What is it that we *actually* believe, and what is it that we've adopted by osmosis? What *actually* makes a culture and which parts of it are we free to cherish or discard? As poet Jamie Varon wrote, 'I want us all to make sure that whatever we're yearning for and whatever we're fighting for and whatever we're suffering for makes sense in our souls . . . That we . . . separate out what is expected of us from what we expect from ourselves – and to truly, intuitively, strongly know the difference.'[291]

There were so many ideas for what the title of this book should be. *The Greater Freedom* was the clear winner because this is ultimately what is most important to me, and ultimately what the book is about. Freedom to be oneself. Or, as poet James Merrill wrote in his memoir, to *not* be oneself. 'Freedom to be oneself is all very well,' he wrote. 'The greater freedom is not to be oneself.'[292]

Indeed. The freedom to not be oneself. To not be restricted by the notion of who 'yourself' is supposed to be, whether those ideas are imposed by culture, by family, by society, by gender, by the media or by you. The greater freedom is to be who you actually are; to be able to live your life in the way you deem best, free from any sort of restriction to do that, or fear of repercussions for doing so.

To be free, we first have to be able to *name* our constraints and the ways in which we are held back from exploring our identities and from expressing our truest selves. That is what I have tried to do throughout the course of this book. Only after we have grappled with these questions can we enjoy a *greater freedom*.

May we all be able to act and love and be and grow and flourish, with the greatest of freedoms. That is my final thought. My final hope.

For now.

BIBLIOGRAPHY

Ahmed, L. *Women and Gender in Islam: Historical Roots of a Modern Debate* (Yale University Press, 1993)

Akala. *Natives: Race and Class in the Ruins of Empire* (Two Roads, 2019)

Al-Khatahtbeh, A. *Muslim Girl: A Coming of Age* (Simon & Schuster, 2017)

Aly, R. *Becoming Arab in London: Performativity and the Undoing of Identity* (Pluto Press, 2015)

Awad, A. *Beyond Veiled Clichés: The Real Lives of Arab Women* (Penguin Random House Australia, 2017)

Bergner, D. *What Do Women Want?: Adventures in the Science of Female Desire* (Ecco Press, 2014)

Eddo-Lodge, Reni. *Why I'm No Longer Talking to White People About Race* (Bloomsbury Publishing, 2018)

El Feki, S. *Sex and the Citadel* (Vintage Books, 2014)

El Saadawi, N. and Hetata, S. *A Daughter of Isis: The Early Life of Nawal El Saadawi, In Her Own Words*, 3rd ed. (Zed Books, 2018)

El Saadawi, N. and Hetata, S. *The Hidden Face of Eve: Women in the Arab World*, 3rd ed. (Zed Books, 2017)

El Saadawi, N. and Hetata, S. *Walking Through Fire: The Later Years of Nawal El Saadawi, In Her Own Words*, 3rd ed. (Zed Books, 2018)

Elnoury, T. *American Radical: Inside the World of an Undercover Muslim FBI Agent* (Bantam Press, 2017)

Eltahawy, M. *Headscarves and Hymens: Why the Middle East Needs a Sexual Revolution* (W&N, 2016)

Haddad, Joumana. *I Killed Scheherazade: Confessions of an Angry Arab Woman* (Saqi Books, 2010)

Hirsch, A. *Brit(ish): On Race, Identity and Belonging* (Jonathan Cape, 2018)

Janmohamed, S. *Generation M: Young Muslims Changing the World* (I. B. Tauris, 2016)

Khan, Mariam. *It's Not About the Burqa: Muslim Women on Faith, Feminism, Sexuality and Race* (Picador, 2019)

Mahfouz, S. *The Things I Would Tell You: British Muslim Women Write* (Saqi Books, 2017)

Mahlouf, A. *On Identity* (Vintage, 2000)

Mokeddem, M. *My Men* (University of Nebraska Press, 2009)

Nasr, S. *The Heart of Islam: Enduring Values for Humanity* (HarperOne, 2004)

Noor, Queen. *A Leap of Faith: Memoir of an Unexpected Life* (W&N, 2004)

O'Hearn, C. *Half and Half* (Random House USA, 1998)

Raassi, T. *Fashion is Freedom: How a Girl from Tehran Broke the Rules to Change Her World* (Sourcebooks, 2016)

Rizvi, A. *The Atheist Muslim* (St Martin's Press, 2016)

Said, E. *Orientalism* (Vintage Books, 2003)

Salbi, Z. *Between Two Worlds: Escape from Tyranny: Growing Up in the Shadow of Saddam* (Avery Publishing Group, 2006)

Sharif, M. *Daring to Drive: A Saudi Woman's Awakening* (Simon & Schuster UK, 2017)

Shukla, N. and Suleyman, C. *The Good Immigrant* (Unbound, 2017)

Yaqub, N. and Quawas, R. *Bad Girls of the Arab World* (University of Texas Press, 2017)

Yousafzai, M. and Lamb, C. *I Am Malala: The Girl Who Stood Up for Education and Was Shot by the Taliban* (W&N, 2014)

Zoepf, K. *Excellent Daughters: The Secret Lives of Young Women Who Are Transforming the Arab World* (Penguin Books, 2017)

ACKNOWLEDGMENTS

Thank you for reading this book. That is the first acknowledgement to make. A book only becomes real by being read, so thank you for making this real.

Thank you to my literary agent, Imogen Pelham, who understood what I was trying to say even when I didn't, and for finding that story a good home. Thank you to Alex Carr, who first took a chance on this book, Victoria Pepe for your vision and support, Arzu Tahsin for understanding my language and knowing how and which threads to pull to get the best out of me. To the entire team at Amazon Publishing, I feel privileged to have had your expertise at all stages of this process.

Thank you to all the women who spoke to me, and who I've quoted in these pages. I hope I did you proud.

Thank you to all the people I mentioned in this book and all those I didn't mention but who played a pivotal role in the making of me. Yes, even Satan. Because of you I am who I am today, and I love that person, so all's well that ends well. CM, you believed in me first and because of you I learnt how to believe in myself, I will be forever grateful.

'Thank you' is likely not enough to my parents but I say it all the same. Thank you for loving me, for supporting me, for granting me the greater freedom and encouraging me to fly. I hope there is nothing too shocking in these pages; I am your daughter, after all, and you know me well. I love you for that. I feel privileged to be able to call you my friends.

To my brother, who was in many ways my first reader and listener, and to my grandfather for your love and your charm and your wisdom.

Thank you to my friend Laura Jane Williams. Since I first met you, you have encouraged and inspired me in countless ways. In being yourself and in sharing your story, you made me think I could too, could maybe write a book too! You are a living embodiment of one of my favourite sentiments: 'a candle loses nothing by lighting another candle.'

Thank you to Nich Panchal for taking me seriously and for believing I had a worthy story to tell, long before I was even able to vocalise it. In doing so you made my desire to one day write a book into something tangible and immediate.

My Gs, thank you for supporting me and encouraging me and understanding that I basically needed to disappear off the face of the earth to write this. In no particular order: Sabreen, Rox, Soupy, Habiba, Julie, Nadia, Marina, Lana, Tash, Ons, Yamina, Lauren, Joss, Nat, Rachael, Hailey and Monique. Love you!

To all my Instagram friends, for your support and your 'likes' and your messages and encouragement, for all the 'YASS's you sent that let me know I was on the right path, that I was writing this for you too. I hope at least some of what you read in these pages is what you wanted this book to be.

Ali Malik, thank you for keeping me sane with our three weekly sessions and sometimes being the only reason I left the house that week. The endorphins and conversation you provided often carried me through.

Thank you to Nawal El Saadawi whose words have been a huge inspiration and to all those like her who speak and have spoken the truth and who have sought to achieve greater freedom. We wouldn't be here without you.

ABOUT THE AUTHOR

Photo © 2017 Hanna Hillier

Alya Mooro was born in Cairo in 1989. She has written for publications including *Grazia*, *Refinery29*, the *Washington Post* and the *Telegraph* on everything from social commentary and fashion to lifestyle. She holds a BA in Sociology and Psychology from City University and a Masters in Journalism from Westminster.

Alya runs the cult blog alyamooro.com and has collaborated with brands including Nike, ASOS and Absolut. She has guested on numerous national radio stations including BBC Radio 4 *Woman's Hour*, BBC Radio 1 and BBC 1Xtra, where she was invited to speak about topics including the need for increased diversity in the media.

She is a representative voice both for her generation and for multi-cultural women everywhere and was featured in a spread in the August 2017 issue of *Harper's Bazaar* Arabia, where she was selected as part of a new generation of 'globetrotting Arab women who embody [a] cosmopolitan legacy'.

(ENDNOTES)

1   Let's banish the term 'Arab world'. What does it mean anyway?, Neheda Barakat. [online] the Guardian. Available at: https://www.theguardian.com/commentisfree/2018/apr/18/lets-banish-the-term-arab-world-what-does-it-mean-anyway 01.05.18

2   Awad, A. (2017). *Beyond Veiled Clichés: The Real Lives of Arab Women*. Penguin Random House Australia.

3   My Search for Belonging as a Young, Middle Eastern American Woman. Elbarmawi, S. (2018). [online] Yellow Co. Available at: https://yellowco.co/blog/2018/03/07/search-to-belong-middle-eastern-american-young-woman/ [Accessed 2 Jul. 2019].

4   Shukla, N. (2016). *The Good Immigrant*. Unbound.

5   'They All Look Alike': The Other-Race Effect. Pomeroy, S. (2014). [online] Forbes.com. Available at: https://www.forbes.com/sites/rosspomeroy/2014/01/28/think-they-all-look-alike-thats-just-the-other-race-effect/#6d49209e3819 10.05.18

6   'I don't find this funny': Stormzy fuming after newspaper photo mix-up. Gillett, F. (2017). [online] Evening Standard. Available at: https://www.standard.co.uk/news/uk/i-dont-find-this-funny-

stormzy-fuming-after-newspaper-mixup-with-footballer-romelu-lukaku-a3584361.html

7   Golden Globes Twitter Account Misidentifies America Ferrera as Jane the Virgin Nominee Gina Rodriguez. Johnson, Z. (2015). 10.05.18 [online] E! News. Available at: https://www.eonline.com/uk/news/722887/golden-globes-twitter-account-misidentifies-announcer-america-ferrera-as-jane-the-virgin-nominee-gina-rodriguez

8   Can You Name the Arab States? Briney, A. (2018). [online] ThoughtCo. Available at: https://www.thoughtco.com/list-of-arab-states-1435128 [Accessed 5 Mar. 2019].

9   Arab Unity: Nasser's Revolution. Aljazeera.com. (2008). [online] Available at: https://www.aljazeera.com/focus/arabunity/2008/02/200852517252821627.html [Accessed 5 Mar. 2019].

10 Aly, R. (2015). *Becoming Arab in London: Performativity and the Undoing of Identity*. Pluto Press.

11 Ons.gov.uk. (2012). Ethnicity and National Identity in England and Wales. [online] Office for National Statistics. Available at: https://www.ons.gov.uk/peoplepopulationandcommunity/culturalidentity/ethnicity/articles/ethnicityandnationalidentityinenglandandwales/2012-12-11

12 Arab-Americans: A 'Growing' Community, But By How Much? Wang, H. (2013). [online] Npr.org. Available at: https://www.npr.org/sections/codeswitch/2013/05/30/187096445/arab-americans-a-growing-community-but-by-how-much?t=1539623370388 [Accessed 5 Mar. 2019].

13 US Census fails to add MENA category: Arabs to remain 'white' in count. Harb, A. (2018). 12.05.18 [online] Middle East Eye. Available at: https://www.middleeasteye.net/news/us-census-continue-count-arabs-white-1206288795

14 I'm Not Your Stereotype: One Middle Eastern Girl Talks Growing Up in America. Syed, A. (2015). 12.05.18 [online] Teen Vogue. Available at: https://www.teenvogue.com/story/middle-eastern-stereotypes

15 Said, E. (2003). *Orientalism*. Vintage Books.

16 The leaves of one tree: Religious minorities in Lebanon. El Rajji, R. (n.d.). 15.05.18 [online] Reliefweb.int. Available at: https://reliefweb.int/sites/reliefweb.int/files/resources/mrg-briefing-religious-minorities-in-lebanon.pdf

17 Shora, N. (2008). *The Arab-American handbook*. Cune Press.

18 You May Know These Muslim-American Actors From Such Roles as Terrorist. Jon Ronson, P. (2015). 15.05.18 [online] GQ. Available at: https://www.gq.com/story/muslim-american-typecasting-hollywood

19 Study Shows Bleak Middle Eastern & North African Representation, Reinforced Stereotypes On Primetime TV. Ramos, D. (2018). [online] Deadline. Available at: https://deadline.com/2018/09/middle-eastern-north-african-representation-primetime-tv-mena-quantico-blacklist-tyrant-diversity-1202458101/ [Accessed 7 Mar. 2019].

20 How One Woman Is Fighting To Get More Latinos Onscreen. Cheng, S. (2018). 15.05.18 [online] Buzzfeednews.com. Available

at: https://www.buzzfeednews.com/article/susancheng/carla-hool-coco-narcos-casting-director-latino-actors#.gpwwALWxY

21 Wohlford, K., Lochman, J. and Barry, T. (2004). The Relation Between Chosen Role Models and the Self-Esteem of Men and Women. *Sex Roles*, 50(7/8), pp.575–582.

22 Riz Ahmed: 'Black Panther,' 'Crazy Rich Asians' Aren't Just Wins For Blacks And Asians. [online] Huffingtonpost. co.uk. (2018). Available at: https://www.huffingtonpost. co.uk/entry/riz-ahmed-black-panther-crazy-rich-asians_ us_5bbf6499e4b040bb4e7fd883 [Accessed 5 Mar. 2019].

23 Smith, Stacy L., Mark Choueiti and Katherine Pieper, 'Inclusion or Invisibility? Comprehensive Annenberg Report on Diversity in Entertainment,' Media, Diversity, & Social Change Initiative, University of Southern California, February 2016.

24 I'm an Arab actor who's been asked to play a terrorist 30 times. If La La Lands cleans up at the Oscars, I'm done. Al-Kadhi, A. (2017). [online] The Independent. Available at: https://www. independent.co.uk/voices/oscars-la-la-land-moonlight-arab-mus-lim-actor-audition-terrorist-i-am-done-a7595261.html [Accessed 8 Jul. 2019].

25 Little girl awestruck by Michelle Obama's portrait believes she's 'a queen'. Zaru, D. (2018). 25.08.18 [online] CNN. Available at: https://edition.cnn.com/2018/03/03/politics/michelle-obama-portrait-girl-parker-curry/index.html

26 Michelle Obama on Instagram: 'As a young girl, even in my wild-est dreams, I never could have imagined this moment. Nobody in my family has ever had a portrait - there . . .' 25.08.18

[online] Instagram. Available at: https://www.instagram.com/p/
BfGxoaUgZ1i/?hl=en&taken-by=michelleobama

27   Footballer Mo Salah is tackling Islamophobia head-on
(2018) 28.05.18. [online] The National. Available at: https://
www.thenational.ae/opinion/editorial/footballer-mo-
salah-is-tackling-islamophobia-head-on-1.724010

28   Mo Salah Song Sheet. (2018). 25.05.18 [online] The Redmen TV.
Available at: https://theredmentv.com/mo-salah-song-sheet/

29   Exactly How Much Appearance Matters, According to Our
National Judgment Survey. Pergament D. (2016). [online] Allure.
Available at: https://www.allure.com/story/national-judgement-
survey-statistics?verso=true [Accessed 5 Mar. 2019].

30   How the Halo Effect Influences the Way We Perceive Attractive
People. Cherry, K. (2018). [online] Verywell Mind. Available at:
https://www.verywellmind.com/what-is-the-halo-effect-2795906
[Accessed 5 Mar. 2019].

31   From Instagram to Balmain: The rise of CGI models. Cresci, E.
(2018). [online] BBC News. Available at: https://www.bbc.co.uk/
news/newsbeat-45474286 [Accessed 5 Mar. 2019].

32   A Media Education Foundation production; writer, producer,
cinematographer and director, Elena Rossini. (2015). The illusionists. Northampton, MA: Media Education Foundation.

33   It's Time We Decolonize Our Beauty Standards. Kaabi, A. (n.d.).
05.06.18 [online] Mille World. Available at: http://www.mille-
world.com/time-we-decolonize-our-beauty-standards/

34 Whitaker, I., Karoo, R., Spyrou, G. and Fenton, O. (2007). The Birth of Plastic Surgery: The Story of Nasal Reconstruction from the Edwin Smith Papyrus to the Twenty-First Century. *Plastic and Reconstructive Surgery*, 120(1).

35 Lebanon emerges as Mideast's 'mecca' for cosmetic surgery. Neild, B. (2010). 05.06.18 [online] Edition.cnn.com. Available at: http://edition.cnn.com/2010/WORLD/meast/11/19/Lebanon.plastic.surgery/index.html (inactive). Archived on 12.04.18 at http://web.archive.org/web/20181204232003/http://edition.cnn.com/2010/WORLD/meast/11/19/Lebanon.plastic.surgery/index.html

36 Global Cosmetics Products Market expected to reach USD 805.61 billion by 2023 (2018). 02.06.18 [online] Reuters.com. Available at: https://www.reuters.com/brandfeatures/venture-capital/article?id=30351

37 Saudi Women Spend Big on Makeup, Even If It's Just a Glimpse. Press, A. (2018). 02.06.18 [online] The Business of Fashion. Available at: https://www.businessoffashion.com/articles/news-analysis/saudi-women-spend-big-on-makeup-even-if-its-just-a-glimpse

38 Mooro, A. (2016). How & Why Fashion Brands Are Catering More To Muslim Consumers. [online] Refinery29.com. Available at: https://www.refinery29.com/en-gb/muslim-fashion-dolce-gabanna-uniqlo [Accessed 9 Jul. 2019].

39 The Good Hair Study, Perception Institute, 2016.

40 Dove Wants You To 'Love Your Curls'. Bahadur, N. (2015). 07.06.18 [online] HuffPost UK. Available at: https://www.huffingtonpost.co.uk/entry/dove-love-your-curls-campaign_n_6506930

41 The Psychology Behind A 'Good Hair Day'. Diller, Ph.D., V. (2012). 07.06.18 [online] HuffPost. Available at: https://www.huffingtonpost.com/vivian-diller-phd/good-hair-day_b_1191203.html

42 Good Hair Documentary, HBO Films, LD Entertainment, Chris Rock Productions, 2009.

43 Is Yuko Hair Straightening the key to smooth hair? (2017). 09.06.18 [online] Marieclaire.co.uk. Available at: https://www.marieclaire.co.uk/beauty/hair/yuko-hair-straightening-463894-463894

44 Zota, A. and Shamasunder, B. (2017). The environmental injustice of beauty: framing chemical exposures from beauty products as a health disparities concern. *American Journal of Obstetrics and Gynecology*, 217(4).

45 Shetty, V., Shetty, N. and Nair, D. (2013). Chemical hair relaxers have adverse effects a myth or reality. *International Journal of Trichology*, 5(1).

46 Personal Hygiene (All parts) – The Religion of Islam. Stacey, A. (2009). 20.06.28 [online] Islamreligion.com. Available at: https://www.islamreligion.com/articles/2149/viewall/personal-hygiene/

47 My Mom Wanted to Anoint Me with Bat's Blood to Make Me Hairless. Abi-Najem, N. (2015).[online] Vice. Available at: https://www.vice.com/en_us/article/d3ggb7/my-mom-wanted-to-anoint-me-with-bats-blood-to-make-me-hairless [Accessed 9 Jul. 2019].

48 America's hair-removal insanity M. HERZIG, R. (2015). 28.06.18 [online] Salon. Available at: https://www.salon.com/2015/02/15/americas_hair_removal_insanity/

49   Rise of young women going 'au naturel' as nearly a quarter now don't shave their underarms. Rudgard, O. (2017). 01.07.18 [online] The Telegraph. Available at: https://www.telegraph.co.uk/news/2017/05/18/rise-young-women-going-au-naturel-nearly-quarter-now-dont-shave/

50   American Apparel Debuts Mannequins With Pubic Hair. Adams, R. (2017). 01.07.18 [online] HuffPost UK. Available at: https://www.huffingtonpost.co.uk/entry/american-apparel-pubic-hair-mannequins_n_4610688

51   Swedish model gets rape threats after ad shows her unshaved legs. Siddique, H. (2017). 01.07.18 [online] the Guardian. Available at: https://www.theguardian.com/lifeandstyle/2017/oct/06/swedish-model-gets-threats-after-ad-shows-her-unshaved-legs

52   Emma Watson Oils Her Pubes And Isn't Afraid To Talk About It. Strutner, S. (2017). 01.07.18 [online] HuffPost UK. Available at: https://www.huffingtonpost.co.uk/entry/emma-watson-pubic-hair_us_58bd9a0be4b033be14670e3d

53   Why Is Pubic Hair Such A Hairy Topic For Instagram? Hinde, N. (2015). 01.07.18 [online] HuffPost UK. Available at: https://www.huffingtonpost.co.uk/2015/01/21/instagram-ban-the-bush_n_6508694.html

54   My body shape may be in fashion just now, but for how long?. Brinkhurst-Cuff, C. (2017). [online] the Guardian. Available at: https://www.theguardian.com/global/2017/jul/30/my-body-shape-is-in-vogue-but-for-how-long-charlie-brinkhust-cuff [Accessed 5 Jul. 2019].

55 New study shows impact of social media on beauty standards. Katz, B. (2015). [online] Women in the World. Available at: https://womenintheworld.com/2015/04/03/new-study-shows-impact-of-social-media-on-beauty-standards/ [Accessed 8 Jul. 2019].

56 Why so many young women are obsessed with getting a bigger bottom. Carey, T. (2017). [online] Mail Online. Available at: https://www.dailymail.co.uk/femail/article-4449368/Why-young-women-want-bigger-bottom.html [Accessed 5 Mar. 2019].

57 Average age of world's most beautiful people is now 38 – up from 33 in 1990. Sarah Knapton (2017). 05.07.18 [online] The Telegraph. Available at: https://www.telegraph.co.uk/science/2017/10/11/average-age-worlds-beautiful-people-now-38-33-1990/

58 El Saadawi, N. and Hetata, S. (2015). *The Hidden Face of Eve: Women in the Arab World*. London: Zed Books.

59 Love and Badness in America and the Arab World. Abdo, D. (2017). 04.06.18 [online] Paris Review. Available at: https://www.theparisreview.org/blog/2017/10/02/love-and-badness-in-america-and-the-arab-world/

60 Bad Girls of the Arab World, Nadia Yaqub and Rula Quawas, University of Texas Press, 2017.

61 Zoepf, K. (2016). *Excellent Daughters: The secret lives of young women who are transforming the Arab world*. Penguin Press.

62 Let's talk about sex in . . . the Arab world. Green, G. (2014). 04.06.18 [online] New Internationalist. Available at: https://newint.org/features/2014/03/01/middle-east-personal-politics

63 Let's talk about sex in . . . the Arab world. El Feki, S. (2014). [online] New Internationalist. Available at: https://newint.org/features/2014/03/01/middle-east-personal-politics [Accessed 10 Jul. 2019].

64 In Egypt, 99 Percent of Women Have Been Sexually Harassed. Schultz, C. (2014). [online] Smithsonian. Available at: https://www.smithsonianmag.com/smart-news/egypt-99-women-have-been-sexually-harassed-180951726/ [Accessed 5 Mar. 2019].

65 The surprise place where hijab can spell trouble. Aboughazala, D. (2018). 06.06.18 [online] BBC News. Available at: https://www.bbc.co.uk/news/world-middle-east-44411333

66 The world's heaviest drinkers. 06.06.18 [online] Geographical. co.uk. Available at: http://geographical.co.uk/people/cultures/item/522-the-world-s-heaviest-drinkers

67 Egypt fights a losing battle against drugs. Menawy, M. (2018). 06.06.18 [online] Arab News. Available at: http://www.arabnews.com/node/1254306/middle-east#photo/0

68 Mapped: The countries that smoke the most cannabis. Gavin Haines (2017). 06.06.18 [online] The Telegraph. Available at: https://www.telegraph.co.uk/travel/maps-and-graphics/mapped-the-countries-that-smoke-the-most-cannabis/

69 Native Born, Foreign Raised: The Frustrations and Comfort Behind Strict Parents. Sulz, N. (2013). 08.06.18 [online] Elite Daily. Available at: https://www.elitedaily.com/life/culture/native-born-foreign-raised

70   Why People Often Do the Exact Opposite Of What They're Told. Grant, A. (2013). 07.06.18 [online] Business Insider. Available at: https://www.businessinsider.com/why-people-dont-follow-directions-2013-8?IR=T

71   Bushman, B. and Stack, A. (1996). Forbidden fruit versus tainted fruit: Effects of warning labels on attraction to television violence. *Journal of Experimental Psychology: Applied*, 2(3), pp.207–226.

72   Want to Popularize a Book? Ban It. Charles, R. (2012). 07.06.18 [online] Washington Post. Available at: https://www.washingtonpost.com/blogs/under-god/post/sister-farleys-revenge-want-to-popularize-a-book-ban-it/2012/06/06/gJQAihARJV_blog.html?utm_term=.dc86ce652559 [Accessed 24 Aug. 2018].

73   'Spare the rod': Arab world needs to change attitudes towards physical child discipline. Badam, R. (2017). [online] The National. Available at: https://www.thenational.ae/uae/spare-the-rod-arab-world-needs-to-change-attitudes-towards-physical-child-discipline-1.677407 [Accessed 5 Mar. 2019].

74   Banning spanking, corporal punishment tied to less youth violence. Lamotte, S. (2018). [online] WSLS. Available at: https://www.wsls.com/health/banning-spanking-corporal-punishment-tied-to-less-youth-violence [Accessed 5 Mar. 2019].

75   Aly, R. (2015). *Becoming Arab in London: Performativity and the Undoing of Identity*. Pluto Press.

76   What people in the Middle East say in private about the West. Salbi, Z. (2015). [online] Women in the World. Available at: https://womenintheworld.com/2015/05/26/what-people-in-

the-middle-east-are-saying-in-private-about-the-west/ [Accessed 2 Jul. 2019].

77 Naber, N. (2006). Arab American Femininities: Beyond Arab Virgin/ American(ized) Whore. *Feminist Studies*, 32(1), p.87.

78 THIS is the average age Brits lose their virginity – it will shock you. Mitchell, L. (2017). 10.07.18 [online] Daily Star. Available at: https://www.dailystar.co.uk/love-sex/608722/Average-age-lose-virginity-UK-sex-habits-statistics-Britain

79 Sex education in schools is from an era when the Spice Girls were equality icons. McInerney, L. (2018). [online] the Guardian. Available at: https://www.theguardian.com/education/2018/may/15/sex-education-schools-from-era-spice-girls-equality-icons [Accessed 5 Mar. 2019].

80 Schools to teach about same-sex relationships and gender identity under new sex ed plan. Duffy, N. (2018). [online] PinkNews. Available at: https://www.pinknews.co.uk/2018/07/19/sex-and-relationship-education-gay-relationships-gender-identity/ [Accessed 5 Mar. 2019].

81 5,000 women a year are still being killed in the name of 'honour'. Thompson, S. (2016). [online] World Economic Forum. Available at: https://www.weforum.org/agenda/2016/07/honour-killings-pakistan-qandeel-baloch/ [Accessed 5 Mar. 2019].

82 In Europe, Debate Over Islam and Virginity. Mekhennet, E. (2008). [online] Nytimes.com. Available at: https://www.nytimes.com/2008/06/11/world/europe/11virgin.html [Accessed 5 Mar. 2019].

83   Eltahawy, M. (2016). *Headscarves and Hymens: Why the Middle East Needs a Sexual Revolution.* W&N.

84   Court blames 'promiscuous' rape survivor. BBC News. (2017). 10.07.18 [online] Available at: https://www.bbc.co.uk/news/world-asia-india-41383459

85   Aly, R. (2015). *Becoming Arab in London: Performativity and the Undoing of Identity.* Pluto Press.

86   El Saadawi, N. and Hetata, S. (2015). *The Hidden Face of Eve: Women in the Arab World.* London: Zed Books.

87   How Women Are Taught To View Themselves As Objects. Weiss, S. (2016). [online] Bustle. Available at: https://www.bustle.com/articles/167897-9-subtle-ways-women-are-taught-to-view-themselves-as-objects [Accessed 9 Jul. 2019].

88   Lewis, R. and Marston, C. (2016). Oral Sex, Young People, and Gendered Narratives of Reciprocity. *The Journal of Sex Research,* 53(7), pp.776–787.

89   Wood, J., McKay, A., Komarnicky, T. and Milhausen, R. (2016). Was it good for you too?: An analysis of gender differences in oral sex practices and pleasure ratings among heterosexual Canadian university students. *The Canadian Journal of Human Sexuality,* 25(1), pp.21–29.

90   Doctors Created Vibrators After Growing Tired of Masturbating 'Hysterical' Women. (2017). 12.07.18 [online] Broadly. Available at: https://broadly.vice.com/en_us/article/paeb9k/doctors-created-vibrators-after-growing-tired-of-masturbating-hysterical-women

91 El Saadawi, N. and Hetata, S. (2015). *The Hidden Face of Eve: Women in the Arab World*. London: Zed Books.

92 What We Teach Women When We Tell Them Not to Be Easy. Weiss, S. (2018). [online] Kinkly.com. Available at: https://www. kinkly.com/what-we-teach-women-when-we-tell-them-not-to-be-easy/2/17150 [Accessed 9 Jul. 2019].

93 What We Teach Women When We Tell Them Not to Be Easy. Weiss, S. (2018). [online] Kinkly.com. Available at: https://www. kinkly.com/what-we-teach-women-when-we-tell-them-not-to-be-easy/2/17150 [Accessed 9 Jul. 2019].

94 Eltahawy, M. (2016). *Headscarves and Hymens: Why the Middle East Needs a Sexual Revolution*. W&N.

95 Bergner, D. (2014). *What Do Women Want?: Adventures in the Science of Female Desire*. Ecco Press.

96 *Liberated: The New Sexual Revolution*. (2018). Netflix.

97 2011 Census analysis – Office for National Statistics. (2014). 14.07.18 [online] ONS.gov.uk. Available at: https://www.ons. gov.uk/peoplepopulationandcommunity/birthsdeathsandmar-riages/marriagecohabitationandcivilpartnerships/articles/whatdo-esthe2011censustellusaboutinterethnicrelationships/2014-07-03

98 Love across the divide: interracial relationships growing in Britain. Bingham, J. (2014). 20.07.18 [online] The Telegraph. Available at: https://www.telegraph.co.uk/news/politics/10943807/Love-across-the-divide-interracial-relationships-growing-in-Britain. html

99   I wrote an article about this for Broadly in 2015: Where Maids Are Treated Like Slaves. [online] Broadly. Available at: https://broadly.vice.com/en_us/article/9ae4qd/where-maids-are-treated-like-slaves

100 The UK's Windrush generation: What's the scandal about? (2018). 28.07.18 [online] Aljazeera.com. Available at: https://www.aljazeera.com/news/2018/04/uk-windrush-generation-scandal-180418074648878.html

101 London nightclub accused of charging black women twice as much as white women to enter. (2018). 27.07.18 [online] The Independent. Available at: https://www.independent.co.uk/news/uk/home-news/drama-park-lane-racism-nightclub-black-women-mayfair-london-entrance-charged-black-a8393476.html

102 Stephen Lawrence murder 25 years on: what happened, and did it really change a nation? (2018). 27.07.18 [online] The Independent. Available at: https://www.independent.co.uk/news/uk/home-news/stephen-lawrence-murder-25-years-changed-a-nation-police-institutional-racism-macpherson-anniversary-a8307871.html

103 Egypt: The forbidden love of interfaith romances. BBC News. (2014). 20.07.18 [online] Available at: https://www.bbc.co.uk/news/world-middle-east-29932094

104 Lebanese Women Can't Pass Citizenship to Kids, Spouses. Human Rights Watch. (2018). [online] Available at: https://www.hrw.org/video-photos/video/2018/10/02/lebanese-women-cant-pass-citizenship-kids-spouses [Accessed 5 Mar. 2019].

105 El Saadawi, N. and Hetata, S. (2015). *The Hidden Face of Eve: Women in the Arab World*. London: Zed Books.

106 Child Custody in the Middle East. Wikigender.org. (n.d.). [online] Available at: https://www.wikigender.org/wiki/child-custody-in-the-middle-east/ [Accessed 5 Mar. 2019].

107 Women are still too often the losers in divorce matters. Salem, O. (2013). [online] The National. Available at: https://www.thenational.ae/women-are-still-too-often-the-losers-in-divorce-matters-1.300377 [Accessed 5 Mar. 2019].

108 Divorce parties are now a trend in Saudi Arabia. Bashraheel, A. (2018). [online] Arab News. Available at: http://www.arabnews.com/node/1235681/saudi-arabia [Accessed 5 Mar. 2019].

109 Mail Online. (2018). *Average age for women to marry is now over 35, figures reveal.* [online] Available at: https://www.dailymail.co.uk/news/article-5447491/Average-age-women-marry-35.html [Accessed 8 Apr. 2019].

110 Marriages between men and women hit lowest rate on record in England and Wales. (2018). 01.08.18 [online] The Independent. Available at: https://www.independent.co.uk/news/uk/home-news/marriages-men-women-lowest-record-heterosexual-lgbt-ons-a8232751.html

111 As U.S. marriage rate hovers at 50%, education gap in marital status widens. Parker, K. and Stepler, R. (2017). 01.01.18 [online] Pew Research Center. Available at: http://www.pewresearch.org/fact-tank/2017/09/14/as-u-s-marriage-rate-hovers-at-50-education-gap-in-marital-status-widens/

112 Amal Clooney has the wrong idea about the word 'spinster'. Bolick, K. (2018). *Grazia Magazine*, June 19th 2018

113 Child Marriage in the Middle East and North Africa – Population Reference Bureau. (2010). 03.08.18 [online] prb.org. Available at: https://www.prb.org/menachildmarriage/

114 *Yes, Arab women marry later these days.* Hedengren, A. (2013). 03.08.18 [online] Your Middle East. Available at: https://yourmiddleeast.com/2013/06/06/yes-arab-women-marry-later-these-days/

115 Egypt: Six men facing anal examinations for 'debauchery' amid homophobic crackdown. [online] Amnesty.org. (2017). Available at: https://www.amnesty.org/en/press-releases/2017/09/egypt-six-men-facing-anal-examinations-for-debauchery-amid-homopho-bic-crackdown/ [Accessed 6 Mar. 2019].

116 Countries That Allow Gay Marriage Around The World. [online] Pew Research Center's Religion & Public Life Project. (2017). Available at: http://www.pewforum.org/2017/08/08/gay-mar-riage-around-the-world-2013/ [Accessed 6 Mar. 2019].

117 Lavish weddings costing Emiratis more than money. Al Hinai, M. (2011). [online] The National. Available at: https://www.the-national.ae/lavish-weddings-costing-emiratis-more-than-mon-ey-1.409625 [Accessed 5 Mar. 2019].

118 Arab News. (2018). *Why are Saudi weddings so expensive?*. [online] Available at: http://www.arabnews.com/node/1238466/saudi-arabia [Accessed 10 Apr. 2019].

119 Allam, R. (2008) Countering the Negative Image of Arab Women in the Arab Media: Toward a 'Pan Arab Eye' Media Watch Project, Middle East Institute.

120 'In Arabic, the word for single woman means withered branch'. (2016). 02.08.18 [online] haaretz.com. Available at: https://www. haaretz.com/israel-news/.premium.MAGAZINE-in-arabic-the-word-for-single-woman-means-withered-branch-1.5474345

121 Divorces in England and Wales – Office for National Statistics. (2017). 04.08.18 [online] Ons.gov.uk. Available at: https://www.ons.gov. uk/peoplepopulationandcommunity/birthsdeathsandmarriages/ divorce/bulletins/divorcesinenglandandwales/2016

122 Mapped: The countries with the highest divorce rate. Oliver Smith (2017). 04.08.18 [online] The Telegraph. Available at: https://www.telegraph.co.uk/travel/maps-and-graphics/mapped-countries-with-highest-divorce-rate/

123 Divorce Rate in Egypt Increases by 83% in the Past 20 Years. (2016). 04.08.18 [online] Cairo Scene. Available at: http:// www.cairoscene.com/Buzz/Divorce-Rate-in-Egypt-Increases-by-83-in-the-Past-20-Years

124 Most Movies' Portrayal of Love Is Sick and Inaccurate. [online] Tonic. (2018). Available at: https://tonic.vice.com/en_us/article/ kzp5av/movies-music-confuse-love-with-obsession [Accessed 6 Mar. 2019].

125 How Movies And TV Shows Are Changing The Way You Think About Love. Hillin, T. (2014). [online] Huffingtonpost.co.uk. Available at: https://www.huffingtonpost.co.uk/entry/love-study_ us_5508965 [Accessed 5 Mar. 2019].

126 Amal Clooney has the wrong idea about the word 'spinster'. Bolick, K. (2018). *Grazia Magazine*, June 19th 2018

127 Middle East and North Africa: Women in the Workforce. (2010). 08.08.18 [online] World Bank. Available at: http://www.worldbank.org/en/news/feature/2010/03/10/middle-east-and-north-africa-women-in-the-workforce

128 EgyptToday. (2018). Women are breadwinners of 3.3M families in Egypt: CAPMAS. [online] Available at: http://www.egypttoday.com/Article/1/44718/Women-are-breadwinners-of-3-3M-families-in-Egypt-CAPMAS [Accessed 8 Apr. 2019].

129 Despite high education levels, Arab women still don't have jobs. (2016). 08.08.18 [online] World Bank. Available at: http://blogs.worldbank.org/arabvoices/despite-high-education-levels-arab-women-still-don-t-have-jobs

130 Despite high education levels, Arab women still don't have jobs. (2016). 08.08.18 [online] World Bank. Available at: http://blogs.worldbank.org/arabvoices/despite-high-education-levels-arab-women-still-don-t-have-jobs

131 Why do so few women work (for pay) in Jordan? (2017). 08.08.18 [online] Public Radio International. Available at: https://www.pri.org/stories/2017-03-08/why-do-so-few-women-work-pay-jordan

132 Majority of men in Middle East survey believe a woman's place is in the home. Lyons, K. (2017). 02.05.18 [online] the Guardian. Available at: https://www.theguardian.com/global-development/2017/may/02/majority-of-men-in-middle-east-north-africa-survey-believe-a-womans-place-is-in-the-home

133 Majority of men in Middle East survey believe a woman's place is in the home. Lyons, K. (2017). 02.05.18 [online] the Guardian. Available at: https://www.theguardian.com/

global-development/2017/may/02/majority-of-men-in-middle-east-north-africa-survey-believe-a-womans-place-is-in-the-home

134 Majority of men in Middle East survey believe a woman's place is in the home. Lyons, K. (2017). 02.05.18 [online] the Guardian. Available at: https://www.theguardian.com/global-development/2017/may/02/majority-of-men-in-middle-east-north-africa-survey-believe-a-womans-place-is-in-the-home

135 El Saadawi, N. and Hetata, S. (2015). *The Hidden Face of Eve: Women in the Arab World*. London: Zed Books.

136 El Saadawi, N. and Hetata, S. (2015). *The Hidden Face of Eve: Women in the Arab World*. London: Zed Books.

137 Do Women Lack Ambition? Fels, A. (2004). 05.05.18 [online] Harvard Business Review. Available at: https://hbr.org/2004/04/do-women-lack-ambition

138 'I feel a lot of pressure': Meet Shadia Bseiso, the first Middle Eastern woman to join the WWE. (2017). 06.05.18 [online] The Telegraph. Available at: https://www.telegraph.co.uk/women/life/feel-lot-pressure-meet-shadia-bseiso-first-middle-eastern-woman/

139 75 per cent of children want to be YouTubers and vloggers. (2017). 10.08.18 [online] Mail Online. Available at: http://www.dailymail.co.uk/news/article-4532266/75-cent-children-want-YouTubers-vloggers.html

140 The 25 Most Influential People on the Internet. (2017). 10.05.18 [online] Time. Available at: http://time.com/4815217/most-influential-people-internet/

141 World's 10 Most Powerful Arab Women. (2018). 10.05.18 [online] Forbes Middle East. Available at: https://www.forbesmiddleeast.com/en/list/the-10-worlds-most-powerful-arab-women/

142 Female Entrepreneurs in the Middle East. Sayyed, M. (2017). 10.08.18 [online] Payfort.com. Available at: https://www.payfort.com/blog/2017/01/24/female-entrepreneurs-in-the-middle-east/ [Accessed 24 Aug. 2018].

143 Hala Hattab, (2012) 'Towards understanding female entrepreneurship in Middle Eastern and North African countries: A cross-country comparison of female entrepreneurship', Education, Business and Society: Contemporary Middle Eastern Issues, Vol. 5 Issue: 3, pp.171-186, https://doi.org/10.1108/17537981211265561

144 The future of female tech leadership is thriving—in the United Arab Emirates. (2017). 10.08.18 [online] Quartz. Available at: https://qz.com/1018217/the-future-of-female-tech-leadership-is-thriving-in-the-united-arab-emirates/

145 India 'fails' victims of abuse. (2014). 06.08.18 [online] BBC News. Available at: https://www.bbc.co.uk/news/world-asia-india-29708612

146 How Pakistani and Indian women confront marital economic abuse. (2017). 06.08.18 [online] The Conversation. Available at: https://theconversation.com/how-pakistani-and-indian-women-confront-marital-economic-abuse-75250

147 Chang, L. (2018). *Egyptian Women and the Fight for the Right to Work*. [online] The New Yorker. Available at: https://www.newyorker.com/news/news-desk/egyptian-women-and-the-fight-for-the-right-to-work [Accessed 8 Apr. 2019].

148 Gender discrimination comes in many forms for today's working women. Parker, K. (2017). 10.08.18 [online] Pew Research Center. Available at: http://www.pewresearch.org/fact-tank/2017/12/14/gender-discrimination-comes-in-many-forms-for-todays-working-women/

149 Here's what's holding working women back in 2018. Bruce-Lockhart, A. (2018). [online] World Economic Forum. Available at: https://www.weforum.org/agenda/2018/03/working-women-challenges-2018/ [Accessed 9 Jul. 2019].

150 Women work for free for a fifth of the year, says TUC. (2017). 10.08.18 [online] TUC. Available at: https://www.tuc.org.uk/news/women-work-free-fifth-year-says-tuc

151 Beydoun, K. (2018). Twitter. [online] Twitter.com. Available at: https://twitter.com/khaledbeydoun/status/1058523963494727685 [Accessed 6 Mar. 2019].

152 Mahlouf, A. (2000). *On Identity*. Vintage.

153 Rizvi, A. (2016). *The Atheist Muslim*. St Martin's Press.

154 Why Will No One Let the Muslim World Be Secular?. Time. (2015). [online] Available at: https://time.com/3675429/muslim-world-secularization/ [Accessed 2 Jul. 2019].

155 *Not All Arabs Are Muslims*. Suarez, E. (2017). 05.05.18 [online] Inter Press Service/News Agency. Available at: https://www.linkedin.com/pulse/arabs-muslims-big-ban-enrique-suarez [Accessed 26 Aug. 2018].

156 Why is Islam so different in different countries?. Hughes, A. (2016). [online] The Conversation. Available at: https://the-conversation.com/why-is-islam-so-different-in-different-countries-51804 [Accessed 2 Jul. 2019].

157 Why Muslims are the world's fastest-growing religious group. (2017). 13.08.18 [online] Pew Research Center. Available at: http://www.pewresearch.org/fact-tank/2017/04/06/why-muslims-are-the-worlds-fastest-growing-religious-group/

158 Invisible Atheists. Benchemsi, A. (2015). 13.08.18 [online] The New Republic. Available at: https://newrepublic.com/article/121559/rise-arab-atheists

159 Why is Islam so different in different countries? (2016). 15.08.18 [online] The Conversation. Available at: https://theconversation.com/why-is-islam-so-different-in-different-countries-51804

160 Boxed In | Women and Saudi Arabia's Male Guardianship System. (2016). 11.08.18 [online] Human Rights Watch. Available at: https://www.hrw.org/report/2016/07/16/boxed/women-and-saudi-arabias-male-guardianship-system

161 The rules are clear, says lawyer: no kissing allowed in Dubai. (2013). 11.08.18 [online] The National. Available at: https://www.thenational.ae/uae/heritage/the-rules-are-clear-says-lawyer-no-kissing-allowed-in-dubai-1.462242

162 Eating in public during Ramadan is a crime. Bassam Za'za', L. (2018). 11.08.18 [online] GulfNews. Available at: https://gulfnews.com/guides/ask-the-law/eating-in-public-during-ramadan-is-a-crime-1.2233387

163 Moroccan women on trial for indecency after wearing skirts to market. (2015). 11.08.18 [online] Mail Online. Available at: http://www.dailymail.co.uk/news/article-3151636/Moroccan-women-trial-gross-indecency-wearing-skirts-market-Case-leads-protests-country-sparks-outrage-globe.html

164 The World's Newest Major Religion: No Religion. (2016). 13.08.18 [online] National Geographic. Available at: https://news.nationalgeographic.com/2016/04/160422-atheism-agnostic-secular-nones-rising-religion/

165 Hijab Policing Is Sexual Harassment, Period. Al-Khatahtbeh, A. (2019). [online] Muslim Girl. Available at: http://muslimgirl.com/52170/hijab-policing-sexual-harassment-period/ [Accessed 5 Mar. 2019].

166 Opinion | How Islamism Drives Muslims to Convert. Akyol, M. (2018). 12.08.18 [online] Nytimes.com. Available at: https://www.nytimes.com/2018/03/25/opinion/islam-conversion.html

167 Opinion | How Islamism Drives Muslims to Convert. Akyol, M. (2018). 12.08.18 [online] Nytimes.com. Available at: https://www.nytimes.com/2018/03/25/opinion/islam-conversion.html

168 The share of Americans who leave Islam is offset by those who become Muslim. (2018). 13.08.18 [online] Pew Research Center. Available at: http://www.pewresearch.org/fact-tank/2018/01/26/the-share-of-americans-who-leave-islam-is-offset-by-those-who-become-muslim/

169 Surveying U.S. And French Muslims. (2011). 13.08.18 [online] HuffPost. Available at: https://www.huffingtonpost.com/nidhal-guessoum/surveys-of-us-muslims-and_b_959894.html

170 Which is the world's fastest growing major religion? (2016). 13.08.18 [online] World Economic Forum. Available at: https://www.weforum.org/agenda/2016/05/fastest-growing-major-religion/

171 Most popular Twitter accounts in Egypt. (2018). [online] Socialbakers.com. Available at: https://www.socialbakers.com/statistics/twitter/profiles/egypt/ [Accessed 25 Aug. 2018].

172 Most popular YouTube Channels in Saudi Arabia. (2018). [online] Socialbakers.com. Available at: https://www.socialbakers.com/statistics/youtube/channels/saudi-arabia/ [Accessed 25 Aug. 2018].

173 Don't be Fooled by Appearances, Liberal Values are Spreading in the Arab World. (2104). [online] Middle East Institute. Available at: http://www.mei.edu/content/article/don%E2%80%99t-be-fooled-appearances-liberal-values-are-spreading-arab-world [Accessed 25 Aug. 2018].

174 *Reza Aslan's response to 'Does Islam Promote Violence?'* (2015). CNN.

175 3 students killed in Chapel Hill shooting. (2105). [online] CNN. Available at: https://edition.cnn.com/2015/02/11/us/chapel-hill-shooting/ [Accessed 25 Aug. 2018].

176 BBC News. (2019). *New Zealand mosque shootings kill 49.* [online] Available at: https://www.bbc.co.uk/news/world-asia-47578798 [Accessed 10 Apr. 2019].

177 New York imam, his assistant killed near mosque. (2016). [online] CNN. Available at: https://edition.cnn.com/2016/08/13/us/new-york-imam-shooting/ [Accessed 25 Aug. 2018].

178 Mohammad, N. (2016). I didn't realize how often Muslims get kicked off planes, until it happened to me. [online] the Guardian. Available at: https://www.theguardian.com/world/2016/sep/08/muslim-woman-kicked-off-american-airlines-flight-islamophobia [Accessed 25 Aug. 2018].

179 WNYW. (2016). Muslim woman's clothes set on fire: NYPD. [online] Available at: http://www.fox5ny.com/news/muslim-womans-clothes-set-on-fire-police [Accessed 25 Aug. 2018].

180 CNN. (n.d.). Muslim Congressman: I received a death threat yesterday - CNN Video. [online] CNN. Available at: https://edition.cnn.com/videos/tv/2015/12/08/trump-ban-muslims-andre-carson-reaction-lead.cnn [Accessed 25 Aug. 2018].

181 2015 Hate Crime Statistics. (2015). [online] FBI. Available at: https://ucr.fbi.gov/hate-crime/2015/tables-and-data-declarations/1tabledatadecpdf [Accessed 25 Aug. 2018].

182 Manchester attack: Islamophobic hate crime reports increase by 500%. (2017). [online] BBC News. Available at: https://www.bbc.co.uk/news/uk-england-manchester-40368668 [Accessed 25 Aug. 2018].

183 Hate crime targeting UK mosques more than doubled in past year. (2017). [online] The Independent. Available at: https://www.independent.co.uk/news/uk/home-news/hate-crime-muslims-mosques-islamist-extremism-terrorism-terror-attacks-a7989746.html [Accessed 25 Aug. 2018].

184 Everything you need to know about the travel ban. (2018). [online] CNN. Available at: https://edition.cnn.com/2018/06/26/politics/timeline-travel-ban/index.html [Accessed 25 Aug. 2018].

185 Britain voted to leave the EU to stop immigration, definitive study finds. (2017). [online] The Independent. Available at: https://www.independent.co.uk/news/uk/home-news/brexit-latest-news-leave-eu-immigration-main-reason-european-union-survey-a7811651.html [Accessed 25 Aug. 2018].

186 *Why we need to talk about the media's role in far-right hate.* Jones, O. (2019). [online] the Guardian. Available at: https://www.theguardian.com/commentisfree/2019/mar/28/media-far-right-radicalisation-politics-hatred [Accessed 10 Apr. 2019].

187 Versi, M. (2015). It's time the media treated Muslims fairly | Miqdaad Versi. [online] The Guardian. Available at: https://www.theguardian.com/commentisfree/2015/sep/23/media-muslims-study [Accessed 25 Aug. 2018].

188 Study: 'NYT' Portrays Islam More Negatively than Alcohol, Cancer, and Cocaine | Mondialisation - Centre de Recherche sur la Mondialisation. (2016). [online] Mondialisation.ca. Available at: https://www.mondialisation.ca/study-nyt-portrays-islam-more-negatively-than-alcohol-cancer-and-cocaine/5513340 [Accessed 25 Aug. 2018].

189 *Why we need to talk about the media's role in far-right hate.* Jones, O. (2019). [online] the Guardian. Available at: https://www.theguardian.com/commentisfree/2019/mar/28/media-far-right-radicalisation-politics-hatred [Accessed 10 Apr. 2019].

190 Rizvi, A. (2016). *The Atheist Muslim.* St. Martin's Press.

191 Kumail Nanjiani's Culture-Clash Comedy. Marantz, A. (2017). [online] The New Yorker. Available at: https://www.newyorker.com/magazine/2017/05/08/kumail-nanjianis-culture-clash-comedy [Accessed 25 Aug. 2018].

192 CoverGirl Signs Its First Ambassador in a Hijab. (2016). [online] Nytimes.com. Available at: https://www.nytimes.com/2016/11/09/fashion/covergirl-beauty-hijab.html [Accessed 25 Aug. 2018].

193 Nike is now selling a sports hijab. (2017). [online] Evening Standard. Available at: https://www.standard.co.uk/fashion/news/nike-has-launched-the-worlds-first-sports-hijab-a3707896.html [Accessed 25 Aug. 2018].

194 L'Oréal launches first ever hair ad with headscarf-wearing model. (2018). [online] DailySabah. Available at: https://www.dailysabah.com/life/2018/01/20/loral-launches-first-ever-hair-ad-with-headscarf-wearing-model [Accessed 25 Aug. 2018].

195 Ahmed, Q. (2018). *A Tale of Two Veils: The Struggle for Muslim Identity*. [online] OZY. Available at: https://www.ozy.com/opinion/a-tale-of-two-veils-the-struggle-for-muslim-identity/83822 [Accessed 25 Aug. 2018].

196 Eltahawy, M. (2018). *Tweet*. Available at: https://twitter.com/monaeltahawy/status/996795426425704448?lang=en-gb [Accessed 26 Aug. 2018].

197 Why Muslim nations shouldn't make the Ramadan fast a matter of law. Diab, K. (2015). [online] haaretz.com. Available at: https://www.haaretz.com/opinion/.

premium-why-muslim-nations-shouldn-t-make-the-ramadan-fast-a-matter-of-law-1.5305782 [Accessed 2 Jul. 2019].

198 The 'masculine mystique' – why men can't ditch the baggage of being a bloke. (2017). [online] the Guardian. Available at: https://www.theguardian.com/money/2017/nov/21/the-masculine-mystique-why-men-cant-ditch-the-baggage-of-being-a-bloke [Accessed 25 Aug. 2018].

199 Girls believe brilliance is a male trait, research into gender stereotypes shows. (2017). [online] the Guardian. Available at: https://www.theguardian.com/education/2017/jan/26/girls-believe-brilliance-is-a-male-trait-research-into-gender-stereotypes-shows [Accessed 25 Aug. 2018].

200 You are your looks: that's what society tells girls. No wonder they're depressed | Natasha Devon. (2017). [online] the Guardian. Available at: https://www.theguardian.com/commentisfree/2017/sep/22/girls-looks-teach-children-appearance-stereotypes [Accessed 25 Aug. 2018].

201 Awad, A. (2017). *Beyond Veiled Clichés: The Real Lives of Arab Women*. Penguin Random House Australia.

202 Sexist stereotypes dominate front pages of British newspapers, research finds. (2012). [online] the Guardian. Available at: https://www.theguardian.com/media/2012/oct/14/sexist-stereotypes-front-pages-newspapers [Accessed 25 Aug. 2018].

203 *The New Congress Is 80 Percent White*. (2015). [online] Washington Post. Available at: https://www.washingtonpost.com/news/the-fix/wp/2015/01/05/the-new-congress-is-80-percent-

white-80-percent-male-and-92-percent-christian/?utm_term=.7482aadb965b [Accessed 26 Aug. 2018].

204 *'Sad truths' about women in US media – it's still dominated by men.* (2015). [online] the Guardian. Available at: https://www.theguardian.com/media/greenslade/2015/jun/04/sad-truths-about-women-in-us-media-its-still-dominated-by-men [Accessed 25 Aug. 2018].

205 Why Wikipedia often overlooks stories of women in history. (2018). [online] The Conversation. Available at: https://theconversation.com/why-wikipedia-often-overlooks-stories-of-women-in-history-92555 [Accessed 25 Aug. 2018].

206 *Gender equality report: not one country has fully closed the gap yet.* (2014). [online] the Guardian. Available at: https://www.theguardian.com/news/datablog/2014/oct/28/not-one-country-has-fully-closed-gender-gap-yet-report-shows [Accessed 25 Aug. 2018].

207 *Women 'won't have equality' for 100 years.* (2017). [online] BBC News. Available at: https://www.bbc.co.uk/news/world-41844875 [Accessed 25 Aug. 2018]. .

208 Men Appear in Ads 4 Times More Than Women, According to Research Revealed at Cannes. (2017). [online] Adweek.com. Available at: https://www.adweek.com/brand-marketing/men-appear-in-ads-4-times-more-than-women-according-to-research-revealed-at-cannes/ [Accessed 25 Aug. 2018].

209 See Jane. (n.d.). Geena Davis Inclusion Quotient. [online] Available at: https://seejane.org/research-informs-empowers/data/ [Accessed 25 Aug. 2018].

210 Smith, D. (n.d.). Gender Stereotypes an Analysis of Popular Films and TV. *Geena Davis institute on gender in media.*

211 Wood, J. (n.d.). Gendered Media: The Influence of Media on Views of Gender. *Department of Communication, University of North Carolina at Chapel Hill.*

212 *Three Percent of Women Portrayed in Leadership Roles in Ads.* (2016). [online] MarketandSelltoWomen. Available at: https://www.marketandselltowomen.com/three-percent-of-women-portrayed-in-leadership-roles-in-ads/ [Accessed 25 Aug. 2018].

213 *Daily Mail 'Legs-it' front page criticised as 'sexist, offensive and moronic'.* (2017). [online] the Guardian. Available at: https://www.theguardian.com/media/2017/mar/28/daily-mail-legs-it-front-page-sexist [Accessed 25 Aug. 2018].

214 *Gender stereotypes are destroying girls, and they're killing boys.* (2017). [online] Eu.usatoday.com. Available at: https://eu.usatoday.com/story/news/2017/09/21/gender-stereotypes-destroying-girls-and-theyre-killing-boys/688317001/ [Accessed 26 Aug. 2018].

215 *Geena Davis: 'We Are Enculturating Kids to See Women and Girls as Not Taking Up Half the Space'.* (2013). [online] IndieWire. Available at: https://www.indiewire.com/2013/12/geena-davis-we-are-enculturating-kids-to-see-women-and-girls-as-not-taking-up-half-the-space-207653/ [Accessed 25 Aug. 2018].

216 *Anne Hathaway accuses herself of misogyny: 'I've treated female directors unfairly'.* (2017). [online] The Telegraph. Available at: https://www.telegraph.co.uk/films/0/anne-hathaway-internalised-misogyny-treated-female-directors/ [Accessed 25 Aug. 2018].

217 Gallup, I. *Americans Still Prefer a Male Boss.* (2013). [online] Gallup.com. Available at: https://news.gallup.com/poll/165791/americans-prefer-male-boss.aspx [Accessed 25 Aug. 2018].

218 *On Twitter, women are more misogynistic than men.* (2016). [online] Mashable. Available at: https://mashable.com/2016/10/18/women-misogynistic-language/?europe=true [Accessed 25 Aug. 2018].

219 *White Women Helped Elect Donald Trump.* (2016). [online] Nytimes. com. Available at: https://www.nytimes.com/2016/12/01/us/politics/white-women-helped-elect-donald-trump.html [Accessed 25 Aug. 2018].

220 *Women Pitching the Same Exact Ideas As Men Still Get Less Funding From Venture Capitalists.* (2014). [online] Smithsonian. Available at: https://www.smithsonianmag.com/smart-news/venture-capitalists-are-less-likely-invest-identical-companies-if-theyre-pitched-women-180950048/ [Accessed 25 Aug. 2018].

221 *Japanese Medical School Admits To Rigging Entrance Exams To Hurt Women Candidates.* (2018). [online] Npr.org. Available at: https://www.npr.org/2018/08/10/637614700/japanese-medical-school-admits-to-rigging-entrance-exams-to-hurt-women-candidate [Accessed 25 Aug. 2018].

222 El Saadawi, N. and Hetata, S. (2015). *The Hidden Face of Eve: Women in the Arab World.* London: Zed Books.

223 *Mapped: The best (and worst) countries for gender equality.* (2017). [online] The Telegraph. Available at: https://www.telegraph.co.uk/travel/maps-and-graphics/mapped-the-best-and-worst-countries-for-gender-equality/ [Accessed 25 Aug. 2018].

224 *Women Inherit Less Under Islam. One Country's Changing the Rules.* (2017). [online] Bloomberg. Available at: https://www.bloomberg.com/news/articles/2017-09-07/women-inherit-less-under-islam-one-country-s-changing-the-rules [Accessed 25 Aug. 2018].

225 *One by One, Marry-Your-Rapist Laws Are Falling in the Middle East.* (2017). [online] Nytimes.com. Available at: https://www.nytimes.com/2017/07/22/world/middleeast/marry-your-rapist-laws-middle-east.html [Accessed 25 Aug. 2018].

226 *The 16 worst countries for gender equality.* (2017). [online] Business Insider. Available at: https://nordic.businessinsider.com/the-16-worst-countries-for-gender-equality-2017-11/ [Accessed 25 Aug. 2018].

227 Awad, A. (2017). *Beyond Veiled Clichés: The Real Lives of Arab Women.* Penguin Random House Australia.

228 *19th Amendment - Women's History.* (n.d.). [online] HISTORY.com. Available at: https://www.history.com/topics/womens-history/19th-amendment [Accessed 25 Aug. 2018].

229 *Battle Lines Drawn As Abortion-Rights Activists Leave Their Mark Outside Clinics.* (n.d.). [online] Thelundreport.org. Available at: https://www.thelundreport.org/content/battle-lines-drawn-abortion-rights-activists-leave-their-mark-outside-clinics [Accessed 25 Aug. 2018].

230 *'It may still be legal, but women's access to abortion is under attack in Trump's America'.* (2018). [online] The Independent. Available at: https://www.independent.co.uk/voices/abortion-america-planned-parenthood-title-x-donald-trump-arkansas-roe-vs-wade-a8381181.html [Accessed 25 Aug. 2018].

231 *The World is Getting Better at Paid Maternity Leave. The US is Not.* (2016). [online] Washington Post. Available at: https://www. washingtonpost.com/news/worldviews/wp/2016/08/13/the-world-is-getting-better-at-paid-maternity-leave-the-u-s-is-not/ [Accessed 26 Aug. 2018].

232 *Domestic violence's real cost: Nearly three women die every day.* (2017). [online] NBC News. Available at: https://www.nbcnews. com/news/us-news/domestic-violence-nearly-three-u-s-women-killed-every-day-n745166 [Accessed 25 Aug. 2018].

233 Unequal pay for women remains a norm in Western 'liberal' coun-tries. Aziz, S. (2017). [online] Cgpolicy.org. Available at: https:// www.cgpolicy.org/articles/unequal-pay-for-women-remains-a-norm-in-western-liberal-countries/ [Accessed 9 Jul. 2019].

234 *Women shoulder the responsibility of 'unpaid work' - Office for National Statistics.* (2016). [online] Ons.gov.uk. Available at: https://www.ons.gov.uk/employmentandlabourmarket/peo-pleinwork/earningsandworkinghours/articles/womenshoulder-theresponsibilityofunpaidwork/2016-11-10 [Accessed 25 Aug. 2018].

235 *Many Famous Suffragists Were Actually Working to Advance White Supremacy.* (2017). [online] Teen Vogue. Available at: https:// www.teenvogue.com/story/womens-suffrage-leaders-left-out-black-women [Accessed 25 Aug. 2018].

236 Ahmed, L. (1993). *Women and Gender in Islam: Historical Roots of a Modern Debate.* Yale University Press.

237 *This is how Islam led the world with women's rights.* (2017). [on-line] StepFeed. Available at: https://stepfeed.com/this-is-how-

islam-led-the-world-with-women-s-rights-0090 [Accessed 25 Aug. 2018].

238 *Can you be a Muslim and a feminist?* (2013). [online] Newstatesman. com. Available at: https://www.newstatesman.com/religion/2013/11/can-you-be-muslim-and-feminist [Accessed 25 Aug. 2018].

239 Murabit, A. (2015). *What My Religion Really Says About Women.* TED Talk

240 *Woman, 38, defied Saudi Arabia's female driving ban speaks out.* (2017). [online] Mail Online. Available at: http://www.dailymail. co.uk/femail/article-4669840/Manal-Al-Sharif-defied-Saudi-Arabia-s-female-driving-ban.html [Accessed 25 Aug. 2018].

241 *Remembering Pioneering Women.* (n.d.). [online] The Women and Memory Forum. Available at: http://www.wmf.org.eg/en/project/remembering-pioneering-women/ [Accessed 25 Aug. 2018].

242 *Tunisian president to seek equal inheritance rights for women.* (2018). [online] Financial Times. Available at: https://www.ft.com/content/182b05f0-9efc-11e8-85da-eeb7a9ce36e4 [Accessed 25 Aug. 2018].

243 *Tunisian women free to marry non-Muslims.* (2017). [online] BBC News. Available at: https://www.bbc.co.uk/news/world-africa-41278610 [Accessed 25 Aug. 2018].

244 *Victory for girls' rights as Lebanon abolishes 'rape law'.* (2017). [online] Plan International. Available at: https://plan-international. org/2017-08-16-victory-girls-rights-lebanon-abolishes-rape-law [Accessed 25 Aug. 2018].

245 *On Women's Rights, Uneven Progress in the Middle East.* Alexander, C. (2019). [online] Bloomberg.com. Available at: https://www.bloomberg.com/news/articles/2019-01-11/on-women-s-rights-uneven-progress-in-the-middle-east-quicktake [Accessed 6 Mar. 2019].

246 Leïla Slimani: the author who dared to ask Arab women about sex. Sage, A. (2017). [online] Thetimes.co.uk. Available at: https://www.thetimes.co.uk/article/leila-slimani-the-author-who-dared-to-ask-arab-women-about-sex-xbp9npm5v [Accessed 10 Jul. 2019].

247 Chimamanda Ngozi Adichie. (2017). We Should All Be Feminists [Video file]. Retrieved from https://www.ted.com/talks/chimamanda_ngozi_adichie_we_should_all_be_feminists

248 *Report shows 137,000 Women and Girls with FGM in England and Wales.* (2014). [online] City, University of London. Available at: https://www.city.ac.uk/news/2014/jul/new-report-shows-137,000-women-and-girls-with-fgm-in-england-and-wales [Accessed 25 Aug. 2018].

249 *FGM is banned but very much alive in the UK.* (2014). [online] the Guardian. Available at: https://www.theguardian.com/society/2014/feb/06/female-genital-mutilation-foreign-crime-common-uk [Accessed 25 Aug. 2018].

250 *'Those involved in FGM will find ways to evade UK law'.* (2018). [online] the Guardian. Available at: https://www.theguardian.com/society/2018/mar/07/reported-cases-fgm-rise-sharply-uk-no-court-convictions [Accessed 25 Aug. 2018].

251 *First ever forced marriage conviction in UK.* (2015). [online] Telegraph.co.uk. Available at: https://www.telegraph.co.uk/news/

uknews/crime/11665908/First-ever-forced-marriage-conviction-in-UK.html [Accessed 25 Aug. 2018].

252 *Doctors, nurses and teachers 'still fear raising alarm over FGM'.* (2018). [online] Evening Standard. Available at: https://www. standard.co.uk/news/health/doctors-nurses-and-teachers-still-fear-raising-alarm-over-fgm-a3825156.html [Accessed 25 Aug. 2018].

253 Mahlouf, A. (2000). *On Identity.* Vintage.

254 El Saadawi, N. and Hetata, S. (2015). *The Hidden Face of Eve: Women in the Arab World.* London: Zed Books.

255 January Cover Star Emily Ratajkowski Talks Feminism, Criticism & Being Controversial. [online] Harper's BAZAAR Arabia. (2017). Available at: https://www.harpersbazaararabia.com/editorials/january-cover-star-emily-ratajkowski-talks-feminism-criticism-being-controversial [Accessed 5 Mar. 2019].

256 Gokova, J. (1998). Challenging men to reject gender stereotypes. *Sex Health Exch.*, [online] 1998(2), pp.1-3. Available at: https://www. ncbi.nlm.nih.gov/pubmed/12294333 [Accessed 5 Mar. 2019].

257 *World Population 2018.* (2018). [online] Worldpopulationreview. com. Available at: http://worldpopulationreview.com/world-cities/london-population/ [Accessed 25 Aug. 2018].

258 Hirsch, A. (2018). *Brit(ish): On Race, Identity and Belonging.* Jonathan Cape.

259 Hirsch, A. (2018). *Brit(ish): On Race, Identity and Belonging.* Jonathan Cape.

260 IS schoolgirl wants to return to UK. [online] BBC News. (2019). Available at: https://www.bbc.co.uk/news/uk-47229181 [Accessed 5 Mar. 2019].

261 Isis runaway Shamima Begum stripped of her British citizenship. Simpson, J. (2019). [online] Thetimes.co.uk. Available at: https://www.thetimes.co.uk/article/isis-runaway-shamima-begum-stripped-of-her-british-citizenship-w97nlm9x3 [Accessed 5 Mar. 2019].

262 *Javid criticised as IS bride's baby dies.* [online] BBC News. (2019). Available at: https://www.bbc.co.uk/news/uk-47506145 [Accessed 9 Apr. 2019].

263 Yates, K. (2019). 'You Can Be Saddened . . .'. [online] Twitter. com. Available at: https://twitter.com/kieran_yates/status/1097950028541370368 [Accessed 5 Mar. 2019].

264 Al-Othman, H. (2019). *If I did a v horrible crime* . . . [online] Twitter.com. Available at: https://twitter.com/HannahAlOthman/status/1097990817522872321 [Accessed 9 Apr. 2019].

265 Exiled: the disturbing story of a citizen made unBritish. Shamsie, K. (2018). [online] the Guardian. Available at: https://www.theguardian.com/books/2018/nov/17/unbecoming-british-kamila-shamsie-citizens-exile [Accessed 5 Mar. 2019].

266 ITV News. (2013). Home Office: British citizenship is a privilege, not a right. [online] Available at: https://www.itv.com/news/update/2013-12-22/home-office-british-citizenship-is-a-privilege-not-a-right/ [Accessed 10 Jul. 2019].

267 Exiled: the disturbing story of a citizen made unBritish. Shamsie, K. (2018). [online] the Guardian. Available at: https://www.theguardian.com/books/2018/nov/17/unbecoming-british-kamila-shamsie-citizens-exile [Accessed 5 Mar. 2019].

268 *Sajid Javid: 770,000 people in England unable to speak English well.* (2018). [online] the Guardian. Available at: https://www.theguardian.com/politics/2018/mar/14/sajid-javid-770000-people-in-england-not-able-to-speak-english [Accessed 25 Aug. 2018].

269 *For immigration to work, migrants should be encouraged to settle.* (2015). [online] Telegraph.co.uk. Available at: https://www.telegraph.co.uk/news/uknews/immigration/11972803/For-immigration-to-work-migrants-should-be-encouraged-to-settle.html [Accessed 25 Aug. 2018].

270 *Britain needs immigrants, but not a 'swarm' of them.* (2015). [online] Telegraph.co.uk. Available at: https://www.telegraph.co.uk/news/politics/11776411/Britain-needs-immigrants-but-not-a-swarm-of-them.html [Accessed 25 Aug. 2018].

271 *For immigration to work, migrants should be encouraged to settle.* (2015). [online] Telegraph.co.uk. Available at: https://www.telegraph.co.uk/news/uknews/immigration/11972803/For-immigration-to-work-migrants-should-be-encouraged-to-settle.html [Accessed 25 Aug. 2018].

272 Mahlouf, A. (2000). *On Identity.* Vintage.

273 EU referendum: youth turnout almost twice as high as first thought. (2016). [online] the Guardian. Available at: https://

www.theguardian.com/politics/2016/jul/09/young-people-refer-endum-turnout-brexit-twice-as-high [Accessed 25 Aug. 2018].

274 *The U.K.'s Old Decided for the Young in the Brexit Vote.* (2016). [online] Time. Available at: http://time.com/4381878/brexit-generation-gap-older-younger-voters/ [Accessed 25 Aug. 2018].

275 *Has Brexit increased the political engagement of Britain's youth?* (2017). [online] Cardiff University. Available at: https://blogs.cardiff.ac.uk/wiserd/2017/06/16/has-brexit-increased-the-political-engagement-of-britains-youth/ [Accessed 25 Aug. 2018].

276 *People are reporting hate crimes sparked by the EU Referendum result.* (2016). [online] The Independent. Available at: https://www.independent.co.uk/news/uk/home-news/brexit-eu-referendum-racial-racism-abuse-hate-crime-reported-latest-leave-immigration-a7104191.html [Accessed 25 Aug. 2018].

277 *After Brexit vote, wave of racist and xenophobic threats reported across U.K.* (2016). [online] Yahoo News. Available at: https://uk.news.yahoo.com/brexit-post-ref-racism-000000858.html [Accessed 25 Aug. 2018].

278 *Half of skilled EU workers that Britain will need after Brexit now plan to leave.* (2017). [online] The Independent. Available at: https://www.independent.co.uk/news/business/news/brexit-half-of-skilled-eu-workers-in-uk-to-leave-healthcare-brain-drain-a7790341.html [Accessed 25 Aug. 2018].

279 *EU citizens explain why they are leaving the UK.* (2017). [online] The Independent. Available at: https://www.independent.co.uk/news/uk/home-news/

eu-migration-uk-brexit-referendum-latest-net-fall-figures-why-racism-hate-crime-brexodus-government-a7911196.html [Accessed 25 Aug. 2018].

280 UK gains £20bn from European migrants, UCL economists reveal. (2014). [online] the Guardian. Available at: https://www. theguardian.com/uk-news/2014/nov/05/eu-migrants-uk-gains-20bn-ucl-study [Accessed 25 Aug. 2018].

281 *How Immigrants Positively Affect the Business Community and the U.S. Economy.* (2016). [online] Center for American Progress. Available at: https://www.americanprogress.org/issues/immigration/news/2016/06/22/140124/how-immigrants-positively-affect-the-business-community-and-the-u-s-economy/ [Accessed 25 Aug. 2018].

282 *Why Brits are feeling better about immigration.* (2018). [online] The Week UK. Available at: http://www.theweek.co.uk/brexit/94936/why-brits-are-feeling-better-about-immigration [Accessed 25 Aug. 2018].

283 *Pico Iyer: 'Where Is Home?'* (2013). TEDGlobal.

284 Andreas, B. (1997). *Story people.* Decorah, IA: StoryPeople.

285 Fee, M. (2018). *Places I Stopped On The Way Home.* Icon Books.

286 *Where Aren't You From? A Third Culture Kid's Identity Crisis.* (2016). [online] HuffPost. Available at: https://www.huffingtonpost.com/rasha-rushdy/where-arent-you-from-a-th_b_10043978.html [Accessed 25 Aug. 2018].

287 *Pico Iyer: 'Where Is Home?'* (2013). TEDGlobal.

288 Pico Iyer: 'Where Is Home?' (2013). TEDGlobal.

289 Yaqub, N., Quawas, R. and Abdo, D. (2017). *Bad girls of the Arab World*. University of Texas Press.

290 Mahlouf, A. (2000). *On Identity*. Vintage.

291 Varon, J. (2018). *Hook Magazine*, (4), p.82.

292 Merrill, J. (1994). *A different person*. HarperSanFrancisco.